UNION AND CONFEDERATE SOLDIERS AND SYMPATHIZERS
OF
BARBOUR COUNTY
WEST VIRGINIA

by
John W. Shaffer

CLEARFIELD

Copyright © 2005 by John W. Shaffer
All Rights Reserved.

Printed for
Clearfield Company, Inc. by
Genealogical Publishing Co., Inc.
Baltimore, Maryland
2005

International Standard Book Number: 0-8063-5264-7

Made in the United States of America

TABLE OF CONTENTS

Introduction	1
Unionists	8
Confederates	126
Appendix A Units in Which Barbour's Union and Confederate Soldiers Served	210
Appendix B Battle and Engagements Referenced in Union and Confederate Biographies	215
Appendix C War-Related Deaths	222

INTRODUCTION

The state of West Virginia owes its existence to the Civil War. When Virginia seceded from the Union, the majority of the population of its western counties refused to follow the Old Dominion into the Confederacy and remained loyal to the Union. Immediately upon passage of the Ordinance of Secession at Richmond in April, 1861, pro-Union leaders in the west met at Wheeling, declared the ordinance null and void and took the first steps on the path that would lead to the formation of West Virginia as a separate state.

Over the course of the war, West Virginia would furnish some 30,000 men for the Union army. Yet within its territory a large segment of the population just as wholeheartedly remained loyal to a seceded Virginia and the Confederacy. It has been estimated that some 15,000 men from what is now West Virginia served in the Confederate army, a figure that is almost certainly an undercount of the true number. Beyond these were hundreds of civilians who supported the Confederacy by whatever means were available to them. The result was a civil war within the Civil War, a struggle that divided the loyalties of West Virginia's people not only during the war but for many years afterward.

This volume is intended as a supplement to A Clash of Loyalties: A Border County in the Civil War that examined the conflict in Barbour County, West Virginia. Like much of the rest of West Virginia, the people of Barbour were evenly divided between Union loyalists and Confederate sympathizers. In order to determine the true extent of those divisions, the study undertook to identify all those who either served in the armed forces of both sides or whose sympathies could be confirmed. The aim was to test the various theories hitherto put forward as to the basis of both Union loyalism and secessionist sentiment in West Virginia. Towards that end, information was gathered on each individual's property, religion and political affiliation.

One overriding factor found to have influenced the direction of loyalties in Barbour was the degree to which an individual identified him or herself as being a Virginian and, by extension, the degree to which loyalty to Virginia demanded they support both their state's secession and its adherence to the Confederacy. This sense of loyalty was itself found to have been strongly influenced by the length of time an individual's family had resided in Virginia. That is, those who had recently settled in the county from outside the state – principally from the North – or whose family had done so in the decades prior to the war by and large remained loyal to the Union. In contrast, those who were not only themselves native Virginians but whose families had lived in Virginia for several generations by and large supported secession.

The results of that research constitute a resource not only for those interested in Barbour's local history, but for the genealogist as well. Altogether it was possible to identify 718 Unionists and 529 Confederates. However, the actual total came to 1,207 as one of the more remarkable findings of the study revealed that twenty men switched loyalties during the war. Most were Confederate soldiers who deserted the army and re-enlisted in Federal regiments, but there were some who served for a time in the Union army and later deserted to the Confederacy.

The vast majority of both groups consisted of men who served in the armed forces: 553 in Federal regiments, the West Virginia State Home Guard and militia; and 399 who served in the Confederate army. The remainder were civilians who could be positively identified as sympathizing with either the Union or Confederate causes. These included those who held public office, were arrested for their professed loyalties, were named in contemporary public or private sources as supporting one side or the other, or whose sympathies were recorded in post-war histories.

Despite every effort to include as many people as possible, the individuals listed here almost certainly do not constitute the total of Barbour's Union and Confederate sympathizers. The most glaring omission is that of women, only twenty-three of whom were identified. That women held very definite views on secession and the war cannot be doubted. Yet local histories only rarely note the important role women played in the war. By the same token, the large percentage of soldiers among both groups necessarily skews any results towards men of military age. However, the men included here totaled nearly half the adult male population of the county and without question constituted the hard core of Union and Confederate activists.

A wide variety of sources were utilized to identify those included in the study. Local histories provided a wealth of information on individuals, church membership and political party affiliation. One of the most important is Hugh Maxwell's <u>History of Barbour County</u>, published in 1899. Amassing a wealth of information on the county's history and its citizens, it is the work to which one must first turn when studying Barbour County. Included are biographies, roster of units of the Confederate army raised in Barbour and lists of public officials who served during the war.

Yet as informative as Maxwell's history is, it serves only as a starting point. The company rosters he provides are incomplete and included many who served in a particular unit but were not residents of Barbour. Reference to other Confederate units raised in the county is omitted entirely. Other than a list of Barbour Home Guardsmen – incomplete and including several who were not Barbour residents – and another of Union soldiers who received bounty payments for army service – most of whom were not Barbour men – no reference at all is made of Union companies raised in Barbour. These omissions are certainly at the base of subsequent conclusions in which Barbour has been incorrectly perceived to have been a secessionist stronghold.

The true extent of Unionist sentiment and the degree to which the county was divided during the war is revealed only when military service records are consulted. The principal sources examined were: Francis P. Pierpont, Annual Reports of the Adjutant General of the State of West Virginia; Compiled Service Records of Confederate Soldiers Serving in Organizations from the State of Virginia; War Department Records of the Confederate Army; and the 1890 Federal Census of Union Veterans and Widows. The main sources utilized to identify civilian sympathizers were newspapers, published biographies, county court records and contemporary letters and diaries. Of several newspapers consulted, by far the most important was the Wheeling Intelligencer, the preeminent pro-Union newspaper in West Virginia that devoted considerable space to war-time activities at the local level.

Several problems were encountered during the course of the investigation. One was posed by the Barbour Light Horse, a militia company called into the Confederate service at the beginning of the war and disbanded a few months later. The only extant list of its members is given by Maxwell. The company was actually formed in 1858 and the roll recorded by Maxwell evidently dates from about that time. Indeed, the roll not only includes five men known to have left the county before the war, but one man reported in court records as having been murdered in 1860. It cannot be assumed that those listed actually turned out in the spring of 1861.

Another problem was posed by Barbour's militia. By law, the state militia was composed of every able-bodied male between the ages of eighteen and forty-five. Decades after the war dozens of Barbour men filed claims for back pay for alleged wartime service in the county militia. All were rejected as Barbour's militia regiments – the 139th and 169th – were never called into service despite repeated demands by their officers that they be armed. There is little doubt those who filed claims did so simply to obtain some quick cash from the state. In fact, a good many of the claims were filed by men who had served in the Confederate army! In short, membership in Barbour's militia was not, in and of itself, proof of one's loyalty to the Union. However, it was decided to include officers commissioned during the war whose allegiance could not be questioned as well as a handful of men who moved to other counties during the war and served in militia units there when these were called into service.

Yet another problem are the twenty individuals who switched loyalties during the war. It was decided to list them as both Unionists and Confederates. Five other Confederate soldiers served in the U.S. Army, but were not counted among Unionists. One served in the Confederate army, came home towards the end of the war and was soon after drafted into the Federal army. He promptly deserted. Four others joined the United States Volunteers while prisoners of war. These regiments were recruited from Confederate prisoners with the specific understanding they would serve only on the frontier protecting settlers from Indian attack. In most cases the decision to join the U.S. Volunteers represented not so much a change in one's allegiance as simply a desire to escape the horrors of Federal prison camps.

Published family histories and individual biographies provided genealogical information for approximately half those listed here. For the rest, recourse was made to Federal censuses, county marriage records and wills. Anyone conversant with these sources, particularly census records, is well aware of the problems they pose. Census enumerators, either through carelessness or inaccurate information given them, often recorded incorrect data on ages and places of birth. It is not at all uncommon for a particular person to be listed in one census as having been born in Maryland, in Virginia in another and in Pennsylvania in yet another. Unfortunately for this study, the 1860 census for Barbour appears to have been the most carelessly one compiled for the entire century. Indeed, there is very good evidence that a number of people living in the county weren't included in the returns at all.

A further problem presented by census lists is the inability to distinguish from them whether an individual was born in Virginia or in what is now West Virginia. Obviously, no such distinction was made in the 1860 census. After the war, some enumerators listed persons born in West Virginia as natives of the state. Others listed persons born in West Virginia before the war as having been born in Virginia – technically correct, but frustrating to the researcher trying to make the distinction. While it was possible to establish the county of birth for most of the people listed here, there are some for whom this could not be determined. This was especially the case for a subject's parents and grandparents. In these cases, the individuals are simply noted as having been born in Virginia.

The method of presentation is alphabetical by surname with an individual's immediate relatives following the entry for that person. Occupations and property values are taken from the 1860 census, the first figure representing the value of real property, the second that of personal property. Property values for an individual's parents are given if the subject was listed as residing with them. Church affiliation was derived from both the 1860 census and sources for the period under consideration with changes noted for the post-war period. Political affiliation is given for the war-time period.

If this study has proven anything, it is the divisiveness of the Civil War in places such as Barbour County. Members of one family often chose opposite sides while others had close relatives fighting in opposing armies or supporting the opposite cause. The biographies therefore include information on relatives who also served in the armed forces or whose allegiance could be ascertained. The names of those relatives also listed here are noted with an asterisk.

No pretense is made to the complete accuracy of the information presented. But while accuracy cannot be guaranteed, the information provided is based on as careful a reading of the source material as was possible.

ABBREVIATIONS

Art.	artillery
AWOL	absent without leave
b.	born
Btln.	battalion
Calif.	California
Capt.	Captain
Cav.	Cavalry
Cf.	compare
Co.	company
Co.	county
Col.	colonel
Com.	commissioned
Conn.	Connecticut
cpl.	corporal
CSA	Confederate States Army
d.	died
Del.	Delaware
disch.	discharged
elec.	elected
enl.	enlisted
exch.	exchanged
Ga.	Georgia
Ill.	Illinois
Ind.	Indiana
Inf.	infantry
Kan.	Kansas
KIA	killed in action
Ky.	Kentucky
Lt.	lieutenant
Lt.-Col.	Lieutenant Colonel
m.	married
Mass.	Massachusetts
Md.	Maryland
MIA	missing in action
Mich.	Michigan
Mil.	militia
Mo.	Missouri
Neb.	Nebraska
NFR	no further record
N.H.	New Hampshire

N.J.	New Jersey
N.Y.	New York
Ore.	Oregon
Ok.	Oklahoma
Pa.	Pennsylvania
POW	prisoner of war
prom.	promoted
R.I.	Rhode Island
sgt.	sergeant
sur.	surrendered
transf.	transferred
USA	United States Army
Va.	Virginia
Vols.	Volunteers
Vt.	Vermont
W. Va.	West Virginia
wd.	wounded

UNIONISTS

ADAMS, John C.
Enl. Co. C, 17th W. Va. Inf. 9-10-64; served as musician; disch. 6-30-65; brother-in-law *Flavius Lipscomb served Co. D, 20th Va. Cav. (CSA). Farmer; $600/200 (parents); b. Barbour 1846; living Barbour 1880. Son of Jonathon and Margaret Adams; grandson of David and Nancy (Reed) Adams, b. Barbour; great-grandson of Jonathon and Margaret (Trenton) Adams, b. N.J., settled Barbour 1790's.

ADAMS, Abraham
Enl. Co. A, 7th W. Va. Inf. 3-15-65 as substitute; disch. 7-1-65. Farmer; $3,000/404 (parents); b. Barbour 1848; m. Matilda Reed Costolow 1867; moved to Harrison Co., W. Va. 1870's where listed Union veterans 1890. Son of Hiram and Delila (Lipscomb) Adams; grandson of David and Nancy (Reed) Adams.

ALDERMAN, James Cicero
Co. F, 133rd W. Va. Mil., called into service 9-63 for three months; com. Lt., 169th W. Va. Mil. 11-5-64, never called into service; brother-in-law *Martin Helmick Lt., 169th W. Va. Mil.; brother-in-law *William Helmick served Co. C, 1st W. Va. Cav. (USA). Farmer; $N/G; b. Highland Co., Va. 1827; m. Sydney Helmick 1848; came to Upshur Co., W. Va. 1850's; to Barbour during war; returned to Upshur Co. after war where living 1880. Son of Daniel and Susan (Wade) Alderman; parents b. Highland Co., settled Pocahontas Co., W. Va. 1830's; grandson of Ezekiel and Elisabeth (Holcomb) Alderman; grandfather b. Conn., settled Highland Co.

ANDERSON, John Siron
Sympathizer; brothers William, James and Lorenzo served Union Army. Farm laborer; $0/190; b. Upshur Co., W. Va. 1833; Methodist-Episcopal Church; came to Barbour 1850's with wife Sarah; d. Barbour 1867. Son of James and Sarah (Siron) Anderson; father b. Rockingham Co., Va., settled Uphsur Co. 1830; grandson of Joseph Anderson, b. Pa.

ANDERSON, James B.
Enl. Co. H, 10th W. Va. Inf. 7-5-64; disch. 8-9-65; brother *George served Co. D, 20th Va. Cav. (CSA). Farmer; $0/153 (parents); b. Loudoun Co., Va. 1845. Son of Eli and Sarah (Stillings) Anderson, b. Loudoun Co., settled Barbour 1850's; grandson of James and Sarah Anderson, b. Va.

ANGLIN, William B.
Enl. Co. L, 6th W. Va. Inf. 3-7-65; disch. 6-30-65; brothers-in-law *Jacob and *John Swartz served Co. K, 6th W. Va. Inf. (USA). Tenant; $0/53 (parents); b. Barbour 1841; m. Hannah Swartz 1860; moved to Kan. after war where living 1880. Son of Garret and Sarah Anglin; grandson of William and Nancy (Cade) Anglin; great-grandson of William and Susanna Anglin, b. Bath Co., Va., settled Barbour 1780's.

ARBOGAST, George Washington
Enl. Co. F, 15th W. Va. Inf. 8-27-62; d. of typhoid fever Meadow Bluff, Va. 5-19-64; brother-in-law *William Yeager served same company. Farmer; $300/264; b. Randolph Co., W. Va. 1836; m. Margaret Lunceford Mace 1855; widow listed Barbour Union veterans 1890. Son of John and Mary (Wood) Arbogast; grandson of John and Hannah (Davis) Arbogast; great-grandson of Michael and Mary Arbogast, immigrants from Germany, settled Augusta Co., Va. 1770's.

ATHERTON, Milton C.
Elec. Constable 1861. Farmer; $228/200; b. N.Y. 1824; m. Elisabeth Holden 1859; moved to Tucker Co., W. Va. after war where living 1880. Son of Cornelius and Mary (Delano) Atherton; father b. Pa.

ATHERTON, Elisabeth (Holden)
Sympathizer; brother *John served Co. H, 31st Va. Inf. and Co. D, 20th Va. Cav. (CSA); brother *Franklin served Co. G, 62nd Va. Mtd. Inf. (CSA). $228/200; b. Barbour 1832, wife of Milton Atherton; Baptist; living Tucker Co., W. Va. 1880. Daughter of John and Prudence (Kittle) Holden; father b. Harrison Co., W. Va.; granddaughter of Alexander Holden, b. N.J., settled Harrison Co. 1790's.

AUVIL, Daniel
Sympathizer; arrested Tucker Co., W. Va. 1863 by 20th Va. Cav. Farmer; $1,000/345; b. Pa. 1818; m. Catherine Hovatter 1838; German Baptist; d. Barbour 1899. Son of Daniel and Susannah (Hatfield) Auvil; father b. Frederick Co., Md., settled Barbour; grandson of John and Magdelena (Ditlo) Auvil, b. Md.

AUVIL, Christopher Columbus
Enl. Co. F, 15th W. Va. Inf. 9-12-64; disch. 6-15-65. Farmer; $1,000/345 (parents); b. Barbour 1842, son of Daniel and Catherine (Hovatter) Auvil; m. Louisa Jane Stewart 1866; listed Barbour Union veterans 1890.

BAKER, Jacob Thomas Melker
Guided Union forces to Philippi 6-2-61; enl. Co. F, 15th W. Va. Inf.; prom. to sgt.; wd. in shoulder Winchester 9-19-64; prom. to Lt. 2-7-65; disch. 6-15-65; NFR. Farmer; $3,000/817 (parents); b. Monongalia Co., W. Va. 1840; Methodist-Episcopal Church. Son of Joseph and Matilda (Thomas) Baker, settled Barbour from Monongalia Co. 1840's; grandparents b. Pa.

BAKER, John
Enl. Co. N, 6th W. Va. Inf. 10-15-64; disch. 6-30-65. Tenant; $0/116; b. Md. 1829; Republican; came to Barbour 1850's with wife Mary; moved to Braxton Co., W. Va after war where widow listed Union veterans 1890.

BALL, John D.
Enl. Co. F, 15th W. Va. Inf. 9-1-62; disch. 6-14-65. Farmer; $0/105; b. Barbour 1831; m. Harriet England 1863; German Baptist Church; listed Barbour Union veterans 1890. Son of Isaac and Ruth (Moats) Ball; grandson of John and Nancy Ball, b. Loudoun Co., Va., settled Barbour 1803.

BARTLETT, Hamilton Goss
Sympathizer, described as "a good Union man." Farmer; $3,000/618; b. Taylor Co., W. Va. 1824; m. Catherine McKinney 1843; Baptist; Democrat; d. Barbour 1887. Son of Eppa and Rebecca (Barron) Bartlett; grandson of William and Elisabeth (Hathaway) Bartlett, b. Loudoun Co., Va., settled Taylor Co.

BARTLETT, William E.
Listed Barbour Light Horse; com. Lt., 169th W. Va. Mil. 8-16-62, never called into service; brothers-in-law *Ephraim and *Simon Johnson 169th W. Va. Mil.; brother-in-law Benjamin Robinson served Co. C, 4th W. Va. Cav. (USA); sister-in-law *Margaret Reed Confederate sympathizer. Farmer; $1,500/465; b. Barbour 1828; Democrat; m. 1) Mariann Johnson 1854; 2) Sarah F. Reed 1863; living Barbour 1870. Son of Daniel and Sarah (Cole) Bartlett; grandson of Eppa and Rebecca (Barron) Bartlett.

BARTLETT, James Fleming
Enl. Co. B, 3rd W. Va. Cav. 3-1-64; disch. 6-30-65. Farmer; $1,000/311; b. Barbour 1827; Baptist; m. Zelda Newlon; moved to Ritchie Co., W. Va. after war where living 1880. Son of Samuel and Mary (Fleming) Bartlett; grandson of Thomas and Malinda (Bartlett) Bartlett; great-grandson of William and Elisabeth (Hathaway) Bartlett.

BARTLETT, Lorenzo Dow
Enl. Co. K, 17th W. Va. Inf. 2-16-65; disch. 6-30-65. Farmer; $1,000/311 (parents); b. Barbour 1848, son of James and Zelda (Newlon) Bartlett; m. Matilda Hall 1871; moved to Ritchie Co., W. Va. after war where listed Union veterans 1890.

BEAN, William Thomas
Enl. Co. H, 10th W. Va. Inf. 11-12-62; d. of wounds received at Winchester 9-19-64. Tenant; $0/35 (parents); b. Hampshire Co., W. Va. 1837. Son of Solomon and Elisabeth (Shillingburg) Bean, b. Hampshire Co.; grandson of Wamsley and Elisabeth Bean, b. Md., settled Barbour 1840's.

BEAN, John H.
Enl. Co. H, 10th W. Va. Inf. 5-20-63; disch. 8-9-65. Tenant; $0/35 (parents); b. Hampshire Co., W. Va. 1840, brother of William; moved to Lewis Co., W. Va. 1870's where listed Union veterans 1890; d. 1899.

BEAN, James Francis
Enl. Co. A, 10th W. Va. Inf. 2-1-62; prom. to cpl.; wd. in chest; disch. 5-7-65. Tenant; $0/35 (parents); b. Hampshire Co., W. Va. 1843, brother of William; m. Caroline Simon 1866; moved to Upshur Co., W. Va. 1870's where listed Barbour Union veterans 1890.

BEAN, Benjamin Franklin
Enl. Co. H, 10th W. Va. Inf. 8-5-63; wd. Winchester 9-19-64; disch. 5-7-65; brother-in-law Nathan Fowler served Co. E, 3rd W. Va. Cav. (USA). Farm laborer; $0/100 (parents); b. Harrison Co., W. Va. 1840; came to Barbour during war; living Barbour 1870. Son of Thomas and Rebecca Bean, b. Va.; grandfather b. Md.

BEAVERS, Moses B.
Com. Lt., 139th W. Va. Mil. 10-18-62, never called into service; NFR. Farmer; $3,500/1,297 (parents); b. Barbour 1839; Methodist-Episcopal Church. Son of John and Susanna (Losher) Beavers; father b. Preston Co., W. Va.; grandson of Moses and Nancy (Holbert) Beavers; grandfather b. N.J., settled Loudoun Co., Va., then Preston Co.

BEAVERS, John Washington
Enl. Co. I, 6th W. Va. Inf. 9-27-61; disch. 11-25-64; elec. Constable 1864 and 1865. Farmer; $3,500/1,297 (parents); b. Barbour 1842, brother of Moses; Methodist-Episcopal Church; m. Catherine McDaniel 1867; moved to Taylor

Co., W. Va. 1870's, then returned to Barbour 1880's where listed Union veterans 1890.

BENNETT, Silas
Elec. Justice of the Peace 1863; son Abraham served Bat. E, 1st W.Va Art. Farmer; $3,500/1,297; b. Upshur Co., W. Va. 1818; m. Rebecca Crites 1836; returned to Upshur Co. after war where living 1880. Son of Moses and Phoebe (Queen) Bennett; father b. Pendleton Co., W. Va., settled Upshur 1798; grandson of Joseph and Hannah (Ellsworth) Bennett; grandfather b. N. J., settled Pendleton Co.

BENNETT, Levi
Com. Lt., 169th W.Va. Mil. 8-16-62; prom. to Capt; never called into service; elec. Constable 1863. Farmer; $500/330; b. Rockingham Co., Va. 1826; settled Barbour 1830's; m. Malinda Campbell 1847; Campbellite Church; d. Barbour 1892; son of John and Sarah (Raines) Bennett; grandson of Joseph and Hannah (Ellsworth) Bennett.

BENNETT, Raleigh C.
Enl. Co. A, 168th Pa. Inf. 6-25-63; prom. to cpl.; disch. 6-28-65. Farmer; $700/390 (parents); b. York Co., Pa. 1840; m. Margaret ___; listed Barbour Union Veterans 1890; d. Harrison Co., W. Va. 193-. Son of John and Malinda (Everly) Bennett, b. Pa., settled Barbour from Preston Co., W. Va. 1850's; grandson of James and ___ (Stewart), Bennett; grandfather immigrant to Pa.

BENNETT, John W.
Enl. Co. H, 10th W. Va. Inf. 6-25-63; disch. 8-9-65. Farmer; $700/390 (parents); b. York Co., Pa. 1843, brother of Raleigh; m. 1) Mary Jane ___ 2); Amanda Wolfe; moved to Taylor Co., W. Va. after war.

BENNETT, Jacob
Elec. Justice of the Peace 1863; son *Laban and brother *James Confederate sympathizers; brother-in-law *Richard Philips Unionist. Farmer; $1,000/527; b. Barbour 1808; m. Sarah Philips 1827; d. Barbour 1882. Son of Jesse and Phoebe Bennett; grandson of Jacob and Sarah Bennett, b. Va., settled Barbour from Loudoun Co.,Va.

BIGGS, William
Arrested Barbour 7-61; escaped with aid of *William Bibey. Physician; $4,800/1,120; b. N.Y. 1821; settled Barbour 1850's with wife Lucy; moved to Mo. 1864 where living 1880. Father immigrant from England.

BISHOP, Carmichael McCurdy
Appointed U.S. Postmaster Kasson 9-30-62; brother Adam served Co. B, 17th W. Va. Inf. (USA); another brother (William?) served CSA. $0/1,700; b. Hardy Co., W. Va. 1836; Republican; m. Rachel Hanway; settled Barbour from Preston Co., W. Va. during war; listed as patient Weston Insane Asylum 1880. Son of Adam and Rebecca (Riley) Bishop, settled Hardy Co. from Allegany Co., Md., then Preston Co. 1843.

BLACK, Andrew
Enl. Bat. E, 1st W. Va. Art. 8-14-62; wd. in stomach Buckhannon, W. Va. 8-30-62; disch. 5-18-65. Farmer; $1,000/278 (parents); b. Upshur Co., W. Va. 1835; m. Sophia ____; returned to Upshur Co. 1880's where listed Union veterans 1890. Son of Thomas and Mary Ann Black, b. Va.; grandson of Samuel Black, b. Va., settled Barbour.

BLACK, George
Enl. Bat. E, 1st W. Va. Art. 8-14-62; KIA Buckhannon, W. Va. 8-30-62. Farmer; $1,000/278 (parents); b. Upshur Co., W. Va. 1842, brother of Andrew.

BLAKE, John Thomas
Enl. Co. F, 15th W. Va. Inf. 8-27-62; disch. 6-14-65. Shoemaker; $0/135; b. Harrison Co., W. Va. 1822; Methodist-Episcopal Church; settled Barbour 1850's; m. Emily Bussy 1860; moved to Calhoun Co.,W. Va. 1870's where listed Union veterans 1890; d. 1911. Son of William and Elisabeth (Reed) Blake; father b. Fauquier Co., Va.; grandparents b. Va.

BLAKE, George W.
Enl. Co. H, 12th W. Va. Inf. 8-27-62; disch. 6-16-65. Farmer; $0/42; b. Harrison Co., W. Va. 1827, brother of John; m. 1) Elisabeth ____; 2) Edith ____; widow listed Barbour Union Veterans 1890.

BOLTON, Stephen
Elec. Constable 1863; drafted 3-65, never inducted; claim for war-time service in 169th Mil. rejected 1902. Tenant; $0/161; b. Barbour 1831; Methodist-Episcopal Church; m. Martha Ellen Jones 1848; moved to Utah after 1880. Son of William and Clarinda (Jones) Bolton; father b. N.Y.; grandfather b. Conn.

BOLTON, Wesley
Enl. Co. H, 10th W. Va. Inf. 3-10-62 for two years; re-enlisted 3-15-64; disch. 8-9-65; father-in-law *Dyer Kelley served Co. K, 6th W. Va. Inf. (USA). Farmer; $1,000/534 (parents); b. Barbour 1844, brother of Stephen; Methodist-Episcopal

Church; m. Martha E. Kelley 1864; d. Barbour 1880's; widow listed Barbour Union veterans 1890.

BOLYARD, Jacob R.
Enl. Barbour Home Guard 11-10-63; listed sick with typhoid fever 4-64; disch. for disability 5-15-64. Farmer; $600/254; b. Preston Co., W. Va. 1827; Methodist-Episcopal Church; m. Christine Brooks; came to Barbour 1850's; moved to Monongalia Co., W. Va. after war where listed Union veterans 1890. Son of Stephen and Barbara (Rosier) Bolyard, b. Pa., settled Preston Co.

BOOTH, James
Elec. Overseer of Poor 1865; brother-in-law *Jacob Cox served Co. F, 15th W. Va. Inf. (USA); brother-in-law *Daniel Cox served Barbour Home Guard; brother-in-law *Henry Cox Unionist. Farmer; $800/430; b. Barbour 1816; m. 1) Malinda Yeager; 2) Susanna Cox 1863; d. Barbour 1870's. Son of James and Phoebe (Osburn) Booth; grandson of Daniel and Jean (Houston) Booth; grandfather b. Berkeley or Monongalia Co., W. Va., settled Barbour 1780's; great-grandson of James and Nancy (Stalnaker) Booth; James immigrant from England, settled Monongalia Co. from Berkeley Co. 1770's.

BOOTH, William H.
Enl. Co. F, 15th W. Va. Inf. 8-27-62; d. of typhoid fever Belington, Barbour Co. 3-10-64. Farmer; $800/430 (parents); b. Barbour 1842, son of James and Malinda (Yeager) Booth.

BOOTH, Isaac
Enl. Co. H, 10th W. Va. Inf. 5-8-62; disch. 8-9-65. Shoemaker; $0/70; b. Barbour 1825; m. Charlotte ____; d. Barbour 1877. Son of William and Debra (Hart) Booth; grandson of Daniel and Jean (Houston) Booth;

BOSWORTH, Harlan Perry
Com. Capt., 169th W. Va. Mil. 8-16-62, never called into service; drafted 2-65; never inducted. Farmer; $1,000/300 (parents); b. Barbour 1842; Presbyterian; Republican; m. Jane ____; living Barbour 1870. Son of Joshua and Fanny (Perry) Bosworth; father b. Mass.; grandson of James and Rueben Bosworth, settled Upshur Co., W. Va.

BOWMAN, Peter
Enl. Co. F, 15th W. Va. Inf. 8-27-62; KIA Berryville 9-3-64. Farm laborer; $0/0; b. Pa. 1840; son of Daniel and Mary (Bogers) Bowman, b. Pa., settled Barbour 1853; grandson of John and Elisabeth (Beeghly) Bowman.

BOWMAN, Michael
Enl. Co. F, 15th W. Va. Inf. 2-17-63; disch. 6-14-65. Farmer; $800/459 (parents); b. Pa. 1840, brother of Peter; m. Sarah Shanabarger 1865; returned to Pa. 1870's where living 1880.

BOWMAN, Moses
Enl. Co. F, 15th W. Va. Inf. 8-23-62; wd. right thigh Kernstown 7-24-64; wd. in thigh Petersburg 4-2-65; disch. 6-14-65. Farmer; $800/459 (parents); b. Pa. 1845, brother of Peter; m. Elisabeth Hovatter 1869; moved to Monongalia Co., W. Va. 1880's where listed Union veterans 1890; d. 1896.

BOWMAN, Joseph
Enl. Co. I, 6th W. Va. Inf. 10-30-63; disch. 6-30-65. Farmer; $2,500/775 (parents); b. Allegany Co., Md. 1841; m. Anna Bowman 1866; moved to Texas 1870's, then to Ok. where d. 1894. Son of Samuel and Mary (Myers) Bowman, b. Pa., settled Barbour 1850's; grandson of John and Elisabeth (Beeghly) Bowman.

BOWMAN, Cornelius
Enl. Barbour Home Guard 1-3-64 for one year; enl. Co. D, 4th Pa. Cav. 2-19-65; disch. 7-1-65. Farmer; $2,500/775 (parents); b. Somerset Co., Pa. 1843, brother of Joseph; m. Elisabeth Bowman 1866; moved to Ind. 1870's where d. 1894.

BOYLEN, John
Sympathizer; attempted to enlist in army but rejected by mustering officer as physically unfit; claim for war-time service in 169th Mil. rejected 1902. Farmer; $1,000/342; b. Barbour 1834; Methodist-Episcopal Church; Republican; m. Elisabeth Ann Reed 1862; d. Barbour 1908. Son of Abner and Margaret (Glascock) Boylen, b. Va., believed to have settled Barbour from Fauquier Co., Va.; grandfather b. Pa.

BOYLEN, Daniel
Com. Lt., 169th W. Va. Mil. 8-16-62, never called into service. Farmer; $1,000/217; b. Barbour 1835, brother of John. Methodist-Episcopal Church; m. 1) Sarah ____ ; 2) Mary A. ____ ; living Barbour 1880.

BOYLEN, Chapin
Com. Capt., 169th W. Va. Mil. 4-64, never called into service. Farmer; $10,000/1,187 (parents); b. Barbour 1841, brother of John; Methodist-Episcopal Church; m. Phoebe Robinson 1865; NFR.

BOYLES, James
Elec. Supervisor for Glade Township 1864; member District Nominating Committee Union Party 1864. Farmer; $2,000/731; b. Barbour 1808; Methodist-Episcopal Church; Republican; m. 1) Catherine Wotring; 2) Margaret Weaver 1866; d. Barbour 1872. Son of Gilbert and Eleanor (Goff) Boyles; father b. N. J., settled Barbour 1800; grandson of Charles and Ester Boyles, immigrants from Ireland.

BOYLES, Daniel
Elec. Justice of the Peace 1861; com. Capt., 169th W. Va. Mil. 8-16-62, never called into service; enl. Co. F, 15th W.Va. Inf. 8-27-62; prom. to Lt.; dismissed from the service 2-25-64; elec. Assessor 1864. Farmer; $400/50; b. Barbour 1830, son of James and Catherine (Wotring) Boyles; Methodist-Episcopal Church; Republican; m. 1) Joanna Smith 1851; 2) Hannah Sharps 1867; 3) Harriet Kittle; listed Barbour Union veterans 1890; d. Barbour 1909.

BOYLES, David A.
Enl. Co. F, 15th W.Va. Inf. 9-10-62; prom. to sgt.; wd. Kernstown 7-24-64; wd. Petersburg 3-31-65; disch. 6-14-65. Farmer; $450/260; b. Barbour 1832, brother of Daniel; Methodist-Episcopal Church; m. 1) Rebecca _____; 2) Emmuette Kelley; moved to Calhoun Co., W. Va. after war where d. 1889; widow listed Union veterans Calhoun Co. 1890.

BOYLES, Barnett B.
Enl. Co. B, 17th W.Va. Inf. 10-10-64; served as scout; disch. 6-30-65; father-in-law *John Kelley served Barbour Home Guard. Farmer; $0/430; b. Barbour 1834, brother of Daniel; Methodist-Episcopal Church; Republican; m. 1) Sarah Ann Kelley 1854; 2) Sarah Amanda Trimble 1869; listed Barbour Union veterans 1890.

BOYLES, Samuel W.
Com. Capt., 139th W. Va. Mil. 8-16-62, never called into service; enl. Co. F, 15th W.Va. Inf. 9-1-62; des. Parkersburg, W. Va. 7-10-64. Farmer; $0/125; b. Barbour 1835, brother of Daniel; Methodist-Episcopal Church; Republican; m. Delila Upton 1859; d. Barbour 1875; widow listed Barbour Union veterans 1890.

BOYLES, Andrew Coleman
Com. Capt., 139th W. Va. Mil. 11-20-62, never called into service; enl. Barbour Home Guard 3-1-64; disch. 10-9-64; re-enlisted Co. B, 17th W.Va. Inf. 10-10-64; disch. 6-30-65. Farmer; $2,000/731 (parents); b. Barbour 1838, brother of

Daniel; Methodist-Episcopal Church; m. Caroline Jones 1868; listed Barbour Union veterans 1890.

BOYLES, William H.
Enl. Co. H, 10th W.Va. Inf. 5-8-62; d. of disease 5-4-63. Farmer; $2,000/731 (parents); b. Barbour 1840, brother of Daniel; Methodist-Episcopal Church.

BOYLES, Melker Martin
Enl. Barbour Home Guard 5-15-63; disch. 10-9-64; re-enlisted Co. B, 17th W.Va Inf. 10-10-64; disch. 6-30-65. Farmer; $2,000/731; b. Barbour 1846, brother of Daniel; Methodist-Episcopal Church; m. Susan Gainer 1866; listed Barbour Union veterans 1890; d. Barbour 1915.

BOYLES, Marshall
Com. Lt., 139th W. Va. Mil. 8-16-62, never called into service; enl. Barbour Home Guard 11-10-63 for one year; father-in-law *Abraham Hershman Confederate sympathizer. Farmer; $300/123; b. Barbour 1838; Methodist-Episcopal Church; Republican; m. Mary Ann Hershman; d. Barbour 1876. Son of Charles and Lettice Ann (Nestor) Boyles; parents b. Barbour; grandson of Gilbert and Eleanor (Goff) Boyles.

BOYLES, Jaspar E.
Enl. Co. I, 6th W.Va. Inf. 11-19-61; prom. to cpl.; transf. to Co. F, 1st U.S. Cav. 11-8-62; NFR. Farmer; $3,000/636; b. Barbour 1836. Son of Richard and Agnes (Hardin) Boyles; grandson of Gilbert and Eleanor (Goff) Boyles.

BOYLES, John L.
Com. Lt., 139th W. Va. Mil. 8-16-62, never called into service. Farmer; $3,000/636 (parents); b. Barbour 1838, brother of Jaspar; m. Mary Spring; living Barbour 1880.

BRYER, David Frederick
Sympathizer; "A very active Union man." Farmer; $3,000/710; b. Fayette Co., Pa. 1826; Methodist-Episcopal Church; Republican; m. Mary Lewis 1850; d. Barbour 1899. Son of Frederick and Susanna (Cobaugh) Bryer; father b. Germany; grandson of Caspar and Rosina Bryer, immigrants from Germany.

CADE, John
Sympathizer; drafted 3-65, never inducted. Farmer; $N/G; b. Barbour 1800; m. 1) Ann____; 2) Margaret____. Son of Moses and Elisabeth (Anglin) Cade; father b. Allegany Co., Md.; grandson of Thomas Cade, settled Barbour 1790's.

CADE, William C.
Enl. Co. H, 10th W.Va. Inf. 6-1-62; wd. and erroneously listed as KIA Webster Co., W. Va. 3-26-64; disch. 6-26-65; father-in-law *Isaac Hays Unionist. $N/G; b. Barbour 1829, son of John and Ann Cade; m. Sarah Hays; listed Barbour Union veterans 1890.

CADE, Baylis
Enl. Co. H, 10th W.Va. Inf. 6-1-62; des. 8-22-62 and joined CSA. $N/G; b. Barbour 1843, brother of William; moved to Putnam Co., W. Va. after war where m. Nancy Love; post-war Baptist minister.

CAMPBELL, Reuben W.
Enl. Co. F, 15th W. Va. Inf. 8-15-62; disch. for disability Orleans Ford, Va. 2-26-63; drafted 2-65; never inducted. Farmer; $700/365; b. Pendleton Co., W. Va. 1820; Methodist-Episcopal Church; m. Elisabeth Lane 1843; moved to Upshur Co., W. Va. 1870's where listed Union veterans 1890. Son of James and Jane Campbell; father b. Berkeley Co., W. Va.; grandson of John and Ruth (Hogsdon) Campbell, Scotch-Irish immigrants, settled Frederick Co., Va.

CAMPBELL, Philip R.
Enl. Co. H, 10th W.Va. Inf. 5-8-62; d. of heart disease Barbour 3-29-63. Farmer; $700/365 (parents); b. Barbour 1846, son of Reuben and Elisabeth (Lane) Campbell.

CAMPBELL, Jacob P.
Enl. Co. F, 15th W.Va. Inf. 8-27-62; wd. Lynchburg 6-18-64; elec. Surveyor 1865. Farmer; $153/73; b. Pendleton Co., W. Va. 1831, brother of Reuben; m. Martha Moore; moved to Upshur Co., W. Va. after war where listed Union veterans 1890; d. Upshur Co. 1911.

CAMPBELL, David
Enlisted Co. H, 7th W. Va. Inf. 9-2-61; disch. for disability 4-27-62; drafted 2-65, never inducted. $N/G; b. Lewis Co., W. Va. 1837, brother of Reuben; Methodist-Episcopal Church; m. Bedy Kelley 1871; moved to Taylor Co., W. Va. after war, then to Braxton Co., W. Va. where listed Union veterans 1890.

CAMPBELL, Preston
Enl. Co. H, 7th W. Va. Inf. 9-2-61; re-enlisted 1-4-64 and prom. to sgt. and transf. to Co. D; prom. to Lt. 5-2-65 and transf. to Co. E; disch. 7-1-65. $N/G; b. Barbour 1842, brother of Reuben; Methodist-Episcopal Church; m. Ann R. Stazell 1867; moved to Kan. 1870's where living 1880.

CAMPBELL, George G.
Sympathizer; forced to flee Philippi to escape arrest 6-61. Merchant; $12,000/2,382; b. Md. 1824; came to Barbour 1845; Methodist-Episcopal Church; Democrat; m. Elisabeth A. Bryan 1854; living Barbour 1880. Son of George and Julia (Wyshan Bedford) Campbell; father immigrant from England, settled Mass., then Md., then Barbour.

CANADAY, William C.
Enl. Co. H, 10th W. Va. Inf. 5-8-62; d. of wounds 3-26-64. Farm laborer $0/0; b. Va. 1839; came to Barbour 1850's.

CAPITO, Daniel
Sympathizer; son John served Co. K, 17th W.Va. Inf. (USA); son Christian served Co. H, 17th W. Va. Inf. (USA); daughter *Helen Confederate sympathizer; son-in-law *Thompson Surghnor served Confederate army. Hotel keeper; $500/170; b. Pendleton Co., W. Va. 1802; Baptist; settled Barbour 1820's where m. Jerusha Hart 1827; d. Barbour 1870's. Son of Daniel and Nancy (Herderberg) Capito, b. Va.

CARDER, Albert G.
Enl. Co. B, 7th W.Va. Inf. 2-28-65 as substitute; disch. 7-1-65. Farmer; $3,000/563 (parents); b. Harrison Co., W. Va. 1847; moved to Doddridge Co., W. Va. after war, then to Kanawha Co., W. Va. where listed Union veterans 1890. Son of Noah and Tabitha (Bennett) Carder; father b. Taylor Co., W. Va.; grandson of Isaac and Tabitha (Bennett) Carder; great-grandson of John Carder, b. Va., settled Taylor Co.

CARPENTER, Conrad
Sympathizer; served as scout for Federal troops Laurel Hill, 7-61; step-son *John Hoffman served Co. F, 3rd W. Va. Inf. (USA); step-son *Sanford Hoffman Lt., 139th W. Va. Mil.; son-in-law *Mathew Edmonds served Co. F, 17th W. Va. Inf. (USA). Farmer; $500/246; b. Barbour 1807; m. 1) Elisabeth Harper; 2) Anna Black Hoffman 1863; moved to Upshur Co., W. Va. 1875 where d. 1891. Son of Jacob and Margaret (Borror) Carpenter; father immigrant from Switzerland.

CARPENTER, Allen
Sympathizer, assisting post-war Board of Registration; drafted 3-65, never inducted. Tenant; $0/185; b. Barbour 1834, son of Conrad and Elisabeth (Harper) Carpenter; m. Harriet Hoffman 1857; d. Barbour 1919.

CARPENTER, Ethan
Enl. Co. F, 15th W.Va. Inf. 9-1-62; wd. in left leg Lynchburg 6-18-64; disch. 6-14-65. Farmer; $300/133; b. Marion Co., W. Va. 1824; came to Barbour 1850's with wife Malinda; moved to Upshur Co., W. Va. 1870's where listed Union veterans 1890; d. Upshur Co. 1914. Son of Ashuar and Emily (Martin) Carpenter; parents and grandparents b. Va.

CARPENTER, John
Enl. Co. F, 15th W.Va. Inf. 2-17-63; disch. 6-14-65; another brother Ashuar enlisted in same company from Marion Co., W. Va. Tenant; $0/160; b. Richland Co., Ohio 1828, brother of Ethan; came to Barbour 1850's with wife Abigail; returned to Marion Co. after war where listed Union veterans 1890.

CARTER, Henry Emerson
Enl. Co. B, 10th W.Va. Inf. 3-12-63; disch. for disability; brother Thomas served in same company; brother *Page served Co. D, 20th Va. Cav. (CSA). Tenant; $0/137; b. Nelson Co., Va. 1839; Baptist, post-war minister Methodist-Episcopal Church; m. Samantha Reed 1860; moved to Upshur Co., W. Va. after war where d. 1879; widow listed Barbour Union veterans 1890. Son of Henry and Martha (Emerson) Carter, b. Nelson Co., settled Upshur Co. 1843; grandson of John and Mary S. (Damrin) Carter of Lancaster Co., Va.

CARTER, David G.
Enl. Co. D, 7th W.Va. Inf. 8-1-61; wd. in right hand; re-enlisted 1-4-64; disch. 7-1-65; brother *Charles served Co. H, 31st Va. Inf. (CSA). Farmer; $4,000/1,030 (mother); b. Page Co., Va. 1842; Baptist; m. Virginia Bartlett 1866; listed Barbour Union veterans 1890. Son of Robert and Elisabeth (Coontz) Carter, settled Barbour from Page Co. 1840's; grandson of Nathaniel Carter.

CHAMP, Jahue
Enl. Co. B, 2nd W.Va. Inf. 7-5-63; wd. in mouth near Belington, Barbour 1863; transf. to Co. K upon organization of 5th W. Va. Cav. 1-64; served Co. H, 6th W. Va. Cav. upon consolidation of regiment with 6th W. Va. Cav.; POW New Creek 11-28-64; exch. three months later; disch. Kan. 5-22-66. Apprentice mechanic; $0/0; b. Barbour 1846; m. Amelia Carpenter 1874; listed Barbour Union veterans 1890. Son of Hiram and Matilda (Wingrove) Champ; father b Barbour; grandson of John and Sarah (Borrer) Champ, b. Pendleton Co., W. Va., settled Barbour.

CHAMP, Rufus B.
Enl. Co. H, 10th W.Va. Inf. 11-15-62; disch. 7-3-65. Farm laborer; $0/0; b. Barbour 1843, brother of Jahue; m. Georgiana Ono; d. 1917.

CHAMP, Martin C.
Enl. Co. F, 15th W.Va. Inf. 8-27-62; wd. Kernstown 7-24-64; disch. 6-14-65. Tenant; $0/107; b. Barbour 1821, brother of Hiram; m. Julian Yeager 1848; listed Barbour Union veterans 1890; d. Barbour 1896.

CHAMP, Jackson
Enl. Co. F, 15th W.Va. Inf. 8-27-62; wd. in hip Lynchburg 6-18-64; disch. 6-14-65. Tenant; $0/43 (parents); b. Barbour 1844; m. Mary A. Bailey 1872; moved to Ritchie Co., W. Va. 1880's where listed Union veterans 1890. Son of Nimrod and Rachel Champ; grandson of John and Sarah (Borrer) Champ.

CHAMP, John L.
Enl. Co. F, 15th W. Va. Inf. 9-13-62; wd. in foot Cedar Creek 10-19-64; disch. 6-14-65. Tenant; $0/43 (parents); b. Barbour 1844, brother of Jackson; m. Mary C. Carpenter 1875; moved to Upshur Co., W. Va. 1880's where listed Union veterans 1890.

CHANNEL, Elias
Com. Lt., 139th W. Va. Mil. 8-16-62; never called into service; enl. Co. K, 6th W. Va. Inf. 10-2-62; disch. 6-14-65; brother Coleman served Co. H, 10th W. Va. Inf. (USA); father-in-law *Leonard Stout Unionist; brother-in-law *Henson Stout served Co. K, 6th W. Va. Inf. (USA). Tenant; $0/43; b. Randolph Co., W. Va. 1838; came to Barbour 1850's; m. Harriet Stout 1858; moved to Iowa after war where living 1880. Son of William and Mary (Skidmore) Channel; grandson of Samuel and Sarah (Hornbeck) Channel; great-grandson of Jeremiah and Nancy (Steel) Channel, settled Randolph Co. 1780's from Hardy Co., W. Va.

CHANNEL, Levi
Enl. Co. K, 6th W.Va. Inf. 10-1-62; disch. 6-30-65; step-brother *Enoch Haddix served Co. C, 17th W. Va. Inf. (USA); brother-in-law Daniel Dawson served Co. K, 1st W. Va. Cav. (USA). Farmer; $2,000/460 (parents); b. Randolph Co., W. Va. 1836; Methodist-Episcopal Church; m. 1) Martha Freeman 1863; 2) Nancy McCoy 1874; moved to Wirt Co., W. Va. 1880's where listed Union veterans 1890. Son of Jonathon and Edith (Sayers) Channel; grandson of Samuel and Sarah (Hornbeck) Channel.

CHANNEL, Sylvester
Enl. Co. K, 6th W.Va. Inf. 10-1-62; disch. 6-30-65. Farmer; $2,000/460 (parents); b. Randolph Co., W. Va. 1843, brother of Levi; Methodist-Episcopal Church; m. Marsilla Parsons 1867; moved to Tucker Co., W. Va. 1870's where listed Union veterans 1890.

CHAPMAN, James M.
Enl. Co. H, 10th W.Va. Inf. 1-22-62; disch. 5-7-62; Tenant; $0/0; b. Orange Co., Va. 1842; Baptist; m. Columbia Thrash; listed Barbour Union veterans 1890; d. Barbour 1899. Son of Walter and Hulda Chapman; came to Barbour 1850's with mother and stepfather Clement Wheland.

CHAPMAN, Alonzo
Enl. Co. E, 3rd W. Va. Cav. 10-20-62; wd.; disch. 6-30-65. Tenant; $0/0; b. Orange Co., Va. 1844, brother of James; Baptist; m. Rachel Loretta Thrash 1865; moved to Mason Co., W. Va. 1870's; d. 1880's; widow listed Barbour Union veterans 1890.

CHRISLIP, Peregrine G.
Listed Barbour Light Horse; Delegate Union Party Convention at Grafton 1864; father-in-law *Amos Marple and brother-in-law *Minter Marple served Co. H, 10th W. Va. Inf. (USA). Farmer; $3,000/865 (parents); b. Barbour 1823; Methodist-Episcopal Church; Republican; m. 1) Elisabeth Marple; 2) Barbara A. Marple 1855; moved to Lewis Co., W. Va. after war where d. 1898. Son of William and Hannah (Ward) Chrislip; father b. Pa.; grandson of Jacob and Nancy (Singer) Chrislip, immigrants from Germany.

CHRISLIP, Alvin Demosthenes
Enl. Co. H, 10th W. Va. Inf. 8-5-63; listed sick with typhoid fever 8-64; disch. 8-9-65. Farmer; $3,000/865 (grandparents); b. Barbour 1848 son of Peregrine and Elisabeth (Marple) Chrislip; Methodist-Episcopal Church; m. Mary V. Anderson 1868; moved to Lewis Co., W. Va. after war where d. 1872; widow listed Union veterans Lewis Co. 1890.

CHRISLIP, Johnson W.
Enl. Co. H, 10th W. Va. Inf. 5-8-62; prom. to sgt.; reduced to ranks 5-25-63; disch. 5-7-65. Farmer; $0/255; b. Barbour 1825, brother of Peregrine; Methodist-Episcopal Church; Republican; m. 1) Malinda Gregory 1846; 2) Mary E. J. Montgomery 1872; moved to Ritchie Co., W. Va. 1870's where living 1880.

CHRISLIP, William Turner
Com. Lt., 169th W. Va. Mil. 8-16-62, never called into service. Farmer; $3,000/865; b. Barbour 1835, brother of Peregrine; Methodist-Episcopal Church; m. Mary Catherine Lawson 1859; moved to Upshur Co., W. Va. after war where d. 1923.

CHROSTEN, Charles M.
Enl. Co. C, 17th W. Va. Inf. 9-8-64; disch. 6-30-65. Farmer; $N/G; b. Hampshire Co., W. Va. 1845; came to Barbour 1860's with wife Rachel; moved to Taylor Co., W. Va. after war; listed Barbour Union veterans 1890. Son of Charles and Mary (Isner) Chrosten, b. Hampshire Co., settled Jackson Co., W. Va. 1840's, to Barbour 1860's; grandfather b. Md.

CHROSTEN, Thomas
Drafted into Co. A, 3rd W. Va. Cav. 3-7-65; disch. 6-30-65. Farmer; $N/G; b. Hampshire Co., W. Va. 1846, brother of Charles; m. Nancy Male 1867; listed Barbour Union veterans 1890.

CLEAVENGER, Benjamin James
Listed Barbour Light Horse; com. Lt., 169th Mil. 8-16-62, never called into service; drafted 2-65, never mustered into service. Farmer; $4,000/4,092 (parents); b. Barbour 1838; Baptist; m. Minerva Jane Newlon 1864; d. Barbour 1901. Son of John and Elisabeth (Fleming) Cleavenger; father slave owner, b. Barbour; grandson of Minor and Elisabeth (Goodwin) Cleavenger; grandfather b. Frederick Co., Va., settled Barbour.

CLEAVENGER, Minor Sylvester
Enl. Co. F, 17th W.Va. Inf. 9-1-64; disch. 6-30-65. Farmer; $4,000/4,092 (parents); b. Barbour 1843, brother of Benjamin; Baptist; moved to Harrison Co., W. Va. 1870's; returned to Barbour 1880's where listed Union veterans 1890.

CLEAVENGER, George G.
Com. Capt., 169th Mil. 8-16-62; prom. to major 9-20-62; never called into service. Farmer; $1,400/3,839 (parents); b. Barbour 1844; Baptist; m. Mary C. Lake 1862; living Barbour 1880. Son of Samuel and Comfort (Goodwin) Cleavenger; father slave owner, b. Barbour; grandson of Samuel and Margaret (Ramsey) Cleavenger, settled Barbour from Frederick Co., Va. 1800.

CLINE, Augustus J.
Enl. Barbour Home Guard 11-10-63 for one year; re-enlisted 9-15-64; disch. 5-30-65. Farmer; $300/87 (parents); b. Rockingham Co., Va. 1846; Baptist; m. Margaret Jane Janes 1876; living Barbour 1880. Son of David and Mary (Minnick) Cline, b. Rockingham Co.; grandfather b. Pa.

COBERLY, William
Com. Lt., 139th W. Va. Mil. 10-20-62, never called into service; son-in-law Patrick Fallon served Union army. Farmer; $/285; b. Bath Co., Va. 1820;

German Baptist; m. Mary Wilmoth 1840; living Barbour 1870. Son of Joseph and Nancy Coberly; father b. Bath Co., settled Randolph Co., W. Va.; grandson of James and Mary (Pfaffenberg) Coberly, b. N.J.

COBERLY, Haymond
Enl. Co. F, 15th W. Va. Inf. 9-1-62; wd. in left side Snicker's Ferry 7-17-64; disch. 6-14-65. Farmer; $0/285 (parents); b. Barbour 1844, son of William and Mary (Wilmoth) Coberly; German Baptist; m. Catherine Rinehart 1868; listed Barbour Union veterans 1890.

COBURN, John H.
Enl. Bat. E, 1st W. Va. Art. 8-15-62; prom. to sgt.; disch. 6-28-65. Farmer; $4,600/708 (parents); b. Barbour 1836; Methodist-Protestant Church; Republican; moved to Ritchie Co., W. Va. 1870's, then to Lewis Co., W. Va. where listed Union veterans 1890. Son of James and Ann Marie (White) Coburn; father b. Harrison Co., W. Va.; grandson of Jonathon and Mary (Granger) Coburn.

COBURN, Marshall W.
Com. Capt., Co. H, 10th W. Va. Inf. 4-62; disch. 6-4-65. Farmer; $3,100/1,300 (parents); b. Barbour 1838; Methodist-Protestant Church; Republican; m. Columbia Arnold 1863; listed Barbour Union veterans 1890. Son of Jonathon and Mary (Evans) Coburn; grandson of Jonathon and Mary (Granger) Coburn.

COFFMAN, Solomon Jr.
Elec. Constable 1863; brother-in-law *Daniel Shomo Unionist. Farmer; $700/325; b. Greenbrier Co., W. Va. 1820; Methodist-Episcopal Church; m. Elisabeth Hays; d. Barbour 1897. Father b. Md.

COFFMAN, William
Delegate to Union Party Convention Parkersburg 1863; enl. Barbour Home Guard 11-1-64; prom. to sgt.; disch. 5-30-65; NFR; brother-in-law *Benjamin Ekis served Co. K, 6th W. Va. Inf. (USA); brother-in-law *Henry Wilson Confederate sympathizer; son-in-law *John Bryan served Co. K, 31st Va. Inf. (CSA). Farmer; $1,500/470; b. Pa. 1806; Republican; m. Elisabeth Ekis 1826.

COFFMAN, Benjamin Franklin
Enl. Co. F, 15th W. Va. Inf. 8-27-62; disch. 6-14-65. Farm laborer; $0/50; b. Barbour 1833, son of William and Elisabeth (Ekis) Coffman; m. 1) Jane Corley 1854; 2) Malinda Hovatter 1860; moved to Tucker Co., W. Va. 1870's where listed Union veterans 1890.

COFFMAN, John
Enl. Co. F, 15th W. Va. Inf. 8-27-62; disch. 6-14-65. Farmer; $1,500/470 (parents); b. Barbour 1841, brother of Benjamin; m. Sarah M. Baker 1866; moved to Harrison Co., W. Va. after war where listed Union veterans 1890.

COFFMAN, George W.
Enl. Barbour Home Guard 1-19-65; disch. 5-30-65; NFR. Farmer; $1,500/470 (parents); b. Barbour 1845, brother of Benjamin.

COFFMAN, Elijah
Enl. Co. F, 15th W. Va. Inf. 8-27-62; disch. 6-14-65. Farmer; $1,500/470 (parents); b. Barbour 1843, brother of Benjamin; m. 1) Matilda Bennett 1871; 2) Eva Poling 1881; listed Barbour Union veterans 1890.

COLE, Jesse M.
Enl. Co. C, 4th W. Va. Cav. 8-1-63; disch. 3-9-64; brother-in-law *Lee Moore served same company; brother-in-law *Enoch Sayers Unionist. Farmer; $2,000/1,101 (mother); b. Barbour 1845; Methodist-Episcopal Church; m. Sarah E. Sayers 1867; listed Barbour Union veterans 1890; d. 1926. Son of Joshua W. and Mary (Ball) Cole; mother slave owner; grandson of Joshua and Eleanor (Cole) Cole, b. Md.; great-grandson of William and Elisabeth (Hardesty) Cole, settled Loudoun Co., Va. 1799, Barbour 1812.

COLE, James Knotts
Enl. Co. D, 6th W. Va. Cav. 9-24-64 as substitute; accidentally shot Camp Remount, Md. 4-1-65; disch. 5-22-66. Farmer; $8,000/778 (parents); b. Barbour 1847; m. 1) Mary C. Shroyer 1868; 2) Florence Victoria Washborn 1876; moved to Lewis Co., W. Va. 1869 where living 1880. Son of Jesse and Elisabeth (Knotts) Cole; grandson of Joshua and Eleanor (Cole) Cole.

COLE, Joshua
Enl. Bat. H, 1st W. Va. Art. 11-28-63; disch. 4-15-64; drafted 2-62, never inducted. Farmer; $6,260/2,785 (parents); b. Taylor Co., W. Va. 1842; m. 1) Elisabeth Walden 1871; 2) Malissa Mary Bartlett 1878; living Barbour 1880. Son of William and Mary (Bartlett) Cole; father slave owner; grandson of Joshua and Eleanor (Cole) Cole.

COLE, John W.
Com. Capt., 169th W. Va. Mil. 11-4-64, never called into service. Farmer; $6,260/2,785 (parents); b. Barbour 1843, brother of Joshua; m. 1) Ann Eliza Waldren 1871; 2) Penelope ____; living Barbour 1880.

COMPTON, Greenbury A.
Elec. Assessor 1862; Committee on Recruitment 8-62; elec. County Supervisor 1863; District Committee Union Party 1864; Minister, Methodist-Protestant Church; $1,200/312; b. Va. 1816; Republican; settled Barbour from Pocahontas Co., W. Va. 1840's with wife Sarah; living Barbour 1880. Parents b. Va.

COMPTON, Fielding Stogdon
Enl. Barbour Home Guard 1-1-64; d. of typhoid fever 2-19-64. $1,200/312 (parents); b. Barbour 1845, son of Greenbury and Sarah Compton.

CONLEY, Thomas
Enl. Co. I, 6th W. Va. Inf. 11-16-61; disch. 11-25-64. Farmer; $300/125; b. Ireland 1822; Methodist-Episcopal Church; settled Barbour 1850's with wife Mary; living Barbour 1880.

CONLEY, William H.
Enl. Co. H, 10th W.Va. Inf. 11-15-62; disch. 7-3-65; NFR. Farm laborer; $0/0; b. Ireland 1838, brother of Thomas.

COOK, John M. C.
Com. Capt. 169th W. Va. Mil. 11-23-62; never called into service; drafted 2-65, never inducted. $0/175; b. Pendleton Co., W. Va. 1837; settled Barbour 1860; m. Sarah A. Talbott 1860; living Barbour 1880. Son of William and Nancy Cook; father b. Pendleton Co.; gransdson of William Cook, immigrant from England.

COONTZ, Philip
Enl. Barbour Home Barbour 9-1-63; disch. and re-enlisted Co. F, 15th W. Va. Inf. 12-29-63; KIA Lynchburg 6-20-64. Tenant; $400/100 (parents); b. Barbour 1845. Son of Adam and Emily (Thorn) Coontz; father b. Barbour; grandson of Philip and Barbara (Barnhouse) Coontz; grandfather b. Md., settled Hardy Co., W. Va., then Barbour.

COONTZ, John W.
Enl. Barbour Home Guard 11-1-63; d. of typhoid fever 3-6-64. Tenant; $400/100 (parents); b. Barbour 1847, brother of Philip.

COOPER, Jonas
Elec. County Supervisor 1863 and 1864; District Committee Union Party 1864; drafted 2-65, never inducted; brother *John listed Barbour Light Horse; father-in-law *Noah Corley served Co. H, 10th W. Va. Inf. (USA); brother-in-law

*Gideon Corley Unionist; brother-in-law William Corley served Co. C, 25th Va. Inf. (CSA); brother-in-law William Clem Confederate sympathizer. $900/400; b Hardy Co.,W.Va. 1826; m. Elisabeth Corley; moved to Upshur Co. W. Va. after war. Son of Samuel and Jane (Simon) Cooper; father b. Hardy Co.; grandson of Jeremiah Cooper, b. Hardy Co., settled Randolph Co., W. Va.

CORLEY, Noah Edwin
Scout for Federal army 7-61; enl. Co. H, 10th W. Va. Inf. 11-15-62; POW Cedar Creek 10-19-64; exch.; d. of fever Camp Parole 11-15-64; brother Alan served Co. F, 19th Va. Cav. (CSA); son William served Co. C, 25th Va. Inf. (CSA); son-in-law Abraham Limber served Co. G, 62nd Va. Mtd. Inf. (CSA); son-in-law Jackson Cooper served Co. B, 2nd W. Va. Inf. (USA); son-in-law *Jonas Cooper Unionist; son-in-law William Clem Confederate sympathizer. Farmer; $1,200/43; b. Frederick Co., Va. 1802; Methodist-Episcopal Church; m. Louisa Wilson 1825. Son of William and Caroline (Whiteman) Corley, settled Barbour 1811; father b. Ireland; grandson of Manoah and Jane (Fogg) Corley, immigrants from Ireland.

CORLEY, Gideon Camden
Scout for Federal army; POW 7-61, claiming to have been second prisoner taken in the war. Farmer; $1,200/43 (parents); b. Barbour 1840, son of Noah and Louisa (Wilson) Corley; Methodist-Episcopal Church; m. Lydia Thorn 1866; moved to Randolph Co., W. Va. after 1880 where living 1889.

CORLEY, John Marshall
Ran for State Senate 1863. Farmer; $2,500/533; b. Bath Co., Va. 1813, brother of Noah; m. Anna Marie Wilson 1843; d. Barbour 1877.

COX, Jacob
Enl. Co. F, 15th W. Va. Inf. 9-1-62; POW Cedar Creek 10-19-64; d. in prison 12-30-64; brother-in-law *James Booth Unionist. Farmer; $900/583; b. Barbour 1819; m. Susanna Boyles; widow listed Barbour Union veterans 1890. Son of William and Elisabeth (Nestor) Cox, b. Md.

COX, John William
Enl. Co. G, 3rd W. Va. Inf. 6-27-61; disch. for disability 4-17-63; enl. Barbour Home Guard 1-1-64 for one year; re-enlisted 3-10-65; disch. for disability; elec. Constable 1865; drafted 3-65, never inducted. $0/0; b. Barbour 1843; Republican; m. Virginia Hovatter 1865; d. 1860's. Son of Jacob and Susanna (Boyles) Cox.

COX, David H.
Enl. Co. G, 3rd W. Va. Inf. 6-27-61; re-enlisted 2-1-64, serving Co. B, 6th W.Va. Cav. upon consolidation of regiment with 5th W. Va. Cav; des. Fort Henry, Neb. 10-16-65. $600 (parents); b. Barbour 1845, brother of John William; m. 1) Emily Hovatter; 2) Olive Corrick; listed Barbour Union veterans 1890.

COX, Henry L.
Com. Lt., 139th W. Va. Mil. 10-17-62, never called into service; elec. Township Commissioner 1864; brother-in-law *Robert Hoffman served Barbour Home Guard; brother-in-law *Sanford Hoffman Lt., 139th W. Va. Mil.. Farmer; $400/128 (mother); b. Barbour 1827, brother of Jacob; m. Nancy Hoffman; living Barbour 1880.

COX, Daniel D.
Enl. Barbour Home Guard 1-19-65; disch. 5-30-65; NFR. Farmer; $1,500/470 (parents); b. Barbour 1845, brother of Jacob.

COZAD, John Wesley
Com. Capt., 139th W. Va. Mil. 10-16-62; never called into service. Farmer; $780/325 (parents); b. Preston Co., W. Va. 1830; Methodist-Episcopal Church; m. Catherine Ann Trisler 1863; living Barbour 1880. Son of John and Lydia (Martin) Cozad; grandson of John and Elisabeth (Skidmore) Cozad, settled Preston Co. from Pendleton Co., W. Va. 1814.

COZAD, William H. H.
Enl. Co. I, 6th W. Va. Inf. 11-19-61; prom. to cpl.; d. of consumption Cumberland, Md. 10-8-64. Farmer; $780/325; (parents); b. Barbour or Preston Co., W. Va. 1840, brother of John; Methodist-Episcopal Church.

CRESS, Caleb
Elec. Overseer of Poor 1865; brother-in-law *Eli Painter served Co. F, 15th W. Va. Inf. (USA). Farmer; $900/206; b. Barbour 1839; Methodist-Episcopal Church; m. Eliza M. Painter 1858; d. 1865. Son of Henry and Phebe (Ward) Cress, b. Va.

CRITES, Michael
Sympathizer; District Committee 1866 ensuring voting rights restrictions enforced; claim for war-time service in 169th Mil. rejected 1902; brother Elam served Co. B, 25th Va. Inf. (CSA); brother-in-law *William Haney served Bat. E, 1st W. Va. Art. (USA); brother-in-law John Riblet t served Co. D, 20th Va.

Cav. (CSA). Farmer; $5,000/895; b. Hardy Co., W. Va. 1820; Methodist-Episcopal Church; Republican; m. Ann Amelia Reeder 1840; living Barbour 1880. Son of Jonas and Catherine (McVany) Crites, b. Hardy Co.; grandson of Michael Crites, immigrant from Germany, settled Hardy Co.

CROSS, Levi
Com. Lt., 139th W. Va. Mil. 10-20-62; never called into service; enl. Co. F, 15th W. Va. Inf. 3-1-63; prom. to cpl.; wd. left hand Winchester 9-19-64; disch. 8-1-65; five brothers served Confederate army; brothers-in-law *William and *Isaac Price served Co. F, 15th W. Va. Inf. (USA); brother-in-law *Albert Price served Co. D, 20th Va. Cav. (CSA). Farmer; $400/135; b. Barbour 1836; Republican; m. Angelina Price 1856; post-war minister United Brethren Church; listed Barbour Union veterans 1890. Son of Barton and Deborah (Moore) Cross; grandson of John and Barbara (Boarer) Cross, settled Barbour from Hardy Co., W. Va.

CROUSE, George
Enl. Co. H, 10th W. Va. Inf. 5-8-62; disch. for disability 5-7-64. Farmer; $0/65; b. Va. 1806; United Brethren Church; m. Mary Lyman 1836; d. Barbour 1867. Parents b. Pa.

CROUSE, Squire
Listed Barbour Light Horse; enl. Co. H, 10th W. Va. Inf. 5-8-62; disch. 8-9-65. Farmer; $0/65 (parents); b. Barbour 1838, son of George and Mary (Lyman) Crouse; United Brethren Church; m. Rebecca Ward 1865; listed Barbour Union veterans 1890.

CROUSE, Anthony
Enl. Co. H, 10th W. Va. Inf. 7-22-62; disch. 6-28-65. Farmer; $0/65 (parents); b. Barbour 1841, brother of Squire; United Brethren Church; m. Rebecca _____; moved to Taylor Co., W. Va. 1880's where listed Union veterans 1890.

CROUSER, George W.
Enl. Co. H, 10th W. Va. Inf. 5-8-62; prom. to sgt.; reduced to ranks 11-23-64 for fleeing field at Cedar Creek; disch. 5-7-65. Tenant; $0/65; b. Barbour 1843; moved to Wirt Co., W. Va. after war where listed Union veterans 1890. Son of John and Nancy (Harris) Crouser, b. Va.; grandfather b. Pa.

CROUSER, Lafayette
Enl. Co. A, 7th W. Va. Inf. 4-1-65 as substitute; disch. Fairfax Seminary Hospital 6-3-65. Tenant, $0/90 (parents); b. Barbour 1846, brother of George

W.; m. Mariah McDougal 1870; moved to Marion Co., W. Va. after war where listed Union veterans 1890.

CROUSER, Levi
Enl. Co. M, 4th W. Va. Cav. 12-26-63; transf. to Co. G, 5th W. Va. Cav. 3-1-64; served Co. G, 6th W.Va.Cav. upon consolidation of regiment; POW New Creek 11-28-64; d. of chronic diarrhea Richmond Prison 1-15-65. Farm servant; $0/0; b. Barbour 1847, brother of George W.

CRUTCHER, Richard
Elec. Constable 1865; drafted 2-65, never inducted. $0/175; b. Ky. 1830; Methodist-Episcopal Church; m. Angeline ____; moved to Tyler Co., W. Va. after war where living 1880.

CUMMINGS, Lewis
Enl. Co. H, 10th W. Va. Inf. 5-8-62; disch. for disability 3-14-63, suffering from disease. Tenant; $0/54; b. Va. 1817; Methodist-Episcopal Church; came to Barbour 1850's with wife Mary; listed Barbour Union veterans 1890; parents b. Va.

CURRENCE, Samuel Melvin
Com. Lt., 139th W. Va. Mil. 10-20-62, never called into service; enl. Barbour Home Guard 9-1-63 for one year; brother Adam served Co. I, 3rd W. Va. Cav. (USA); brother-in-law Martin Black served Co. M, 3rd W. Va. Cav. (USA). Farmer; $N/G; b. Randolph Co., W. Va. 1830; m. Mary Jane ____; moved to Upshur Co., W. Va. after war where living 1880. Son of John and Joanna (Harris) Currence; father b. Randolph Co.; grandson of Samuel and Elisabeth (Bogard) Currence; grandfather b. Md.; great-grandson of William and Lydia (Steele) Currence; William, immigrant from Ireland, settled Md., then Randolph Co. 1774.

DALTON, Isaac
Enl. Bat. B, 9th U.S. Art. 8-10-62; disch. 10-10-64. Farmer; $3,000/563; b. Monongalia Co., W. Va. 1834; m. Elisabeth Black; listed Barbour Union veterans 1890. Son of John and Mary Dalton, b. Va., settled Barbour from Monongalia Co.; grandparents b. Md.

DANFORTH, A.W.
Appointed U.S. Postmaster Belington 1-11-65. $500/100; b. Ohio 1828; came to Barbour during war with wife Laura; d. Barbour 1866.

DAUGHERTY, Jacob A.
Enl. Co. N, 6th W. Va. Inf. 10-5-64; disch. 6-30-65; claim for war-time service in 169th Mil. rejected 1902; brother *William served Barbour Light Horse and arrested 1863 as hostage for *James Trayhern. Farmer; $1,200/630; b. Rockingham Co., Va. 1832; came to Barbour 1840's; m. 1) Jane Pittman; 2) Jane Freeman; 3) Jane Workman; listed Barbour Union veterans 1890. Son of Joshua and Hannah (Turkeyheim) Daugherty, b. Va.; grandson of John and Elisabeth (Bryer) Daugherty; grandfather immigrant from Ireland, settled Rockingham Co.

DAVISSON, Alexander Herron
Delegate Union Party Convention, Parkersburg 1863. Farmer; $5,000/365; b. Barbour 1817; Methodist-Episcopal Church; m. 1) Matilda Reed Hite 1838; 2) Susan Griffith; moved to Ill. after war. Son of Jesse and Nancy (McIntosh) Davisson; father b. Rockingham Co., Va., settled Barbour; grandson of Josiah and Edith (Herron) Davisson, b. Rockingham Co.; great-grandson of Daniel and Phoebe (Harrison) Davisson, b. N.J., settled Rockingham Co.

DAYTON, Spencer
Delegate, First and Second Wheeling Conventions, 1861; Committee on Recruitment 8-62; County Union Party Central Committee 2-63; elec. Prosecuting Attorney 1863; Delegate Union Party Convention, Parkersburg 1863 and Grafton 1864; five brothers in Union army, among them Lewis, served Co. D, 11th Conn. Inf., KIA at Antietam. Attorney; $12,000/840; b. Litchfield Co., Conn. 1820; came to Barbour 1847; Republican; m. Sarah Bush Barrett 1849; living Barbour 1880. Son of Henry and Lavina (Calver) Dayton; grandson of Justice and Hannah Dayton.

DAYTON, Charles
Enl. Co. K, 6th W. Va. Inf. 8-20-62; disch. 6-30-65. Farmer; $0/74; b. Litchfield Co., Conn. 1823, brother of Spencer; came to Barbour 1850's with parents and wife Ruhama; Republican; listed Barbour Union veterans 1890.

DENNISON, Jeremiah L.
Drafted Co. K, 17th W. Va. Inf. 2-20-65; prom. to cpl.; disch. 6-30-65. $900 (parents); b. Preston Co., W. Va. 1831; m. 1) Fanny A. Woodard 1853; 2) Mary Rebecca Woodford 1865; listed Barbour Union veterans 1890. Son of James and Nancy (Leach) Dennison; father b. Ireland, settled Preston Co., then Barbour 1840's.

DENNISON, John H.
Enl. Co. B, 2nd W. Va. Inf. 5-25-61; wd. Second Bull Run 8-28-62; disch. 6-4-64. $300/125; b. Barbour 1843, brother of Jeremiah; married Reason ____;

moved to Lewis Co., W. Va. after war where living 1880.

DOUGLAS, John
Elec. Justice of the Peace 1863 and 1865. Farmer; $8,000/1,957; b. Harrison Co., W. Va. 1807; m. Elisabeth Lance; d. Barbour 1874. Son of Levi and Nancy (Haly) Douglas; father b. Harrison Co.; grandson of Levi and Nancy Ann (Merrick) Douglas; grandfather b. Md., settled Harrison Co. 1770's.

DOUGLAS, Simington Clark
Com. Lt., 169th W. Va. Mil. 12-24-64, never called into service. Farmer; $6,000/2,470 (parents); b. Barbour 1845; Methodist-Protestant Church; m. Mary Dickenson 1867; living Barbour 1880. Son of William and Mary (Nutter) Douglas; grandson of Levi and Nancy Ann (Merrick) Douglas.

DOUGLAS, Josiah
Sympathizer, assisting post-war Board of Registration. Tenant; $0/163; b. Harrison Co., W. Va. 1830; came to Barbour 1850's where m. Eleanor Swick 1858; moved to Upshur Co., W. Va. after war where living 1880. Son of _____ and Hannah Douglas; parents b. Va.

DUCKWORTH, Thomas J.
Enl. Co. F, 15th W. Va. Inf. 9-1-62; prom. to cpl.; disc. 6-14-65. Farmer; $1,200/252 (parents); b. Allegany Co., Md. 1836; m. 1) Eliza Ann Mitchell 1871; 2) Mary Ann Poling 1874; d. Barbour 1874. Son of George and Rachel (Kittle) Duckworth, b. Md., settled Barbour; grandson of Henry and Abigail (Tichnell) Duckworth, b. N.J.

DUCKWORTH, Ephraim B.
Enl. Co. F, 3rd W. Va. Inf. 6-25-61; re-enlisted 9-23-64, serving Co. D, 6th W.Va. Cav. upon consolidation of regiment with 5th W. Va. Cav.; disch. 5-19-65. Farmer; $1,200/252 (parents); b. Allegany Co., Md., 1843, brother of Thomas J.; m. Mary Melissa Hathaway 1868; moved to Braxton Co., W. Va. 1878 where listed Union army veterans 1890.

DUCKWORTH, Nathaniel
Com. Lt., 169th W. Va. Militia 8-16-62, never called into service; drafted 3-65, never inducted. Farmer; $3,000/638 (parents); b. Allegany Co., Md. 1835; living Barbour 1880. Son of William and Mary Jane (McGear) Duckworth, b. Md., settled Barbour; grandson of Henry and Abigail (Tichnell) Duckworth.

DUCKWORTH, James H.
Enl. Co. F, 15th W. Va. Inf. 9-2-62; disch. 6-14-65; father-in-law *Josiah Hawkins Unionist; brother-in-law *Leroy Hawkins served Co. N, 6th W. Va. Inf. (USA). Farmer; $3,000/638 (parents); b. Allegany Co., Md. 1838, brother of Nathaniel; m. 1) Mary Hawkins 1860; 2) Mary Royse 1874; listed Barbour Union veterans 1890.

DUCKWORTH, Moses T.
Enl. Co. F, 15th W. Va. Inf. 9-10-62; disch. 6-14-65. Farmer; $3,000/638 (parents); b. Allegany Co., Md. 1842, brother of Nathaniel; m. Anna Haddix 1869; living Barbour 1880.

DUCKWORTH, Lemuel
Enl. Co. M, 4th W. Va. Cav. 12-23-63 for six months; transf. to Co. L, 5th W. Va. Cav. 3-1-64, serving Co. G upon consolidation of regiment with 6th W.Va. Cav; POW New Creek 11-28-64; d. of chronic colitis Richmond Prison 2-4-65. Farmer; $3,000/638 (parents); b. Allegany Co., Md. 1844, brother of Nathaniel.

EDMUNDS, Mathew
Enl. Barbour Home Guards 9-1-63; "left company in consequence of being dismounted;" elec. Overseer of Ppoor 1864; enl. Co. F, 17th W.Va. Inf. 9-25-64; disch. 6-30-65; brother John served Co. E, 31st Va. Inf. (CSA), KIA Fort Stedman; father-in-law *Conrad Carpenter Unionist. Tenant; $0/26; b. Highland Co., Va. 1833; came to Barbour 1850's; m. Hannah Carpenter 1857; listed Barbour Union veterans 1890; d. Barbour 1905. Son of Samuel and Jane Edmunds, b. Bath Co., Va.; grandson of Thomas Edmunds, immigrant from England, settled Highland Co.

EDMUNDS, William
Enl. Co. H, 10th W. Va.. Inf. 5-8-62; disch. 5-7-65. Farm laborer; $0/0; b. Pendleton Co., W. Va. 1842, brother of Mathew; m. Delila Ware 1865; listed Barbour Union veterans 1890.

EKIS, Benjamin
Enl. Co. K, 6th W. Va. Inf. 10-1-61; disch. 12-24-64; brother-in-law *William Coffman served Barbour Home Guard; brother-in-law *Henry Wilson, Confederate sympathizer, killed 1-3-63; brother-in-law *Almander Watkins served Co. F, 15th W. Va. Inf. (USA). Farmer; $1,000/251; b. Md. 1816; m. Marian Hardin; d. Barbour 1879. Son of Peter of Barbara Ekis.

EKIS, Larkin D.
Enl. Co. H, 10th W. Va. Inf. 5-8-62; wd. in chest Cedar Creek 10-19-64; d. Baltimore Hospital 12-13-64. Farmer; $1,000/251 (parents); b. Md. 1839, son of Benjamin and Marian (Hardin) Ekis.

EKIS, Josiah Henry
Enl. Barbour Home Guard 11-7-64; disch. 5-30-65. Farmer; $1,200/251 (parents); b. Md. 1845, brother of Larkin; Republican; m. Sarah Miller 1872; d. Barbour 1923.

ELLIOTT, James
Enl. Barbour Home Guard 3-6-65; disch. 5-30-65; NFR. $N/G; b. White Co., Ga. 1844; came to Barbour during war; m. Lucy Streets 1865. Son of Thomas and Malinda Elliott.

ENGLAND, John Sr.
Enl. Barbour Home Guard 1-25-64; prom. to sgt.; disch. 5-30-65; Farmer; $4,000/1,340; b. Barbour 1803; m. Sarah Boylen; d. 1870's. Son of James and Jane (Hunt) England, b. Pa.; grandson of James and Elisabeth England, b. Pa., settled Barbour 1787.

ENGLAND, Jaspar
Enl. Co. F, 15th W. Va. Inf. 5-1-63; disch. 8-9-65. Farmer; $4,000/1,340 (parents); b. Barbour 1840, son of John and Sarah (Boylen) England; m. Sarah Kines 1866; listed Barbour Union veterans 1890.

ENGLAND, David
Sympathizer, assisting post-war Board of Registration. Tenant; $0/125; b. Barbour 1819; m. Margaret Skidmore 1835; living Barbour 1880. Son of Henry and Mary (Alexander) England; grandson of James and Elisabeth England.

ENGLAND, John W.
Com. Capt., 139th W. Va. Mil. 10-24-62, never called into service; enl. Barbour Home Guard 9-1-63 for one year. Farmer; $1,000/197 (parents); b. Barbour 1842; Methodist-Protestant Church; m. Malinda Wolf 1868; living Barbour 1880. Son of Archibald and Mary (Nestor) England; parents b. Barbour; grandson of John and Sarah (Ryan) England; great-grandson of Henry and Elisabeth (Nestor) England, b. Pa., settled Barbour 1787.

FARRENCE, Elam
Enl. Co. F, 15th W. Va. Inf. 9-17-63; prom. to cpl.; disch. 6-14-65; brother Granville served Co. E, 12th W. Va. Inf. (USA). $N/G; b. Harrison Co., W. Va. 1845; m. Mary Haddix 1869; listed Barbour Union veterans 1890. Son of Abner and Elisabeth Farrence; grandson of Henry and Elisabeth (Lewis) Farrence; grandfather b. Frederick Co., Md., settled Harrison Co.

FELTON, Daniel
Elec. Justice of the Peace 1863; brother Henry served Co. F, 6th W. Va. Inf., killed in train accident at end of war; father-in-law *John England served Barbour Home Guard. Farmer; $5,000/1,500; b. Allegany Co., Md. 1805; Methodist-Episcopal Church; Republican; m. Lucinda England 1856; d. Barbour 1894. Son of John and Mary (McHenry) Felton; father b. Allegany Co., Md., settled Preston Co., W. Va. 1808; grandson of John Felton, immigrant from England, settled Md. 1759.

FISHER, Bernard W.
Enl. Co. C, 7th W.Va. Inf. 9-2-61; re-enlisted 1-4-64; wd. in left leg Cold Harbor 6-30-64; disch. and re-enlisted Co. K, 6th W. Va. Inf. 2-15-65; disch. 7-1-65; brother-in-law *Edgar Elliott served Co. D, 20th Va. Cav. (CSA). Miller; $1,200/680; b. Augusta Co., Va. 1841; m. Mary L. Hill 1865; moved to Tucker Co., W. Va. 1870's where listed Union veterans 1890. Son of Isaac and Catherine (Myers) Fisher; father b. Augusta Co.; grandson of William Fisher, b. Orange Co., Va.; great-grandson of Adam Fisher, immigrant from Germany.

FORD, Frederick George Washington
Enl. Co. F, 15th W. Va. Inf. 8-27-62; com. Lt.; field report by regimental commander on battle of Cedar Creek stated "Among the officers who performed their duty faithfully that day was Lt. F.G. Ford;" prom. to Capt. 1-18-65; disch. 6-14-65; brother Dabney served 6th W. Va. Inf. (USA); brother-in-law *Basil Hovatter served Co. F, 15th W. Va. Inf. (USA). Farmer; $350/80; b. Hardy Co., W. Va. 1834; Methodist-Episcopal Church; Republican; came to Barbour 1840's from Preston Co., W. Va.; m. Jemima Hebb 1856; post-war minister and sheriff, Preston Co. where listed Union veterans 1890; d. Preston Co. 1921. Son of Frederick and Nancy (Williams) Ford; grandson of Dabney Ford, b. Albemarle Co., Va., settled Preston Co., W. Va.

FOSTER, John H.
Enl. Co. H, 10th W. Va. Inf. 5-8-62; prom. to cpl.; reduced to ranks 2-63; POW Cedar Creek 10-19-64; d. of chronic constipation Salisbury Prison, N.C. 12-2-64;

son-in-law Joseph Norris served Co. B, 6th W. Va. Inf. (USA). Farmer; $0/130; b. Rockingham Co., Va. 1800; Methodist-Episcopal Church; m. 1)____; 2) Frances Fisher 1846; settled Barbour 1850's.

FOSTER, John Z. Thomas
Drafted Co. E, 7th W. Va. Inf. 4-1-65; disch. 7-1-65. Farmer; $0/130 (parents); b. Rockingham Co., Va. 1848, son of John and Frances (Fisher) Foster; Methodist-Episcopal Church; m. Vandelia Townsend 1867; d. Barbour 1936.

FOY, David
Elec. Constable 1863. Farmer; $0/100; b. Lewis Co., W. Va. 1830; m. 1) Sophia Teter 1854; 2) Elisabeth O. McCauley 1873; living Barbour 1880. Son of John Foy and Barbara Crites; father b. Md.

FREEMAN, James Davenport
Enl. Co. F, 15th W. Va. Inf. 8-23-62; lost right eye and leg Winchester 9-19-64; brother-in-law *John Kines served same company. Tenant; $0/161; b. Fauquier Co., Va. 1832; m. Cynthia Ann Kines 1858; listed Barbour Union veterans 1890. Son of James and Frances (Hill) Freeman; parents and grandparents b. Va.

FRY, George
Waggoner, Union army; Delegate Union Party Convention, Grafton, 1864; son-in-law *Sanford Hoffman Major, 139th W. Va. Mil. Tenant; $0/65; b. Rockbridge Co., Va. 1810; Methodist-Protestant Church; Republican; m. Jemima Ingram 1830; settled Barbour 1843; living Barbour 1880. Father b. Pa.

FRY, Alexander
Enl. Co. K, 17th W. Va. Inf. 2-15-65; prom. to cpl.; disch. 6-30-65. Tenant; $0/225; b. Rockbridge Co., Va. 1827, son of George and Jemima (Ingram) Fry; Methodist-Protestant Church; m. Nancy ____; moved to Wood Co., W. Va. after war where listed Union veterans 1890.

FRY, James W.
Enl. Barbour Home Guard 2-15-64; disch. 5-30-65; drafted 3-65, never inducted; brother-in-law *John Hoffman served Co. F, 3rd W. Va. Inf. (USA); brother-in-law *James Stemple served Co. K, 31st Va. Inf. (CSA). Tenant; $0/50; b. Rockbridge Co., Va. 1834, brother of Alexander; m. Julie Ann Hoffman 1857; living Barbour 1880.

FRY, Thomas H.
Enl. Barbour Home Guard 1-1-64; disch. 5-15-64. Tenant; $0/65 (parents); b. Rockbridge Co., Va. 1836, brother of Alexander; Methodist-Episcopal Church; m. Margaret Graham 1853; living Barbour 1880.

FRY, George W.
Enl. Barbour Home Guard 11-10-63 for one year. Tenant; $0/65 (parents); b. Barbour 1846, brother of Alexander; Methodist-Protestant Church; m. Arminda Nestor 1874; living Barbour 1880.

FURR, Abraham
Enl. Co. H, 10th W. Va. Inf. 5-8-62 at personal request of regimental commander; served as waggoner; disch. for disability 5-21-65; son-in-law *James Paugh served same company. Tenant; $0/58; b. Barbour 1820; m. Barbara Pifer 1840; d. 1870's. Son of John and Susannah (Martin) Furr, settled Barbour from Shenandoah Valley.

FURR, John M.
Enl. Co. D, 6th W. Va. Inf. 3-29-64; disch. 6-10-65; father-in-law *Wellington Hickman served Barbour Light Horse; brothers-in-law *John and *Marshall Harvey served Co. D, 20th Va. Cav. (CSA). Tenant; $0/52; b. Lewis Co., W. Va. 1840, son of Abraham and Barbara (Pifer) Furr; m. 1) Elisabeth Hickman 1858; 2) Mary Jane Harvey 1863; moved to Harrison Co., W. Va. after war where listed Union veterans 1890.

FURR, Francis Marion
Enl. Co. H, 10th W. Va. Inf. 5-8-62; disch. 5-7-65; brother-in-law *James Paugh served same company. Tenant; $0/52; b. Barbour 1844, brother of John M.; m. Mary Jane Hickman 1869; listed Barbour Union veterans 1890.

GALL, George William
Elec. County Supervisor 1863 and 1864; brothers *Andrew, *Burton and *Lafayette served Confederate army; brothers-in-law *John Talbott, *Robert Talbott and *Jacob Shank Confederate sympathizers. Farmer; $2,500/1,131; b. Pendleton Co., W. Va. 1829; Methodist-Episcopal Church; came to Barbour 1832; Republican; m. Elisabeth Talbott 1840; d. Barbour 1915. Son of John and Margaret (Arbogast) Gall; father b. Rockbridge Co., Va.; grandson of George and Susanna (Nicolas) Gall, b. Rockbridge Co.; great-grandfather immigrant from Germany to Pa., settled Va.

GALL Gustavus Hale
Com. Lt., 169th W. Va. Mil. 11-22-62; prom. to Capt; never called into service; drafted 2-65, never inducted; brother-in-law *Elias Leach served Union army. Farmer; $2,500/1,131 (parents); b. Barbour 1843, son of George and Elisabeth (Talbott) Gall; Methodist-Episcopal Church; m. 1) Martha Leach 1860; 2) Cynthia Jane Saffel 1881; 3) Sarah Henderson 1893.

GEORGE, James Warren
Com. Lt., 169th W. Va. Mil. 8-16-62, never called into service; enl. Co. F, 15th W. Va. Inf. 9-10-62; wd. Kernstown 7-24-64; discharged 6-14-65; elec. Justice of the Peace 1865; brothers-in-law *Noah, *John and *David Sipe served Union army. Farmer; $0/71; b. Barbour 1839; Methodist-Episcopal Church; m. Mary Sipe 1858; moved "West" 1870's. Son of Samuel and Elisabeth (Werner) George, b. Pendleton Co. W. Va.; grandson of Reuben George, b. Culpepper Co., Va.

GEORGE, John Randolph
Enl. Co. B, 2nd W. Va. Inf. 5-21-61; transf. to Co. K upon organization of 5th W. Va. Cav. 1-64; re-enlisted 1-5-64, serving Co. H, 6th W. Va. Cav. upon consolidation of regiment with 6th W. Va. Cav.; POW New Creek 11-28-64; prom. to cpl. 9-1-65; disch. 3-25-66. Farmer; $200/80 (mother); b. Barbour 1841, brother of James W.; Methodist-Episcopal Church; m. 1) Gatura Taylor; 2) Eliza C. Carpenter 1875; 3) Sarah Anderson; d. Barbour 1881; widow listed Barbour Union veterans 1890.

GEORGE, Samuel
Enl. Co. H, 7th W. Va. Inf. 9-2-61; des. 1862; NFR. Miller; $0/117; b. Ill. 1819; United Brethren Church; m. Rebecca Brown; came to Barbour 1850's.

GEORGE, William Marion
Com. Lt., 169th Mil.; never called into service; father-in-law *James Ward Unionist. $0/117 (parents); b. 1842, son of Samuel and Rebecca (Brown) George; United Brethren Church; m. Elisabeth Ward 1863; moved to Tucker Co., W. Va.

GLASCOCK, Joshua
Elec. Constable 1863; District Committee, Union Party 1863; sister *Elisabeth Wood Unionist; son-in-law *Cyrus Robinson served Co. F, 15th W. Va. Inf. (USA). Farmer; $7,000/450; b. Fauquier Co., Va. 1801; Republican; m. 1) Polly Booth 1822; 2) Mary Estelle Hathaway; d. Barbour 1881. Son of William and Alsie (Cole) Glascock, b. Fauquier Co., settled Barbour; grandson of Thomas and Agnes (Rector) Glascock, b. Fauquier Co.

GLASCOCK, Hansford
Elec. County Supervisor 1865; drafted 2-65, never inducted. Farmer; $7,000/450 (parents); b. Barbour 1832, son of Joshua and Polly (Booth) Glascock; Republican; living Barbour 1880.

GLASCOCK, John Spencer
Elec. Sheriff 1863. Farmer; $5,000/580; b. Barbour 1815, brother of Joshua; m. Pheobe Ann Cochran 1834; moved to Taylor Co., W. Va. 1870's where living 1880.

GLASCOCK, Job H.
Com. Capt., 139th W. Va. Mil. 10-17-62, never called into service; elec. Constable 1863 and 1865; delegate to Union Party convention, Grafton 1864; drafted 3-65, never inducted. Farmer; $5,000/580 (parents); b. Barbour 1840, son of Spencer and Pheobe (Cochran) Glascock; Republican; m. Virginia Ann Chrislip 1864; living Barbour 1880.

GLASCOCK, William H.
Enl. Co. H, 10th W. Va. Inf. 5-8-62; disch. 5-7-65. Farmer; $5,000/580 (parents); b. Barbour 1843, brother of Job H.; m. Martha Barron 1864; moved to Tucker Co., W. Va. 1870's where living 1880.

GOODWIN, Samuel
Com. Capt., 169th Mil.; never called into service; brother William served 13th W. Va. Inf. (USA). Farmer; $3,440/275; b. Harrison Co., W. Va. 1836; Methodist-Episcopal Church; m. 1) Jane Harrison 1853; 2) Malinda Cole 1863; came to Barbour during war; moved to Lewis Co., W. Va. 1870's where living 1880. Son of George and Ingaby (Bartlett) Goodwin, b. Harrison Co.; grandson of John and Elisabeth (Wells) Goodwin; grandfather b. Montgomery Co., Md., settled Harrison Co.

GRANT, Edward Francis
Elec. Justice of the Peace 1861; brother William Delegate, First Wheeling Convention and surgeon 9th W. Va. Inf. (USA). Mechanic; $1,350/275; b. Harrison Co., W. Va. 1812; came to Barbour 1840's; Baptist; Republican; m. 1) Amanda Bartlett 1839; 2) Elgintine Jarvis 1846; 3) Lydia Skidmore 1861; d. Barbour 1880. Son of Chapman and Mary (Jett) Grant, b. Culpepper Co., settled Barbour 1806.

GRANT, Granville A.
Enl. Co. F, 7th W. Va. Inf. 4-7-65; disch. 7-1-65; $1,350/275 (parents); b.

Barbour 1847, son of Edward and Elgintine (Jarvis) Grant; Baptist; listed Barbour Union veterans 1890.

GREATHOUSE, John
Enl. Co. B, 14th W. Va. Inf. 8-25-62; disch. 6-26-65. Laborer; $0/0; born Preston Co., W. Va. 1839; came to Barbour 1850's; returned to Preston Co. where listed Union veterans 1890. Son of William and Eunice (Zweyer) Greathouse, b. Pa.

GRIFFITH, Hiram
Enl. Co. K, 17th W. Va. Inf. 2-16-65; disch. 6-30-65. Tenant; $0/50; b. Augusta Co., Va. 1842; came to Barbour 1840's; m. 1) Susan _____; 2) Elisabeth Trayhern 1869; d. Barbour 1876. Son of Caleb and Mary Griffith; father b. Augusta Co.; grandson of Abel and Magdelena (Johnston) Griffith; grandfather immigrant from England, settled Augusta Co.

GROVES, Charles M.
Elec. Constable 1861; com. Capt., 139th W. Va. Mil. 8-16-62, never called into service; enl. Co. F, 15th W. Va. Inf. 8-27-62; prom. to sgt.; prom. to Lt. 1-27-65; disch. 6-14-65; brothers-in-law *James, *Oliver and *Abel Teter served same company; father-in-law *Jacob Teter Confederate sympathizer. Farmer; $350/108; b. Rappahannock Co., Va. 1833; came to Barbour 1850's; Republican; m. Margaret Teter; moved to Upshur Co., W. Va. 1870's where listed Union veterans 1890; d. Upshur Co. 1917. Son of John and Elisabeth (Grant) Groves, b.Va.

HADDIX, Isaac
Enl. Co. B, 17th W. Va. Inf. 8-30-64; disch. 6-30-65; brother-in-law *Nathan McDaniel served same company; brothers-in-law Daniel and Reuben Dillon served Co. B, 2nd W. Va. Inf. (USA). Farmer; $N/G; b. Barbour 1830; m. 1) Malinda Weaver 1847; 2) Elisabeth Dillon 1862; moved to Taylor Co, W. Va. after war where d. 1860's. Son of Adam and Mary (Willet) Haddix; grandson of William and Catherine (Minear) Haddix; grandfather settled Barbour from Fauquier Co., Va.; great-grandson of John and Mary (Taylor) Haddix, b. Fauquier Co..

HADDIX, Elam
Enl. Co. L, 1st W. Va. Cav. as substitute 1-27-65; disch. 7-8-65. Farmer; $N/G; b. Barbour 1849, son of Isaac and Malinda (Weaver) Haddix; m. Lucy McDaniel 1867; NFR.

HADDIX, William
Enl. Co. F, 15th W. Va. Inf. 9-2-62; KIA Kernstown 7-24-64. Tenant; $0/46; b.

Barbour 1834, brother of Isaac; Methodist-Episcopal Church; m. Sarah Moats; widow listed Barbour Union veterans 1890.

HADDIX, Harvey
Enl. Co. H, 12th W. Va. Inf. 8-27-62; cited for bravery for capturing guerrillas near Strasburg, Va. 4-63; KIA Petersburg 4-2-65; brother-in-law Hiram Boner served Co. B, 17th W. Va. Inf. (USA). Farmer; $300/70 (parents); b. Ill. 1839; came to Barbour 1840's. Son of Samuel and Sarah (Poling) Haddix, b. Barbour; grandson of Adam and Sarah (Willet) Haddix.

HADDIX, Adam
Enl. Co. F, 15th W. Va. Inf. 2-17-63; disch. 6-14-65. Tenant; $300/70 (parents); b. Barbour 1845, brother of Harvey; m. Fanny Sinclair 1867; moved to Ritchie Co., W. Va. 1870's; d. 1880's; widow listed Gilmer Co., W. Va. Union veterans 1890.

HADDIX, Philip
Enl. Co. L, 1st W. Va. Cav. 2-3-65; disch. 7-8-65. Farmer; $300/70 (parents); b. Barbour 1846, brother of Harvey; m. Debra Watkins 1869; moved to Preston Co., W. Va. after war where living 1880.

HADDIX, Enoch
Enl. Co. C, 17th W. Va. Inf. 9-24-64; disch. 6-30-65; step-brothers *Levi and *Sylvester Channel served Co. K, 6th W. Va. Inf. (USA); brother-in-law *Elam Weaver served Co. K, 17th W. Va. Inf. (USA). Farmer; $400/45; b. Barbour 1848; m. Matilda Channell 1866; moved to Tucker Co., W. Va. after war where listed Union veterans 1890. Son of John and Elisabeth (Reed) Haddix; grandson of Adam and Mary (Willet) Haddix.

HADDIX, Samuel
Com. Lt., 169th W. Va. Mil. 10-24-62, never called into service; enl. Co. B, 17th W. Va. Inf. 8-30-64; disch. 6-30-65. Farmer; $150/224; b. Barbour 1830; Republican; m. Mary Jane Kennedy; moved to Ritchie Co., W. Va. 1870's where living 1880. Son of Philip and Isabel (Hewey) Haddix; grandson of William and Mary (Minear) Haddix.

HADDIX, Allen P.
Enl. Co. F, 15th W. Va. Inf. 8-23-62; disch. 6-14-65; brother-in-law *Josiah Hawkins Unionist; brother-in-law Orson Duckworth served Co. A, 14th W. Va. Inf. (USA). Farmer; $700/262; b. Barbour 1834, brother of Samuel; m. Nancy H. Duckworth 1854; listed Barbour Union veterans 1890.

HALL, Stephen
Com. Lt., Co. C, 21st W. Va. Mil., called into service 10-64; brother *William Lt., Co. D, 20th Va. Cav. (CSA); brother-in-law George Morris served 25th Va. Inf. and 62nd Va. Mtd. Inf. (CSA). Farmer; $5,000/2,055; b. Barbour 1823; m. 1) Mary McPherson 1844; 2) Cynthia Ann Morris 1863; moved to Harrison Co., W. Va. during war where living 1880. Son of Lewis and Rachel (Johnson) Hall; father b. Pendleton Co., W. Va.; grandson of John and Elisabeth (Gregg) Hall; great-grandson of Thomas and Elisabeth (Dickenson) Hall; Thomas b. Md., settled Barbour.

HALL, William K.
Attended "Shoe Shop" meeting at Myers store, 5-61; Superintendant of Elections 2-63; elec. County Supervisor 1863. Mechanic; $0/125; b. Va. 1795; Methodist-Episcopal Church; Republican; m. Elisabeth Simpson; came to Barbour 1840's; living Barbour 1880. Parents b. Va.

HALLER, Michael Theodore
Com. Capt., 139th W. Va. Mil. 8-16-62, never called into service; enl. Barbour Home Guard 10-13-63; com. Capt., 12-21-63; County Union Party Committee 1863; District Union Party Committee 1864; drafted 3-65, never inducted; KIA Holsberry Farm, Barbour Co. 4-24-65; described as "A man of excellent mind and a great reader and due to the habit of reading was a man of superior education in the county;" brother-in-law *Andrew Nestor served Barbour Home Guard. Farmer; $600/279; b. Barbour 1824; United Brethren Church; Republican; m. Sarah Nestor 1844. Son of Godfrey and Catherine Haller, b. Frederick Co., Md.; grandson of George and Catherine (Ragburn) Haller; great-grandson of William Haller, immigrant from Germany, settled Frederick Co.

HALLER, Elias Francis Marion
Enl. Barbour Home Guard 9-14-64; disch. 5-30-65; brother-in-law *Andrew Nestor served same company. Farmer; $126/84; b. Barbour 1834, brother of Michael; United Brethren Church; Republican; m. Catherine Nestor 1854; d. Barbour 1915.

HAMILTON, Samuel L.
Enl. Co. D, 6th W. Va. Inf. 8-20-61; re-enlisted 3-29-64; disch. 6-30-65; brother Adolpheus served U.S. Army. Farmer; $0/279; b. Monongalia Co., W. Va. 1833; came to Barbour 1850's; m. 1) Susan A. Gainer; 2) Elisabeth Gainer 1857; moved to Taylor Co., W. Va. after war where living 1880. Son of John and Matilda (Costolo) Hamilton; father b. Pa.; grandson of Robert and Sarah (Brocks) Hamilton; grandfather immigrant from Ireland, settled Pa., then Monongalia Co.

HANEY, William F.
Enl. Bat. E, 1st W. Va. Art. 8-15-62; POW Buckhannon 8-30-62; paroled 9-62; disch. 6-28-65; brother-in-law *Michael Crites Unionist; brother-in-law Elam Crites served Co. B, 25th Va. Inf. (CSA). Tenant; $800/108; b. Harrison Co., W. Va. 1833; came to Barbour 1850's; m. Barbara Crites 1852; moved to Randolph Co., W. Va. after war where listed Union veterans 1890; moved to Marion Co., W. Va. where living 1907. Son of John M. and Ann (Poling) Haney; father immigrant from Scotland, settled Augusta Co., Va., then Harrison Co.

HANLINE, John W.
Enl. Co. H, 12th W. Va. Inf. 8-27-62; disch. 6-16-65; brothers-in-law *Benjamin, *William and *Charles Harvey served U.S. Army. Farmer; $1,000/173; b. Hardy Co., W. Va. 1827; m. Sarah Harvey 1848; came to Barbour from Md. in 1850's; d. 1865. Son of Martin and Rebecca (Hays) Hanline; father b. Hardy Co.; grandson of Samuel and Elinor Hanline; grandfather b. Md.

HARDIN, Nestor Jr.
Teamster, U.S. Army; "I am a Union man, soul, body and breeches!"; brother-in-law *Holsberry Stalnaker Unionist. Farmer; $2,600/1,649; b. Barbour 1806; Republican; m. Margaret Stalnaker 1847; d. Barbour 1884. Son of Nestor and Catherine (Hardin) Hardin, b. Fayette Co., Pa., settled Barbour; grandson of John and Isabella Hardin.

HARDIN, John P.
Enl. Co. B, 2nd W. Va. Inf. 7-3-63; transf. to Co. K upon organization of 5th W. Va. Cav.; served Co. H upon consolidation of regiment with 6th W. Va. Cav.; discharged 5-22-66. $0/55; b. Fayette Co., Pa. 1845; came to Barbour 1850's; married Elisabeth ____; moved to Preston Co., W. Va. after war where living 1880. Son of John and Lydia (Hardin) Hardin, distant cousin of Nestor.

HARRIS, Job E.
Elec. Overseer of Poor 1865. Farmer; $2,000/600; b. Barbour 1822; m. Martha Morrison 1850; d. Barbour 1870's. Son of John and Catherine (Hymes) Harris; father b. Barbour; grandson of Simeon and Hannah (Smith) Harris; grandfather settled Barbour from Hardy Co., W. Va.

HARRIS, Barton H.
Com. Capt., 139th W. Va. Mil. 8-16-62; never called into service; NFR; brother-in-law *Solomon Smith Unionist. Tenant; $0/350; b. Barbour 1838; Baptist; m. Barbara ____. Son of George and Christina (Cross) Harris; grandson of Simon and Hannah (Smith) Harris.

HARRIS, Gideon Draper Camden
Enl. Co. K, 31st Va. Inf. (CSA) 5-18-61; des. 4-19-62; com. Lt., 139th W.Va. Mil. 8-16-62, never called into service; father-in-law Abraham Hosaflock served Bat. E, 1st W. Va. Art. Farmer; $5,000/1,317 (parents); Baptist; b. Barbour 1840, brother of Barton; m. Rachel Hosaflock 1862; d. Randolph Co., W. Va. 1916.

HARRIS, James W.
Enl. Barbour Home Guard 4-1-64 for one year; brother-in-law *Daniel Shomo served Co. F, 15th W. Va. Inf. (USA). Farmer; $400/49 (parents); b. Barbour 1846; United Brethren Church; m. Eliza A. Ware 1868; living Barbour 1880. Son of Samuel and Nancy Harris; parents and grandparents b. Va.

HARSH, Samuel F.
Enl. Barbour Home Guard 9-15-64; disch. 5-30-65; brother *Adam served Co. K, 31st Va. Inf. (CSA); brother-in-law *William Nestor served Barbour Home Guard. Tenant; $0/28; b. Barbour 1838; m. Louisa Nestor 1858; living Barbour 1880. Son of Jacob and Sarah (Stemple) Harsh; father b. Preston Co., W. Va.; grandson of Frederick and Sarah (Bolyard) Harsh; grandfather immigrant from Germany, settled Preston Co. from Md.

HARTSOC, Loman
Enl. Co. F, 15th W. Va. Inf. 9-10-62; POW Cedar Creek 10-19-64; d. in prison; step-brother *Israel Canfield served Co. H, 62nd Va. Inf. (CSA). Farmer; $600/180 (parents); b. Barbour 1842. Son of George and Sydney Hartsoc, b. Va.; grandparents settled Barbour from Md.

HARTSOC, George W.
Enl. Co. B, 17th W. Va. Inf. 9-19-64; disch. 6-30-65. Farmer; $600/180 (parents); b. Barbour 1843, brother of Loman; m. 1) Sarah Durst 1865; 2) Lucinda J. Canfield 1887; moved to Randolph Co., W. Va. 1880's where listed Union veterans 1890.

HARTSOC, George
Enl. Co. B, 3rd W. Va. Cav. 10-21-62, prom. to cpl.; disch. 6-30-65. Farmer; $600/180 (parents); b. Taylor Co., W. Va. 1845; came to Barbour 1850's; m. Clarinda _____; returned to Taylor Co. after war where living 1880. Son of William and Amy Hartsoc; parents and grandparents b. Va.

HARVEY, James F.
Com. Major, 169th W. Va. Mil. 9-20-62; never called into service; elec. Justice of the Peace 1863; Delegate Union Party Convention Parkersburg 1863; enl. Co.

B, 3rd W. Va. Cav. 3-31-64; disch. 6-30-65. Farmer; $1,500/565; b. Loudoun Co., Va. 1825; came to Barbour 1850's; Republican; m. Rachel Baker 1865; NFR. Son of William and Mary Harvey, b. Garrett Co., Md.

HARVEY, Benjamin Franklin
Enl. Co. I, 6th W. Va. Inf. 11-19-61; transf. to Co. F, 1st U.S. Cav. 11-8-62; prom. to cpl. Farmer; $30,000/1,619 (parents); b. Garrett Co., Md. 1837; came to Barbour from Preston Co., W. Va. in 1850's; m. Harriet Shaffer 1868; NFR. Son of William and Elisabeth (Wilson) Harvey; parents b. Md., settled Preston Co. 1852, then Barbour; grandson of Rezin and Elisabeth (Queen) Harvey, b. Montgomery Co., Md.

HARVEY, William Fletcher Locke
Enl. Co. H, 12th W. Va. Inf. 8-27-62; prom. to cpl., serving as color-bearer; wd. Berryville 9-3-64, d. next day. Farmer; $30,000/1,619 (parents); b. Garrett Co., Md. 1840, brother of Benjamin; m. Nancy ____; widow listed Preston Co., W. Va. Union veterans 1890.

HARVEY, Charles Crampton
Enl. Co. I, 6th W. Va. Inf. 11-19-61; disch. 11-25-64. Farmer; $30,000/1,619 (parents); b. Garrett Co., Md. 1842, brother of Benjamin; returned to Md. after war where living 1880.

HARVEY, Fielding
Com. Major, 139th W.Va. Mil. 9-20-62; never called into service; brother-in-law *James Trayhern Unionist; NFR. Farmer; $1,500/565; b. Va. 1806; m. Ruth Trayhern 1832; settled Barbour from Loudoun Co., Va.

HAWKINS, Josiah L.
Elect. Assessor 1861 and 1864; Delegate Union Party Convention, Grafton 1864; brother-in-law *Allen Haddix and sons-in-law *James Duckworth and *Aaron Mitchell served Co. F, 15th W. Va. Inf. (USA). Farmer; $500/55; b. Pa. 1814; Methodist-Episcopal Church; settled Marion Co., W. Va. where m. 1) Julie Ann Dearer 1836; moved to Ritchie Co., W. Va. 1848, then Barbour 1850's where m. 2) Nancy Haddix 1859; moved to Upshur Co., W. Va. after war, then to Doddridge Co., W. Va. where d. 1887. Son of William and Catherine (Brumage) Hawkins, b. Md., settled Marion Co.; grandson of Thomas Hawkins, immigrant from England.

HAWKINS, Leroy H.
Enl. Co. N, 6th W. Va. Inf. 10-24-64; disch. 6-10-65. Farmer; $500/55 (parents); b. Marion Co., W. Va. 1849, son of Josiah and Julie Ann (Dearer) Hawkins;

Methodist-Episcopal Church; m. Mary Lucinda Malcom 1866; moved to Upshur Co., W. Va. 1870's where listed Union veterans 1890; d. Upshur Co. 1906.

HAYS, Isaac F.
Elec. Surveyor 1863; elected Constable 1864; son-in-law *William Cade served Co. H, 10th W.Va. Inf. (USA). Farmer; $1,100/207; b. Albemarle Co., Va. 1795; United Brethren Church; m. Ann ____; d. Barbour 1868. Son of James and Mary (Buster) Hays; father b. Augusta Co., Va.; grandson of Moses and Sarah (Petty) Hays, settled Augusta Co. from Frederick Co., Md.

HAYS, William M.
Enl. Co. H, 10th W. Va. Inf. 5-8-62; com. Lt. 5-14-62; disch. 5-7-65. Farmer; $1,100/207 (parents); b. Barbour 1837, son of Isaac and Ann Hays; Republican; m. Mary Wamsley 1866; moved to Marion Co., W. Va. after war where d. 1870's.

HELMICK, Martin James
Com. Lt., 169th W.Va. Mil. 11-1-62, never called into service; brother-in-law *James Alderman Lt. in same regiment. Farm laborer; $0/0; b. Pendleton Co., W. Va. 1835; Baptist; came to Barbour 1850's from Pocahontas Co., W. Va.; m. Lovina Cunningham 1860; moved to Upshur Co., W. Va. 1870's where d. 1909. Son of Peter and Mary (Davis) Helmick, b. Pendleton Co.

HELMICK, William Perry
Enl. Co. C, 1st W. Va. Cav. 2-28-62; disch. 7-8-65. Tenant; $0/0 (mother); b. Pendleton Co., W. Va. 1840, brother of Martin; m. Barbara Echard; moved to Ill. after war, returned in 1870's, moving to Upshur Co., W. Va. where d. 1912.

HENDERSON, Jacob P.
Enl. Co. K, 17th W. Va. Inf. 2-10-65; disch. 6-30-65. Tenant; $0/36; b. Taylor Co., W. Va. 1833; Baptist; came to Barbour 1850's; m. Elisabeth Moss; moved to Randolph Co., W. Va. 1870's, then Upshur Co., W. Va. where listed Union veterans 1890; d. Upshur Co. 1915. Son of Alexander and Mary (Dunham) Henderson, b. Pa.

HENDERSON, Alexander M.
Enl. Co. F, 15th W. Va. Inf. 4-16-64; disch. 6-14-65. Tenant; $0/0 (parents); b. Taylor Co., W. Va. 1836, brother of Jacob; Baptist; m. Mary Crose 1861; returned to Taylor Co. 1880's where listed Union veterans 1890.

HENDERSON, Joseph R.
Enl. Co. F, 15th W. Va. Inf. 8-23-62; disch. 6-14-65; Tenant; $0/0 (parents); b. Taylor Co., W. Va. 1843, brother of Jacob; Baptist; m. Mary E. _____; d. Barbour 1881; widow listed Taylor Co. Union veterans 1890.

HEWITT, Joel
Sympathizer. Farmer; $200/133 (mother); b. Barbour 1834; United Brethren Church; Republican; m. Hulda Hays 1871; d. Barbour 1917. Son of William and Mary (Rosencrantz) Hewitt; father b. Pa.

HEWITT, Hiram
Enl. Co. A, 6th W. Va. Inf. 11-5-61; d. of disease Clarksburg 2-12-63. Farmer; $200/133 (mother); b. Barbour 1840, brother of Joel; United Brethren Church; m. Sarah Wilson.

HILEMAN, Henry W.
Enl. Co. F, 17th W. Va. Inf. 9-14-64; disch. 6-30-65. Farmer; $0/25 (parents); b. Preston Co., W. Va. 1845; came to Barbour 1840's; m. Almira Hall 1866; moved to Calhoun Co., W. Va. after war. Son of Samuel and Harriet (Hennen) Hileman; father b. Greene Co., Pa.; grandson of George Hileman, settled Preston Co. 1830.

HILEMAN, Greenbury A.
Enl. Co. F, 17th W. Va. Inf. 9-14-64; disch. 6-30-65. Farmer; $0/25 (parents); b. Barbour 1849, brother of Henry; moved to Harrison Co., W. Va. after war.

HILKEY, John Lyon K.
District Committee Union Party 1864; appointed U.S. Postmaster Belington 1864; brother-in-law Townsend Goldsberry served Co. H, 12th W. Va. Inf. (USA). Tenant; $0/228; b. Hampshire Co., W. Va. 1828; United Brethren Church; came to Barbour during war; m. 1) Christina Goldsberry 1860; 2) Margaret See 1865; living Barbour 1880; parents b. Va.

HILL, Edmund
Delegate Union Party Convention Grafton, 1864; drafted 3-65; never inducted. Farmer; $2,000/1,172; b. Allegany Co., Md. 1810; m. Emeline Ridgely 1837; came to Barbour 1850's; Republican; d. Barbour 1877.

HILL, John E.
Enl. Co. H, 10th W. Va. Inf. 5-8-62; prom. to cpl.; d. of disease Moorefield, W. Va. 12-28-62. Farmer; $2,000/1,172 (parents); b. Allegany Co., Md. 1842, son of Edmund and Emeline (Ridgely) Hill.

HOFF, Henson Lewis
Attended "Shoe Shop" meeting at Myers' store 5-61; District Committee Union Party 1864; elec. to House of Delegates 1864; elec. Justice of the Peace 1865. Farmer and slave owner; $11,600/2,023; b. Barbour 1805; Baptist; Republican; m. 1) Ann Rightmire 1828; 2) Sarah Rightmire; 3) Emily Johnson Coplin 1858; d. Barbour 1890. Son of Anthony and Leticia Hoff; father b. N.J.; grandson of John Hoff, immigrant from Germany, settled Barbour 1797.

HOFF, Loman M.
Sympathzer. Farrier; $0/370; b. Barbour 1825, son of Henson and Ann (Rightmire) Hoff; Baptist; Republican; m. Malinda Chrislip 1857; d. Barbour 1860's.

HOFF, William Davisson
Com. Capt., 169th W. Va. Mil. 8-16-62; never called into service; enl. Co. F, 15th W. Va. Inf. 9-10-62; prom. to sgt.-mgr.; prom. to 2nd Lt. 6-6-63 and transf. to Co. I; prom. to 1st Lt. 9-4-63 and transf. to Co. D; POW Cedar Creek 10-19-64; sentenced to hard labor in retaliation for two hostages held by Federals; released Richmond 2-7-65. Farmer; $11,600/2,023 (parents); b. Barbour 1839, brother of Loman; Baptist; Republican; moved to Marshall Co., W. Va. after war.

HOFF, Hartzell Eldridge
Elec. County Tax Collector 1863. Farmer; $11,600/2,023 (parents); b. Barbour 1843, half-brother of Loman; Baptist; m. Emily Ann Coplin 1872; post-war Baptist minister; d. Barbour 1895. Son of Henson and Sarah (Rightmire) Hoff.

HOFFMAN, Sanford
Com. Lt., 139th W.Va. Mil. 8-16-62; prom. to Capt., then Major 9-20-62; never called into service; father-in-law *George Fry Unionist; brothers-in-law *Alexander, *James, *Thomas and *George Fry served Union Army and Home Guard. Farmer; $540/312; b. Barbour 1825; United Brethren Church; m. 1) Margaret Ptomey 1848; 2) Elisabeth Fry; living Barbour 1880. Son of John and Osa (Kelley) Hoffman; father b. Loudoun Co., Va.; grandson of John and Margaret (Hoff) Hoffman, b. N.J., settled Allegany Co., Md., then Barbour in 1790's.

HOFFMAN, Robert G.
Enl. Barbour Home Guard 9-1-63 for one year; re-enlisted 9-15-64; disch. 2-4-65 for disability; brother-in-law *William Nestor served same company; brother-in-law *Henry Cox Unionist. Farmer; $2,000/766 (parents); b. Barbour 1840, brother of Sanford; United Brethren Church; Republican; m. Nancy Nestor 1864; d. Barbour 1904.

HOFFMAN, Ebenezer Stingley
Enl. Barbour Home Guard 9-1-63 for one year; re-enlisted 9-15-64; disch. 5-30-65. Farmer; $2,000/766 (parents); b. Barbour 1844, brother of Sanford; United Brethren Church; m. Serena Nestor 1870; living Barbour 1880.

HOFFMAN, John I.
Enl. Co. F, 3rd W. Va. Inf. 1-23-63; served Co. D, 6th W. Va. Cav. upon consolidation of regiment with 5th W. Va. Cav.; des. Fort Leavenworth, Kan. 7-15-65; step-father *Conrad Carpenter Unionist; brother-in-law *James Fry served Barbour Home Guard; brother-in-law *James Stemple served Co. K, 31st Va. Inf. (CSA). Farmer; $500/47 (mother); b. Barbour 1841; Methodist-Episcopal Church; Democrat; m. Elisabeth Trimble 1869; listed Barbour Union veterans 1890; living Barbour 1899. Son of Israel and Anna (Black) Hoffman; grandson of John and Margaret (Hoff) Hoffman.

HOGE, John Armstrong
Enl. Co. N, 6th W. Va. Inf. 10-21-61; prom. to cpl.; re-enlisted 2-26-64; prom. to sgt.; discharged 6-10-65. Tenant; $0/35; b. Highland Co., Va. 1837; came to Barbour 1850's with wife Elisabeth Jane; moved to Ritchie Co., W. Va. after war where listed Union veterans 1890. Son of Jeremiah and Mary (Armstrong) Hoge, b. Highland Co.; grandson of John Hoge, immigrant from England.

HOGE, William H.
Enl. Co. M, 3rd W. Va. Cav. 2-27-64; disch. 5-31-65. Tenant; $0/86 (parents); b. Highland Co., Va. 1838, brother of John; moved to Ritchie Co., W. Va. after war.

HOOKER, William Henry
Enl. Co. H, 10th W. Va. Inf. 5-8-62; may have died during war, but no record; brother *James served Co. K, 19th Va. Cav. (CSA), d. Camp Chase, Ohio. Domestic servant; $0/0 (mother); b. Bath Co., Va. 1843; came to Barbour 1850's. Son of Richard and Nancy Hooker, b. Bath Co.

HOUSE, John C.
Enl. Co. K, 6th W. Va. Inf. 8-20-62; disch. 6-10-65. Farmer; $600/377; b. Barbour 1842; Methodist-Episcopal Church; moved to Webster Co., W. Va. after war where listed Union veterans 1890. Son of Isaac and Elisabeth House; grandson of Abraham and Judith (Simon) House, b. Hardy Co., W. Va., settled Barbour 1817; great-grandson of Jacob House, b. Va.; great-great-grandson of William House, immigrant from Germany.

HOUSE, Simon
Com. Capt., 169th W. Va. Mil. 10-11-62; never called into service; drafted 2-65, never inducted; brother-in-law Luther Sandridge served Co. F, 15th W. Va. Inf. (USA). Blacksmith; $0/237; b. Barbour 1830; Methodist-Episcopal Church; Republican; m. Ruhamy Cool 1852; living Barbour 1880. Son of Abraham and Sarah (Simon) House; grandson of Abraham and Judith (Simon) House.

HOUSE, Abram
Enl. Barbour Home Guard 9-1-63; "left company on account of being dismounted;" drafted 2-65, never inducted. Farmer; $1,700/417 (parents); b. Barbour 1838, brother of Simon; Methodist-Episcopal Church; m. Mary J. Waldron 1865; listed Barbour Union veterans 1890.

HOVATTER, Henry
Wagoner, U. S. Army; appointed U. S. Postmaster Kasson 10-21-62. Wagonmaster; $600/514; b. Barbour 1806; m. Rachel Kittle 1831; moved to Preston Co., W. Va. 1880's where listed Union veterans 1890. Son of Christopher and Catherine (Johnson) Hovatter, b. Pa.

HOVATTER, Henry Jr.
Enl. Co. F, 15th W. Va. Inf. 8-23-62; wd. in right shoulder Lynchburg 6-18-64; disch. 6-14-65. Tenant; $0/17; b. Barbour 1828, son of Henry and Rachel (Kittle) Hovatter; m. Mariny ____; moved to Preston Co., W. Va. 1880's; widow listed Preston Co. Union veterans 1890.

HOVATTER, Isaac
Enl. Co. F, 15th W. Va. Inf. 8-23-62; disch. 6-14-65; brother-in-law *John Kines served same company. Tenant; $600/514 (parents); b. Barbour 1832, brother of Henry Jr.; Methodist-Episcopal Church; m. 1) Elisabeth Bradden 1856; 2) Sydney Kines 1862; listed Barbour Union veterans 1890.

HOVATTER, Christopher Columbus
Sympathizer; forced to flee Philippi 5-61; elec. Justice of the Peace during war; drafted 3-65, never inducted. Boarder; $0/0; b. Barbour 1835, brother of Henry Jr.; Methodist-Episcopal Church; Democrat; m. Amanda Capito; d. Barbour 1900.

HOVATTER, William
Enl. Co. F, 15th W. Va. Inf. 9-10-62; d. of disease Cumberland, Md. 11-25-64. Farmer; $700/216; b. Barbour 1816, brother of Henry; m. Clara Ann Kittle 1838.

HOVATTER, John
Enl. Co. I, 6th W. Va. Inf. 11-19-61; disch. 11-25-64. Farmer; $700/216 (parents); b. Barbour 1842, son of William and Clara Ann (Kittle) Hovatter; m. Elma ____; moved to Mo. after war where living 1880.

HOVATTER, George M.
Enl. Barbour Home Guard 2-26-65; disch. 5-30-65. Farmer; $700/216 (parents); b. Barbour 1846, brother of John; m. Margaret J. Nestor 1868; moved to Tucker Co., W. Va. after war where living 1884.

HOVATTER, Basil
Enl. Co. F, 15th W. Va. Inf. 8-23-62; wd. in side Cedar Creek 10-19-64; disch. 6-14-65; brother-in-law *Frederick Ford served same company. Farmer; $700/70; b. Barbour 1837; m. Nancy Hebb 1859; listed Barbour Union veterans 1890. Son of Andrew and Elisabeth (Moats) Hovatter; grandson of Christopher and Catherine (Johnson) Hovatter.

HOVATTER, Andrew Jackson
Enl. Co. E, 1st W. Va. Cav. 3-10-64; des. Carpenter; $0/0; b. Barbour 1843, brother of Basil; m. Elisabeth Satterfield 1867; NFR.

HOVATTER, Melker J.
Enl. Co. F, 15th W. Va. Inf. 8-23-62; lost right leg Cedar Creek 10-19-64. Tenant; $100/80; b. Barbour 1825; m. Sarah Lohr; d. 1880's; widow listed Barbour Union veterans 1890. Son of Michael and Barbara (Backus) Hovatter.

HOWELL, Nehemiah
Served U. S. Army, unit unknown; son-in-law Lawrence Brozier served Union army. Farmer; $2,000/965; b. Md. 1815; Methodist-Episcopal Church; settled Barbour from Preston Co., W. Va.; m. Rachel Limbers; d. Barbour 1885; widow listed Barbour Union veterans 1890. Son of John Howell, b. Greene Co., Pa.; great-grandfather immigrant from Scotland.

HOWELL, David
Enl. Co. N, 6th W. Va. Inf. 9-15-64; disch. 6-10-65. Farmer; $2,000/965 (parents); b. Barbour 1844, son of Nehemiah and Rachel (Limbers) Howell; Methodist-Episcopal Church; living Barbour 1880.

HOWELL, John
Enl. Co. N, 6th W. Va. Inf. 9-15-64; disch. 6-10-65. Farmer; $2,000/965 (parents); b. Barbour 1843, brother of David ; Methodist-Episcopal Church;

Republican; m. 1) Mary E. Ringer 1866; 2) Mary E. Brown; listed Barbour Union veterans 1890; living Barbour 1899.

HOWELL, William
Enl. Co. H, 10th W. Va. Inf. 11-15-62 for two years; re-enlisted 3-15-64; wd. in hip Cedar Creek 10-19-64; d. 11-14-64. Farmer; $2,000/965 (parents); b. Barbour 1845, brother of David; Methodist-Episcopal Church.

HOWES, Joseph
Elec. County Surveyor 1860, continued to serve during war; District Committee Union Party 1863. Farmer; $1,500/857; b. Maine 1803; Methodist-Episcopal Church; m. Hepzibah Shurtliff 1826; living Barbour 1880. Son of Joseph and Louise (Shurtliff) Howes, settled Upshur Co., W. Va. 1814.

HOWES, Fenelon
Com. Capt., Co. F, 15th W. Va. Inf. 8-22-62; prom. to Major 9-22-64; cited for bravery Cedar Creek, one of only six officers of the regiment to remain with colors; Delegate Union Party Convention Grafton 1864; brothers-in-law *James, *Oliver and *Abel Teter served same company; father-in-law *Jacob Teter Confederate sympathizer. Farmer; $1,000/605; b. Upshur Co., W. Va. 1829, son of Joseph and Hepzibah (Shurtliff) Howes; Methodist-Episcopal Church; Republican; m. Elisabeth Teter; listed Barbour Union veterans 1890.

HOWES, Loren M.
Com. Lt., 139th W. Va. Mil. 8-16-62; never called into service; enl. Co. F, 15th W. Va. Inf. 8-23-62; prom. to cpl.; d. of disease Cherry Run 8-3-63. Farmer; $1,500/857 (parents); b. Upshur Co., W. Va. 1837, brother of Fenelon; Methodist-Episcopal Church.

HUDKINS, Jacob
Elec. County Supervisor 1863; drafted 2-65, never inducted. Farmer; $5,330/243; b. Barbour 1820; Baptist; m. 1) Rachel Holden 1844; 2) Amanda Cropp Holden 1867; living Barbour 1880. Son of Richard and Elisabeth (Ingram) Hudkins; father· b. Barbour; grandson of Bennett and Susan (Serrit) Hudkins, b. Md.

HUGHES, Felix H.
Enl. Co. B, 2nd W. Va. Inf. 5-21-61; prom. to sgt.; prom. to Lt. 9-4-63; cited for bravery Droop Mountain 11-6-63; disch. 1864; brother John secessionist, delegate to Richmond Convention, mistakenly killed by Confederate soldiers Rich Mountain. Attorney; $0/45; b. Green Co., Pa. 1830; came to Barbour

1850's with wife Rosa W.; moved to Wood Co., W. Va. after war where d. 1870's; widow listed Wood Co. Union veterans 1890. Son of Frances Hughes, b. Pa.; grandson of James Hughes, b. Jefferson Co., Va.; great-grandson of immigrant from Ireland to Loudoun Co., Va.

HYMES, Cornelius
Enl. Co. F, 15th W. Va. Inf. 8-27-62; KIA Winchester 9-19-64. Farmer; $0/50; b. Hardy Co., W. Va. 1829; m. Mary ____; widow listed Barbour Union veterans 1890. Son of George and Hulda Hymes; father b. Hardy Co. (?); grandson of John Hymes.

ISNER, Hamilton J.
Enl. Co. F, 15th W. Va. Inf. 8-27-62; wd. in thigh Lynchburg 6-18-64; disch. 6-14-65; brothers *Henry, *Thomas and *William served in Confederate army; brothers-in-law *John and *James Moats served Union army. Tenant; $0/50; b. Barbour 1831; m. Rebecca Moats 1856; moved to Taylor Co., W. Va. after war where listed Union veterans 1890. Son of John and Mary (Hudkins) Isner; father b. Barbour; grandson of William Isner, settled Barbour 1780's.

ISNER, Washington
Enl. Co. F, 3rd W. Va. Inf. 6-25-61; disch. for disability 1863; re-enlisted Co. E, 7th W. Va. Inf. as substitute 3-29-65; disch. 7-1-65. Farmer; $250/45 (mother); b. Barbour 1839, brother of Hamilton; m. Luander ____; moved to Ritchie Co., W. Va. 1870's where listed Union veterans 1890.

JANES, William
Com. Lt., 169th W. Va. Mil. 8-27-62, never called into service; enl. Barbour Home Guard 11-10-63 for one year; Delegate Union Party Convention Grafton, 1864; brother-in-law *John Shaffer Unionist. Farmer; $0/215 (parents); b. Barbour 1844; Methodist-Protestant Church; m. Rebecca Hotsinpillar 1862; moved to Preston Co., W. Va. 1870's where listed Union veterans 1890; d. 1903. Son of Alexander and Louisa (Casteel) Janes; father b. Green Co., Pa.; grandson of Bartholomew and Nancy (Gibson) Janes; grandfather b. Monongalia Co., W. Va., moved to Pa., then Barbour.

JENKINS, Henry Middleton
Listed Barbour Light Horse; com. Lt., 169th W. Va. Mil. 5-15-62; never called into service; brothers-in-law John and Lewis Fleming served Union army; brother-in-law Patrick Fleming served Confederate army. Farmer; $0/30 (parents); b. Harrison Co., W. Va. 1836; came to Barbour 1850's; Baptist;

Democrat; m. Mary Ann Fleming 1863; d. Barbour 1916. Son of Jonathon and Amanda (McKinney) Jenkins, b. Loudoun Co., Va.; grandson of Jesse and Elisabeth (Reed) Jenkins; grandfather immigrant from England, settled Loudoun Co., then Barbour.

JENKINS, Jesse
Sympathizer; drafted 2-65, never inducted. Tenant; $0/16; b. Barbour 1823; m. 1) Ursula Reed 1848; 2) Elisabeth Costolow 1863; moved to Doddridge Co., W. Va. after war. Son of David and Martha (Chrislip) Jenkins; grandson of Jesse and Elisabeth (Reed) Jenkins.

JOHNSON, John
Enl. Co. M, 4th W. Va. Cav. 12-22-63; disch. 6-23-64. Farmer; $300/90 (parents); b. Barbour 1843; m. 1) Magdelina Miller 1868; 2) Mariah Hotsinpillar; listed Barbour Union veterans 1890; d. 1913. Son of Isaac and Elisabeth (Nestor) Johnson, b. Barbour; grandson of Isaac and Elisabeth (Poling) Johnson; grandfather b. Loudoun Co., Va.; great-grandson of Robert and Mary (Vannoy) Johnson; Robert b. N.J., settled Loudoun Co., then Barbour 1797.

JOHNSON, George W.
Enl. Barbour Home Guard 2-3-64 for one year. Farmer; $300/90 (parents); b. Barbour 1846, brother of John; m. Melinda Moats Murphy 1867; d. Barbour 1926.

JOHNSON, Ephraim
Com. Lt., 169th W. Va. Mil. 8-16-62; never called into service; brother-in-law *William Bartlett listed Barbour Light Horse. Farmer; $6,260/2,705 (parents); b. Barbour 1830; Baptist; m. Martha Stickle; living Barbour 1880. Son of Isaac and Cassa (Roberts) Johnson; grandson of Garrett and Mary (England) Johnson; great-grandson of Robert and Mary (Vannoy) Johnson.

JOHNSON, Simon
Com. Lt., 169th W. Va. Mil. 8-16-62; never called into service. Farmer; $6,260/2,705 (parents); b. Barbour 1840, brother of Ephraim; Baptist; m. Elisabeth Ann Rader 1880; living Barbour 1880.

JOHNSON, Harrison W.
Enl. Co. B, 3rd W. Va. Cav. 10-21-62; prom. to sgt.; POW Winchester 6-18-63; exch. 8-63; disch. 6-30-65. Farmer; $400/1,527 (mother); b. Taylor Co., W. Va. 1841; Methodist-Episcopal Church; Republican; came to Barbour from Preston Co., W. Va. 1850's; m. Augusta J. Hull 1866; moved to Marion Co., W. Va. after

war where listed Union veterans 1890. Son of Wick and Clarrisa (Zinn) Johnson, b. Va.; mother listed as slave owner in 1860.

JOHNSON, Levi
Elec. School Commissioner 1864; father-in-law *George Pickens Unionist; NFR. $N/G; b. N.Y. 1830; came to Barbour 1850's where m. Leah Ann Pickens 1858. Son of Levi and Permilia Johnson.

JONES, Solomon S.
Com. Lt., 169th W.Va. Mil. 10-18-62; prom. to Capt.; never called into service; drafted 3-65, never inducted; brother *William served Co. H, 31st Va. Inf. (CSA); brother-in-law *William Malcomb Unionist. Shoemaker; $0/0; b. Bath Co., Va. 1831; Baptist; m. 1) Catherine ____; 2) Virginia Malcomb 1861; living Barbour 1880. Son of John and Delphia Jones, b. Va., settled Barbour 1840's.

JONES, William
Enl. Co. H, 10th W. Va. Inf. 5-8-62; d. of disease 3-16-65. Tenant; $1,350/130 (parents); b. Bath Co., Va. 1841; came to Barbour 1840's. Son of Anderson and Jane Jones; father b. N.Y.

JONES, Joshua
Delegate Union Party Convention Grafton 1864. Farmer; $1,700/220; b. Va. 1827; came to Barbour 1850's with wife Elisabeth; d. Barbour 1870's.

KANE, Patrick
Enl. Co. C, 1st W. Va. Cav. 12-2-61; wd. in left leg; re-enlisted 12-2-64; disch. 7-8-65. Farmer; $200/80 (parents); b. Gallway Co., Ireland 1842; Catholic; m. ____; listed Barbour Union veterans 1890. Son of Michael and Barbara Kane; grandson of Patrick and Mary Kane.

KELLER, John
Superintendant of Elections 2-63; Delegate Union Party Convention Grafton 1864; elec. to House of Delegates 1865; drafted 3-65, never inducted; brothers-in-law *Elijah and William McIntosh served Co. H, 12th W. Va. Inf. (USA). Farmer; $8,500/1,037; b. Randolph Co., W. Va. 1809; Methodist-Episcopal Church; Democrat; m. 1) Lucinda Mitchell 1830; 2) Ellen Jane McIntosh; d. Barbour 1887. Son of Isaac and Sarah (Keller) Keller; grandparents settled Randolph Co. from Shenandoah Valley.

KELLER, Lafayette
Enl. Co. C, 4th W. Va. Cav. 8-26-63; disch. 3-7-64; brother-in-law *John Bryan served Co. K, 31st Va. Inf. (CSA). Farmer; $8,500/1,037 (parents); b. Barbour 1845, son of John and Lucinda (Mitchell) Keller; Methodist-Episcopal Church; m. Rebecca Bryan 1864; moved to Taylor Co., W. Va. 1870's where listed Union veterans 1890; d. 1905.

KELLEY, John L.
Enl. Barbour Home Guard; son-in-law *Barnett Boyles served Co. B, 17th W. Va. Inf. (USA). Farmer; $2,500/557; b. Barbour 1796; Methodist-Episcopal Church; m. Mary Yoke 1822; d. Barbour 1866. Son of Ebenezer and Rachel (Johnson) Kelley; father b. Somerset Co., N.J., moved to Allegany Co., Md., then Barbour 1795; grandson of Samuel and Eunice Kelley, b. N.J.

KELLEY, James Lewis Burbridge
Enl. Barbour Home Guard 4-1-63; re-enlisted 4-1-64; disch. and enl. Co. F, 17th W. Va. Inf. 9-4-64; shot in left leg; disch. 6-30-65; brother Oscar served Co. C, 11th W. Va. Inf. (USA). Farmer; $2,500/557 (parents); b. Barbour 1847, son of John and Mary (Yoke) Kelley; Methodist-Episcopal Church; Republican; m. Ann Boehm 1874; listed Barbour Union veterans 1890; living Barbour 1899.

KELLEY, Samuel
Elec. Justice of the Peace 1861; son *William served Co. H, 31st Va. Inf. (CSA). Farmer; $500/358; b. Barbour 1805, brother of John L.; m. Delila Poling 1827; d. Barbour 1863.

KELLEY, Dyer
Enl. Co. N, 6th W. Va. Inf. 10-17-64; disch. 6-30-65; son-in-law *Wesley Bolton served Co. H, 10th W. Va. Inf. (USA). Farmer; $0/245; b. Barbour 1831, son of Samuel and Delila (Poling) Kelley; m. Melinda ____; listed Barbour Union veterans 1890.

KELLEY, Loman G.
Enl. Co. K, 6th W. Va. Inf. 8-26-62; disch. 6-30-65. Farmer; $500/358 (parents); b. Barbour 1842, brother of Dyer; m. Mary Agnes Moore; moved to Calhoun Co., W. Va. 1870's where listed Union veterans 1890.

KELLEY, Isaiah
Com. Lt., 139th W. Va. Mil. 8-16-62, never called into service; enl. Co. F, 3rd W. Va. Inf. 6-25-61; disch. 8-15-64; NFR; step-brother *David Stevens served Co. C, 4th W. Va. Cav. (USA). Farmer; $300/75 (parents); b. Barbour 1840.

Son of Johnson and Sarah (Yoke) Kelley; father b. Barbour; grandson of Ebenezer and Rachel (Johnson) Kelley.

KELLEY, Jaspar
Com. Lt., 139th W. Va. Mil. 10-20-62; never called into service; enl. Co. H, 10th W. Va. Inf. 8-22-63; KIA Kernstown 7-24-64; brothers-in-law *William and *Isaiah Moore and Marshall Canfield served same company. Tenant; $170/32; b. Randolph Co., W. Va. 1837; came to Barbour 1850's where m. Deborah Moore 1857; widow listed Barbour Union veterans 1890. Son of Absalom and Ruth (Chenowith) Kelly, b. Randolph Co.; grandson of William and Jean (Kittle) Kelly; grandfather b. Pa., settled Randolph Co. 1790's.

KELLEY, William C.
Enl. Co. H, 10th W. Va. Inf. 5-8-62; POW 6-15-64; d. in prison 3-16-65. Farmer; $500/358; b. Randolph Co., W. Va. 1841, brother of Jaspar; m. Agnes Moore 1860; widow listed Barbour Union veterans 1890.

KERANS, David
Enl. Co. F, 15th W. Va. Inf. 9-10-62; wd. Kernstown 7-24-64; disch. 6-14-65. Tenant; $N/G; b. Randolph Co., W. Va. 1814; came to Barbour 1840's with wife Leah; moved to Taylor Co., W. Va. after war where living 1880. Son of Peter and Susannah (Smith) Kerans, b. Randolph Co.; grandson of Bernard and Margaret Kerans; grandfather immigrant from Ireland, settled Hampshire Co., Va., then Randolph Co.

KERANS, Aaron
Enl. Co. B, 10th W. Va. Inf. 10-4-62; des. Webster Co., W. Va. 5-17-64; drafted into Co. I, 17th W. Va. Inf. 2-15-65; disch. 6-30-65; brother-in-law Isaac Gower served Co. E, 4th W. Va. Cav. (USA). Tenant; $N/G; b. Monongalia Co., W. Va. 1843, son of David and Leah Kerans; m. Elisabeth Gower 1864; moved to Taylor Co., W. Va. 1870's where living 1880.

KINES, John Robert
Enl. Co. F, 15th W. Va. Inf. 8-23-62; wd. in shoulder Petersburg 4-2-65; disch. 6-14-65; brothers-in-law *James Freeman and *Isaac Hovatter served same company. Farmer; $0/100 (parents); b. Washington Co., Pa. 1841; m. 1) Amy Catherine Hovatter; 2) Mary Lohr 1872; d. Barbour 1880's; widow listed Barbour Union veterans 1890. Son of Edwin and Sarah Jane (Sealock) Kines, settled Barbour from Fauquier Co., Va.

KIRKENDAHL, Levi
Enl. Co. F, 15th W. Va. Inf. 9-10-62; listed sick Clarysville 8-63; POW Cedar Creek 10-19-64; d. in prison; brother George Lt. Col., 3rd Iowa (USA); brother-in-law *Alexander Greathouse served Co. D, 20th Va. Cav. (CSA). Tenant; $0/55; b. Barbour 1823; United Brethren Church; m. 1) Sarah Ann Cokenour 1846; 2) Keziah Greathouse 1859. Son of Simeon and Prudence (Graham) Kirkendahl, b. Hardy Co., W. Va.; descendant of settlers on South Branch 1750's.

KISNER, Elias M.
Enl. Co. F, 15th W. Va. Inf. 8-23-62; wd. in chest Cedar Creek 10-13-64; disch. 6-14-65. Farmer; $50/175; b. Monongalia Co., W. Va. 1826; m. Nancy Philips 1846; came to Barbour 1850's; listed Barbour Union veterans 1890; d. Barbour 1919. Son of Samuel and Mary (Wooget) Kisner, b. Md.

KNABENSHOE, John W.
Enl. Barbour Home Guard 9-1-63 for one year; "left company in consequence of being dismounted." $0/172 (parents); b. Hampshire Co., W. Va. 1835; Methodist-Episcopal Church; came to Barbour 1840's; m. 1) Hannah Paugh 1866; 2) Rebecca ____; listed Barbour Union veterans 1890. Son of John and Jane (Jenkins) Knabenshoe; father b. Hardy Co., W. Va.; grandson of John Knabenshoe, immigrant from Germany.

KNAPP, Samuel
Com. Capt., 139th W. Va. Mil. 11-9-61; never called into service; enl. Co. F, 7th W. Va. Inf. 9-2-61; injured right knee and disch. for disability 8-12-62; elec. County Supervisor 1863 and 1865; step-brothers *Henry and *George Markeley served Co. N, 6th W. Va. Inf. (USA). Chair maker; $150/80; b. Barbour 1821; Republican; m. Catherine Delawder 1847; d. Barbour 1883. Son of Henry and Anna (Jenkins) Knapp; father b. N.Y.

KNIGHT, William L.
Enl. Co. N, 6th W. Va. Inf. 9-25-61; disch. 11-17-64; brother *Benjamin listed Barbour Light Horse. Farmer; $1,000/238 (parents); b. Taylor Co., W. Va. 1841; Baptist; came to Barbour 1840's; m. Malinda Stockwell 1866; listed Barbour Union veterans 1890. Son of Thomas and Catherine (Rosier) Knight; father b. Monongalia Co., W. Va.; settled Taylor Co. 1830's, then Barbour; grandparents b. Va.

KNOTTS, Ahab
Enl. Co. E, 15th W. Va. Inf. 10-17-62; wd. left leg Kernstown 7-24-64; wd. Winchester 9-19-64; disch. 6-30-65; seven brothers served Union Army.

Laborer; $0/76; b. Preston Co., W. Va. 1825; Methodist-Episcopal Church; came to Barbour 1850's with wife Sarah; returned Preston Co. during war, then Taylor Co., W. Va. 1880's; widow listed Taylor Co. Union veterans 1890. Son of Absalom and Elisabeth (Keller) Knotts; father b. Preston Co.; grandson of Robert Knotts, b. Pa., settled Preston Co. 1814.

LANHAM, Jaspar
Enl. Co. H, 62nd Va. Mtd. Inf. (CSA) 4-24-63; des. Barbour 11-63; enl. Home Guard, Upshur Co. 1-1-64 for one year; disch. and re-enlisted Co. M, 3rd W. Va. Cav. 4-4-64; disch. 6-12-65; brother-in-law John Booth served Confederate army. Farmer; $2,500/300 (parents); b. Taylor Co., W. Va. 1833; Methodist-Episcopal Church; m. Sarah Radabaugh 1860; moved to Harrison Co., W. Va. after war where d.1888. Son of George and Nancy (Orten) Lanham; father b. Clarke Co., Va.; grandson of Jeremiah and Barbara (Bence) Lanham, natives of Va.

LANHAM, Granville
Enl. Home Guard, Upshur Co. 1-1-64 for one year; disch. and re-enlisted Co. M, 3rd W. Va. Cav. 4-4-64; disch. 6-12-65. Farmer; $2,500/300 (parents); b. Barbour 1846, brother of Jaspar; Methodist-Episcopal Church; m. Susan Virginia Osborn 1866; moved to Upshur Co., W. Va. after war where listed Union veterans 1890; d. Upshur Co. 1916.

LANTZ, Seymour
Enl. Co. H, 7th W. Va. Inf. 9-2-61; KIA Antietam 9-17-62. Farmer; $1,000/659 (parents); b. Barbour 1842; United Brethren Church. Son of Joseph and Mary (Crites) Lantz; grandson of George and Mary (Woodford) Lantz, b. Va., settled Barbour 1811 from Shenandoah Valley.

LATHAM, John Thomas
Com. Lt., Bat. E, 1st W. Va. Art. 9-13-62; disch. 6-28-65; three brothers in Union Army, including George R. Latham, Col., 2nd W. Va. Inf. (USA). Farm laborer; $0/0; b. Fauquier Co., Va. 1837; Baptist; m. Mary Virginia Hieronimus 1863; moved to Taylor Co., W. Va. after war, then Marion Co., W. Va. where listed Union veterans 1890; d. Marion Co. 1920. Son of John and Juliet (Newman) Latham, slave owners 1860; father b. Prince William Co., Va. settled Taylor Co. 1849; grandson of Robert Latham; great-grandson of immigrant from England.

LEACH, Elias
Enl. Co. C, 4th W. Va. Cav. 7-14-63; prom. to cpl.; disch. 6-23-64; com. Capt., 169th W. Va. Mil. 11-5-64; never called into service; drafted into Co. K, 17th W.

Va. Inf. 2-13-65; prom. to sgt; disch. 6-30-65; brother-in-law *Gustavus Gall Unionist. Farmer; $700/187 (parents); b. Fauquier Co., Va. 1840; Methodist-Episcopal Church; Republican; came to Barbour 1848; m. Cinderella Gall 1867; listed Barbour Union veterans 1890; d. Barbour 1915. Son of Enoch and Mary (Collins) Leach; father b. Fauquier Co.; grandson of John and Mary (Hall) Leach, b. Fauquier Co.; great-grandson of Anglican minister immigrated from England 1760.

LEESON, Jesse
Enl. Co. F, 15th W. Va. Inf. 4-16-64; wd. in right arm Kernstown 7-23-64; disch. 6-14-65; brother-in-law *Amaziah Reed served Co. K, 6th W. Va. Inf. (USA). Farmer; $3,000/1,000 (mother); b. Barbour 1846; m. Fanny Reed 1865; moved to Ritchie Co., W. Va. after the war, then to Doddridge Co., W. Va. 1880's where listed Union veterans 1890. Son of Thomas and Nancy (Carrol) Leeson; father b. Monongalia Co., W. Va. settled Barbour 1840's; grandson of Richard and Hannah (Pride) Leeson, settled Monongalia Co. from Hardy Co., W. Va. 1790's.

LEMMON, William H.
Listed Barbour Light Horse; enl. Bat. E, 1st W. Va. Art. 8-12-62, serving as buglar; POW Buckhannon 8-30-62; escaped; wd. New Creek 11-28-64; disch. 6-28-65; NFR; brother George served Co. I, 7th W. Va. Inf. (USA). Farm laborer; $0/0; b. Hardy Co., W. Va. 1830; came to Barbour 1850's. Son of John and Elisabeth (Ridgeway) Lemmon; father b. Md.

LEONARD, Bowen Edward
Enl. Co. H, 12th W. Va. Inf. 8-16-62; disch. 6-16-65. Farmer; $2,100/400; b. Monongalia Co., W. Va. 1828; m. Susan Jones; listed Barbour Union veterans 1890; moved to Taylor Co., W. Va. 1895 where d. 1900. Son of John and Josina (Evans) Leonard; father b. Pa.; grandson of Gardner and Sarah (Bowen) Leonard, settled Monongalia Co.

LEONARD, Solomon S.
Co. B, 133rd W. Va. Militia, called into service 9-63 for three months. Farmer and slave owner; $2,000/268; b. Upshur Co., W. Va. 1818; Republican; m. 1) Elisabeth F. Wolfenbarger; 2) Matilda J. Rohrbach 1868; returned to Upshur Co. after war where living 1880. Son of Ebenezer and Elisabeth (Burr) Leonard; father b. Mass., settled Upshur Co. 1810.

LEYMAN, Joel
Elec. Overseer of Poor 1865; drafted 3-65, never inducted; brother-in-law *John Bryan served Co. K, 31st Va. Inf. (CSA), KIA. Farmer; $250/400; b. Marion

Co., W. Va. 1830; Methodist-Episcopal Church; came to Barbour 1840's; m. 1) Margaret Bryan; 2) Mary Jane Wagner 1871; d. Barbour 1900; parents b. Va.

LIMBERS, Andrew
Enl. Co. F, 15th W. Va. Inf. 9-10-62; disch. 6-14-65; brother Abraham served Co. G, 62nd Va. Mtd. Inf. (CSA); brother Johnson arrested for secessionist activity. Tenant; $0/50; b. Barbour 1836; m. Martha Boyles; moved to Upshur Co., W. Va. after war where living 1880. Son of James and and Sarah Limbers, b. Pa., settled Barbour 1830's.

LOCK, Nelinza
Enl. Co. B., 2nd W. Va. Inf. 5-20-61; prom. to cpl.; assigned to duty as scout, working behind enemy lines disguised as a Confederate soldier; injured Droop Mountain 11-3-63; d. 1-5-65; described by regimental historian as "a true soldier, loyal to the heart; was a daring and faithful scout, one that could be trusted in an emergency." Farmer; $750/277 (parents); b. Monongalia Co., W. Va. 1842; Methodist-Episcopal Church. Son of John and Rebecca (Jaco) Lock, b. Md.

LOCK, Isaac W.
Enl. Co. H, 10th W. Va. Inf. 2-7-63; prom. to sgt.; disch. 7-3-65; NFR. Farmer; $750/277 (parents); b. Monongalia Co., W. Va. 1844, brother of Nelinza; Methodist-Episcopal Church.

LOCK, William C.
Enl. Co. K, 6th W. Va. Inf. 2-15-65; disch. 6-30-65; NFR. Farmer; $750/277 (parents); b. Barbour 1847, brother of Nelinza; Methodist-Episcopal Church.

LOCK, Isaac M.
Enl. Co. F, 15th W. Va. Inf. 9-15-62; wd. in foot Snickers Gap 7-17-64; disch. 6-14-65. Farmer; $100/30 (parents); b. Monongalia Co., W. Va. 1846; m. Nancy Frances Kines 1866; listed Barbour Union veterans 1890; d. Barbour 1931. Son of Neal and Elisabeth (Lyman) Lock; father b. Md.

LOCKNEY, Samuel S.
Elec. Assessor 1861 and 1864; Delegate Union Party Convention Parkersburg 1863; District Committee Union Party 1864. Farmer; $300/183; b. Fluvanna Co., Va. 1828; Methodist-Episcopal Church; Republican; came to Barbour from Bath Co., Va. 1837; m. Lucinda Payne 1847; moved to Jackson Co., W. Va. 1870's, then to Gilmer Co., W. Va. where living 1880. Son of Frederick and Lucy (Thomas) Lockney; grandson of John and Dolly (Humphrey) Lockney; grandfather immigrant from Scotland, settled Fluvanna Co.

LOHR, Henry
Enl. Co. K, 31st Va. Inf. 5-18-61 (CSA); des. 4-19-62; enl. Co. H, 10th W. Va. Inf. 5-8-62; des. 9-9-62; rejoined 31st Va. Inf.; wd. Gettysburg 7-3-63; des. 10-10-63 and returned home; brother-in-law *Jesse Poling served Co. E, 62nd Va. Mtd. Inf. (CSA); brother-in-law *William Nestor served Barbour Home Guard. Farmer; $100/82 (parents); b. Shenandoah Co., Va. 1844; came to Barbour 1850's from Preston Co., W. Va.; m. Fannie ____; moved to Ind. 1870's. Son of Jacob and Mary (Futz) Lohr, b. Va.; grandson of John and Margaret Lohr; grandfather immigrant from Germany.

LOHR, George W.
Enl. Barbour Home Guard 1-5-64 for one year. Farmer; $300/108 (parents); b. Va. 1837; Methodist-Protestant Church; m. Eliza ____; d. Barbour 1907. Son of George W. and Judith (Low) Lohr; parents and grandparents b. Va.

LOHR, John J.
Enl. Co. B, 10th W. Va. Inf. 3-62 for two years; re-enlisted 3-16-64; disch. 8-29-65. Farmer; $300/108 (parents); b. Va. 1841, brother of George W.; listed Barbour Union veterans 1890.

LONGUANETTI, James W.
Enl. Co. B, 10th W. Va. Inf. 3-12-62 for two years; re-enlisted 2-29-64; disch. 8-9-65. Tenant; $0/342 (parents); b. Albemarle Co., Va. 1843; came to Barbour 1850's from Upshur Co., W. Va.; m. Margaret McCloud; returned to Upshur Co. 1880's, then to Harrison Co., W. Va. where listed Union veterans 1890; d. Harrison Co. 1926. Son of John and Mary Longuanetti; father immigrant from Italy.

LOUGH, James W.
Enl. Co. H, 10th W. Va. 5-8-62; prom. to cpl.; d. of disease Winchester 6-2-63; brother-in-law Job Musgrave served Co. F, 12th W. Va. Inf. (USA). Tenant; $0/45; b. Barbour 1839. Son of Zebulon and Dorcas (Alexander) Lough; father b. Pendleton Co., W. Va.; grandson of John and Sarah (Harpole) Lough; grandfather immigrant from Germany, settled Pendleton Co.

LOUGH, Elias
Enl. Co. H, 10th W. Va. Inf. 11-15-62; d. of pneumonia Moorefield, W. Va. 1-4-63. Farmer; $2,000/665 (parents); b. Barbour 1845, brother of James W.

LOUGH, William E.
Enl. Co. E, 14th W. Va. Inf. 9-13-62; wd. and POW Cloyd Moutain 5-9-64; d. Andersonville Prison. Tenant; $0/218; b. Rockingham Co., Va. 1839;

Methodist-Episcopal Church; came to Barbour 1843; m. Indiana Talbott; widow listed Barbour Union veterans 1890. Son of John and Mary (Zircle) Lough; father b. Pendleton Co. W. Va.; grandson of John and Sarah (Harpole) Lough.

LOUGH, Jacob J.
Com. Capt., 169th W. Va. Mil. 6-63; never called into service; enl. Co. C, 4th W. Va. Cav. 7-27-63; disch. 6-23-64; re-enlisted Co. D, 6th W. Va. Cav. 9-30-64; disch. 5-19-65. Farmer; $8,000/2,005 (parents); b. Rockingham Co., Va. 1842, brother of William; m. 1) Caroline Melissa ____; 2) Nancy Dennison 1868; 3) Mary Hines 1883; moved to Harrison Co., W. Va. after war where listed Union veterans 1890.

LOVE, Byron
Enl. Co. A, 10th W. Va. Inf. 1-22-62; transf. to Co. H; prom. to sgt. 9-27-62; brother Edward served same company; brother William served Co. A, 133rd W. Va. Mil.; father Delegate Second Wheeling Convention. Tenant; $2,500/450; b. Upshur Co., W. Va. 1836; Methodist-Protestant Church; Republican; m. Mary Jane Arnold 1856; listed Barbour Union veterans 1890. Son of John and Mahala (Rohrbaugh) Love; parents and grandparents b. Va.

LUDWIG, Henry
Enl. Co. F, 15th W. Va. Inf. 9-10-62; prom. to sgt.; disch. 6-14-65. Farmer; $600/220; b. Hardy Co., W. Va. 1823; United Brethren Church; m. Margaret Shoemaker; came to Barbour 1847; moved to Jackson Co., W. Va. 1870's where d. 1909. Son of Jacob and Nancy (Miller) Ludwig; father b. Hardy Co.; grandson of George and Maria (Weirs) Ludwig, b. Pa.; great-grandson of Jacob Ludwig, immigrant from Germany.

LUDWIG, William H.
Enl. Co. F, 3rd W. Va. Inf. 6-25-61; re-enlisted 1-29-64, serving Co. D, 6th W. Va. Cav. upon consolidation of regiment with 5th W. Va. Cav.; des. Fort Leavenworth, Kan. 7-15-65. Farmer; $600/220 (parents); b. Hardy Co., W. Va. 1843, son of Henry and Margaret (Shoemaker) Ludwig; United Brethren Church; m. 1) Margaret Streets 1866; 2) Eliza J. Streets 1879; moved to Jackson Co., W. Va. 1870's where living 1880.

LUNENBARGER, Jacob
Sympathizer; home attacked by rebels 7-63; son-in-law Frederick Dopf served Co. B, 2nd W. Va. Inf. (USA). Farmer; $1,500; born Bavaria 1809; immigrated to Md. where m. Sarah Morrison; moved to Berkeley Co., W. Va. then Taylor Co., W. Va., then Barbour 1861, to Tyler Co. W. Va. 1865 where living 1880.

LUNENBARGER, Sarah (Morrison)
Sympathizer; home attacked by rebels. $1,500; b. Md. 1810, husband of Jacob; living Tyler Co., W. Va. 1880. Parents b. Wittenburg.

LUNENBARGER, John Wesley
Enl. Co. H, 10th W. Va. Inf. 11-15-62; leg shot off; transf. to Veteran Reserve Corps; disch. for disability 7-9-64. Farmer; $1,500 (parents); b. Berkeley Co., W. Va. 1845, son of Jacob and Sarah (Morrison) Lunenbarger; m. Nancy Ellen Moore 1872; moved to Tyler Co., W. Va. 1865 where listed Union veterans 1890.

MALCOMB, William Irving
Wagoner, Union Army; drafted 2-65, never inducted; claim for war-time service in 169th Mil. rejected 1902; brother-in-law *Benjamin Simon Unionist. Farmer; $3,700/465 (parents); b. Barbour 1842; Methodist-Episcopal Church; m. Emily J. Bolten 1864; d. Barbour 1903. Son of James and Catherine (Haddix) Malcomb; parents and grandparents b. Va.

MALE, George W.
Enl. Co. E, 17th W. Va. Inf. 9-26-64; disch. 6-30-65. Farmer; $300/131; b. Barbour 1828; m. 1) Lucinda Kennedy 1858; 2) Nancy Male 1862; listed Barbour Union veterans 1890. Son of Jesse and Eleanor (Cole) Male; father b. Randolph Co., W. Va.; grandson of George and Margaret Male, b. Hampshire Co., Va., settled Barbour 1790's.

MALE, William R.
Enl. Co. B, 17th W. Va. Inf. 8-30-64; disch. 6-30-65. Tenant; $0/15; b. Barbour 1836, brother of George W.; m. Alcinda _____; d. 1880's; widow listed Barbour Union veterans 1890.

MALE, Daniel
Enl. Co. H, 7th W. Va. Inf. 9-2-61; re-enlisted 1-4-64; disch. 7-1-65; NFR. Farmer; $1,000/225 (parents); b. Barbour 1840, brother of George W.

MALE, Andrew J.
Enl. Co. H, 7th W. Va. Inf. 9-2-61; KIA Gettysburg 7-3-63. Farmer; $1,000/225 (parents); b. Barbour 1842, brother of George W.

MALE, George J.
Enl. Co. L, 1st W. Va. Cav. 3-28-65 as substitute; disch. 7-8-65. Farmer; $N/G; b. Barbour 1848; m. Melinda Kennedy 1866; listed Barbour Union veterans

1890. Son of Thomas and Julie Ann (Hardin) Male, b. Barbour; descendant of George and Margaret Male, settled Barbour from Hampshire Co., W. Va.

MANEFEE, E. H.
Delegate First Wheeling Convention 5-61; recommended by Col. George Latham as surgeon for 2nd or 9th W. Va. Inf., never appointed. Doctor; $0/700; b. Va. 1838; came to Barbour 1850's; m. Elisabeth P. Wyatt 1866; NFR.

MANLEY, Matthew
Com. Capt., 169th W. Va. Mil. 10-17-62; never called into service. Shoemaker; $175/20; b. Va. 1835; came to Barbour 1850's; m. Delila Floyd 1860; moved to Upshur Co., W. Va. after war where living 1880. Parents b. Va.

MARKELEY, James C.
Enl. Co. K, 6th W. Va. Inf. 9-22-64 as a substitute; disch. 6-10-65. Farmer; $1,200/393 (parents); b. Barbour 1847; m. Francis C. Murphy 1869; d. Barbour 1929. Son of Jacob and Eliza (Coberly) Markeley; father b. Allegany Co., Md.; grandson of Christian and Margaret (Shockey) Markeley, b. Md., settled Barbour 1835; great-grandson of Jacob Markeley, b. N.J.

MARKELEY, Henry A.
Enl. Co. N, 6th W. Va. Inf. 10-3-64; disch. 6-30-65; step-brother *Samuel Knapp and brother-in-law *Simon Winans served Co. F, 15th W. Va. Inf. (USA). Farmer; $1,500/262; b. Allegany Co., Md. 1835; United Brethren Church; m. 1) Ann Eliza Murphy 1857; 2) Mary Gaither 1880; moved to Kan. 1870's where d. 1912. Son of Christian and Margaret (Shockey) Markeley.

MARKELEY, George Washington
Enl. Co. N, 6th W. Va. Inf. 10-3-64; disch. 6-30-65. Farmer; $200/60 (parents); b. Barbour 1844, brother of Henry; United Brethren Church; m. Sarah M. Ringer 1863; moved to Kan. 1870's where d. 1919.

MARPLE, Amos T.
Enl. Co. H, 10th W. Va. Inf. 11-19-62; served as musician; disch. 5-7-65; son-in-law *Peregrine Chrislip Unionist. Tenant; $0/190; b. Upshur Co., W. Va. 1808; Methodist-Episcopal Church; m. Jemima Cummins 1830; returned to Upshur Co. after war where d. 1880's; widow listed Upshur Co. Union veterans 1890. Son of Abraham and Barbara (Weaver) Marple; parents b. Pa.

MARPLE, Minter Furr
Enl. Co. H, 10th W. Va. Inf. 5-8-62; prom. to sgt., serving as color bearer; wd. right thigh Kernstown 7-24-64; wd. in back Winchester 9-19-64; prom. to Lt. 9-

24-64; disch. 5-8-65. Mechanic; $0/111; b. Upshur Co., W. Va. 1837, son of Amos T. and Jemima (Cummins) Marple; Methodist-Episcopal Church; m. Minerva E. Chrislip 1860; returned to Upshur Co. after war where listed Union veterans 1890; d. Upshur Co. 1905.

MARTIN, William S.
Enl. Barbour Home Guard 11-10-63; re-enlisted 9-15-64; KIA Holsberry Farm, Barbour Co. 4-24-65. Farmer; $100/189; b. Barbour 1844. Son of Joseph and Catherine (Squires) Martin, b. Preston Co., W. Va.; grandson of John Van Meter and Sarah A. (Cassiday) Martin; great-grandson of Thomas Charles and Olive (Van Meter) Martin, b. Va., settled Monongalia Co., W. Va.

MARTIN, Zephania D.
Enl. G, 14th W. Va. Inf. 9-3-62; disch. 12-5-64; brother *Enoch served Co. K, 31st Va. Inf. (CSA), d. in prison. Saddler; $75/75; b. Taylor Co., W. Va. 1834; m. 1) _____; 2) Sarah Poling 1880; listed Barbour Union veterans 1890. Son of Henson and Jane (Currence) Martin; father b. Monongalia Co., W. Va., settled Barbour 1830's.

MARTIN, William H.
Enl. Co. G, 3rd W. Va. Inf. 6-27-61; re-enlisted 2-29-64, serving Co. C, 6th W. Va. Cav. upon consolidation of regiment with 5th W. Va. Cav.; disch. 5-22-66; uncle Gideon Martin, prominent Methodist-Episcopal minister and abolitionist, elec. W. Va. House of Delegates and served as chaplain 15th W. Va. Inf. (USA). Tenant; $0/75 (parents); b. Barbour 1842; Methodist-Episcopal Church; moved to Harrison Co., W. Va. 1870's where listed Union veterans 1890. Son of Nimrod and Elisabeth (Hickman) Martin; parents b. Barbour; grandson of Stephen and Catherine (Reger) Martin; grandfather b. Fauquier Co., Va., settled Barbour 1785; great-grandson of Joseph and Mary (Hitt Strange) Martin, immigrants from England and Scotland.

MARTIN, Joab
Enl. Co. F, 15th W. Va. Inf. 9-1-62; wd. left ankle Snickers Gap 7-17-64; disch. 6-14-65. Farmer; $500/291 (parents); b. Marion Co., W. Va. 1842; m. 1) Mary R. Severe 1869; 2) Lydia Ball 1879; listed Barbour Union veterans 1890. Son of William and Rebecca Martin; parents and grandparents b. Va.

MARTIN, Henry D.
Elec. Township Commissioner 1863; District Committee Union Party 1863; Delegate Union Party Convention Grafton 1864; enl. Barbour Home Guard; elec. Justice of the Peace 1865; son-in-law *William Scott Unionist. Farmer;

$5,000/1,700; b. Fayette Co., Pa. 1806; Methodist-Episcopal Church; Republican; came to Barbour 1810; m. Margaret Means 1821; d. Barbour 1880.

MARTIN, Jacob
Enl. Co. F, 15th W. Va. Inf. 9-10-62; prom. to sgt.; KIA Hobbs Hill 10-13-64. Farmer; $5,000/1,700 (parents); b. Barbour 1836, son of Henry and Margaret (Means) Martin; Methodist-Episcopal Church.

MARTIN, Henry
Enl. Barbour Home Guard; NFR. Farmer; $5,000/1,700 (parents); b. Barbour 1842, brother of Jacob; Methodist-Episcopal Church.

MARTIN, George S.
Enl. Barbour Home Guard. Farmer; $5,000/1,700 (parents); b. Barbour 1842, brother of Jacob; Methodist-Episcopal Church; d. Barbour 1880.

MARTIN, Arthur Wellington
Elec. Justice of the Peace 1865. Farmer; $10,000/3,000; b. Harrison Co., W. Va. 1816; m. Catherine Hart 1864; Republican; came to Barbour during war; returned to Harrison Co. after 1880 where d. 1896. Son of William and Jane Martin; father b. N.J., settled Harrison Co.

MAXWELL, John
District Committee Union Party 1863 and 1864. Farmer; $8,000/1,165; b. Pa. 1816; Methodist-Protestant Church; m. Miranda Vandevort 1839; came to Barbour 1850's from Harrison Co., W. Va.; moved to Taylor Co., W. Va. after war where living 1880.

McBEE, William Porter
Enl. Co. K, 17th W. Va. Inf. 2-18-65 as substitute; disch. 6-30-65. Farmer; $800/286 (parents); b. Monongalia Co., W. Va. 1847; came to Barbour 1850's; m. 1) Irritha Corbin 1867; 2) Alice G. Siger 1883; moved to Harrison Co., W. Va. 1880's where listed Union veterans 1890. Son of William and Elisabeth (Shaffer) McBee, b. Monongalia Co., settled Barbour; grandson of Hezekiah and Mamie (Carl) McBee; grandfather immigrant from Scotland, settled Pa., then Monongalia Co.

McCAULEY, Edward Jackson
Sympathizer; drafted 3-65, never inducted; brother-in-law *Lemuel Marks listed Barbour Light Horse; son-in-law *William Weaver served Home Guard. Tenant;

$0/150; b. Barbour 1823; Methodist-Episcopal Church; m. Catherine Forinash 1841; d. Neb. 1880. Son of John and Eleanor (McCall) McCauley; father b. Md.; grandson of Robert McCauley, settled Barbour.

McCAULEY, Noah
Co. A, 133rd W. Va. Militia, called into service 9-63 for three months; brother-in-law William Bennett served Co. D, 20th Va. Cav. (CSA). Farmer; $1,500/505 (father); b. Barbour 1834, brother of Edward; Methodist-Episcopal Church; m. Phoebe Bennett 1860; moved to Upshur Co., W. Va. where d. 1900.

McCAULEY, Emery C.
Sympathizer, assisting post-war Board of Registration. Farmer; $1,500/505 (father); b. Barbour 1840, brother of Edward; Methodist-Episcopal Church. NFR after 1868.

McCAULEY, Joseph C.
Enl. Bat. H, 1st W. Va. Art. 3-24-64 for six months; re-enlisted 9-64; POW New Creek 11-28-64; disch. 7-11-65; step-brother *Francis Snodgrass Unionist. $0/94 (mother); b. Harrison Co., W. Va. 1846; came to Barbour 1850's; m. Elisabeth Cline 1865; living Barbour 1880. Son of Robert and Nancy (Jenkins) McCauley; grandson of John and Eleanor (McCall) McCauley.

McCOY, Benjamin
District Committee Union Party 1864; brother William served 7th W. Va. Cav. (USA); brother-in-law *Wellington Holland served Co. B, 31st Va. Inf. (CSA). $10,000/1,025; b. Pendleton Co., W. Va. 1823; Republican; m. Matilda Johnson; moved to Upshur Co., W. Va. after 1880 where d. 1909. Son of Joseph and Mildred (Harvey) McCoy, b. Va., grandson of Joseph and Sarah (Olive) McCoy; grandfather immigrant from Scotland.

McDANIEL, William S.
Com. Capt., 169th W. Va. Mil. 10-24-62; never called into service; enl. Co. C, 4th W. Va. Cav. 7-27-63; disch. 3-9-64; re-enlisted Co. B, 17th W. Va. Inf. 8-29-64; disch. 6-30-65; in addition to brothers listed below, brother David served Co. C, 4th W. Va. Cav. (USA). Farmer; $40/120 (parents); b. Taylor Co., W. Va. 1827; came to Barbour 1850's; m. Catherine McWilliams; listed Barbour Union veterans 1890. Son of Isaac and Sarah (McVicker) McDaniel, b. Taylor Co.; grandson of Aaron and Mary (Haddix) McDaniel; grandfather b. Pa., settled Taylor Co.

McDANIEL, Abraham
Appointed U. S. Postmaster Pleasant Creek 1864. Saddler; $800/278; b. Taylor Co., W. Va. 1824, brother of William; came to Barbour 1850's with wife Mary; moved to Upshur Co., W. Va. after 1880 where d. 1905.

McDANIEL, Nathan
Enl. Co. B, 17th W. Va. Inf. 8-29-64; disch. 6-30-65; brother-in-law *Isaac Haddix served same company; son-in-law *Nathaniel Streets served Co. K, 31st Va. Inf. (CSA). Manager; $850/205; b. Taylor Co., W. Va. 1826, brother of William; came to Barbour 1840's; Methodist-Episcopal Church; m. Sarah Haddix; listed Barbour Union veterans 1890; d. 1893.

McDANIEL, Adam
Enl. Co. B, 17th W. Va. Inf. 8-29-64; prom. to cpl.; disch. 6-30-65. $850/205 (brother); b. Taylor Co., W. Va. 1845, son of Nathan and Sarah (Haddix) McDaniel; m. Harriet Pitzer 1865; moved to Ind. 1870's where living 1880.

McDANIEL, Isaac
Drafted Co. K, 17th W. Va. Inf. 2-25-65 ; disch. 6-30-65. Farmer; $900/200; b. Taylor Co., W. Va. 1828, brother of William; Republican; m. Nancy Luzadder 1840; came to Barbour 1850's; living Barbour 1880.

McDANIEL, Alpheus
Com. Capt., 169th W. Va. Mil. 8-16-62; never called into service; enl. Co. H, 12th W. Va. Inf. 8-1-62; wd. Petersburg 3-31-65; disch. 6-16-65. Tenant; $0/18; b. Taylor Co., W. Va. 1833; came to Barbour 1850's from Ritchie Co., W. Va. with wife Lucinda; returned to Taylor Co. after war where listed Union veterans 1890. Son of David and Lydia (Stansberry) McDaniel; grandparents b. Pa., settled Taylor Co. 1790's.

McDANIEL, Martin Van Buren
Enl. Co. K, 17th W. Va. Inf. 2-22-65 as substitute; disch. 6-30-65. Farmer; $650/55 (parents); b. Barbour 1847; moved to Mo. after the war. Son of Aaron and Statira (Glascock) McDaniel; grandson of Aaron and Mariah (Shaw) McDaniel; grandfather b. Pa.

McDONALD, Adoniram
Pre-war Col., 186th Va. Mil., Calhoun Co. W. Va.; State Commissioner of Roads; arrested 7-5-63, held for twelve days Highland Co., Va., then released; Delegate Union Party Convention Grafton 1864; brother-in-law Bailey Cleavenger served Co. C, 11th W. Va. Inf. (USA), killed by guerrillas. Farmer; $5,000/1,000; born Marion Co., W. Va. 1827; m. Elisabeth Ann Bartlett 1842;

moved to Calhoun Co. 1852; forced to flee county in early months of war due to threats on his life by Confederates; moved to Barbour 1863; moved to Taylor Co., W. Va. 1866 where d. 1905. Son of James and Tabitha (Housten) McDonald; father b. Pa.; grandson of Benjamin and Mercy (Nixon Reed) McDonald; grandfather immigrant from Scotland.

McGINNIS, Thomas
Enl. Co. F, 15th W. Va. Inf. 9-10-62; POW Cloyd Mountain 5-9-64; believed to have d. in prison. Farmer; $500/126 (mother); b. Ireland 1838. Son of Peter and Bridgett McGinnis, settled Barbour 1850's from Allegany Co., Md.

McINTOSH, Elijah
Enl. Co. H, 12th W. Va. Inf. 8-27-62; d. of pleurisy Winchester, Va. 10-12-64; brother William served in same company; brothers-in-law *John Keller and *Minor Reynolds Unionists. Apprentice blacksmith; $0/0; b. Taylor Co., W. Va. 1841; Methodist-Episcopal Church; came to Barbour 1849. Son of Elijah and Rebecca (Sayre) McIntosh; father b. Taylor Co.; grandson of Alexander McIntosh.

McNEIL, Moore
Enl. Barbour Home Guard 9-27-64; prom. to sgt. 3-27-65; prom. to Capt. 4-30-65; disch. 5-30-65; brother James Capt., Co. D, 22nd Va. Inf. (CSA); brother Claiborne served Co. G, 31st Va. Inf. (CSA). Methodist-Episcopal minister; $1,900/565 (mother); b. Pocahontas Co., W. Va. 1830; Republican; m. Eliza Caldwell; came to Barbour during war; moved to Preston Co., W. Va. 1869, then to Ritchie Co., W. Va. where living 1922. Son of William and Nancy (Griffey) McNeil, b. Pocahontas Co.; grandson of Jonathon and Phoebe (Moore) McNeil; great-grandson of Thomas and Mary (Hughes) McNeil; Thomas immigrant from Wales.

McVICKER, John
Delegate Union Party Convention Grafton 1864; elec. Overseer of Poor 1865; brother-in-law *Hezekiah Mitchell served Home Guard. Farmer; $1,800/285; b. Md. 1803; Methodist-Episcopal Church; Republican; m. 1) Malinda Mitchell 1824; 2) Phoebe Proudfoot 1867; d. Barbour 1882. Son of John and Elisabeth McVicker.

McVICKER, Absalom
Enl. Co. C, 4th W. Va. Cav. 8-22-63; disch. 3-9-64. Farmer; $3,000/508 (parents); b. Barbour 1844; Methodist-Episcopal Church; m. Catherine Haddix 1865; listed Barbour Union veterans 1890. Son of Levi and Maria (Toothman) McVicker; father b. Md.; grandson of John and Malinda (Mitchell) McVicker.

McWILLIAMS, John A.
Enl. Co. C, 4th W. Va. Cav. 7-27-63; disch. 3-9-64; brother Benjamin served Union army, KIA. Tenant; $0/78; b. Augusta Co., Va 1828; Methodist-Episcopal Church; came to Barbour 1850's with wife Christine; moved to Taylor Co., W. Va. after war, then to Preston Co., W. Va. 1870's where listed Union veterans 1890. Son of John and Isabell (Piatt) McWilliams, settled Taylor Co. 1840's; grandson of John McWilliams, b. Somerset Co., N.J., settled Augusta Co.

MELROSE, Adam A.
Com. Lt., 139th W. Va. Mil. 8-16-62; never called into service; drafted 2-65, never inducted. Mechanic; $2,500/500; b. Scotland 1820; came to Barbour 1850's with wife Elisabeth; moved to Kan. after war where living 1880.

MILLER, Andrew
Enl. Co. H, 10th W. Va. Inf. 5-8-62; disch. 5-7-65. Tenant; $0/50; b. Barbour 1824; Methodist-Episcopal Church; m. Rebecca Nutter 1845; moved to Doddridge Co., W. Va. after war, then Ritchie Co., W. Va. where d. 1888; widow listed Union veterans 1890. Son of Martin and Margaret (Lochrea) Miller; grandson of John and Janet Miller, settled Barbour from South Branch 1780's.

MILLER, Godfrey
Enl. Co. F, 15th W. Va. Inf. 9-10-62; disch. 6-14-65. Farmer; $0/50; b. Barbour 1844; m. Nancy C. Latham 1866; living Barbour 1880. Son of Daniel and Nancy (Boyles) Miller; grandson of Martin and Margaret (Lochrea) Miller.

MILLER, Andrew
Sympathizer. Farmer and slave owner; $24,000/17,119; b. Tucker Co., W. Va. 1794; Methodist-Episcopal Church; m. Hester Ann Poling 1841; d. Barbour 1879. Son of Andrew and Sarah (Miller) Miller, settled Barbour from South Branch 1780's.

MILLER, William L.
Com. Lt., 139th W.Va Mil. 10-24-62; never called into service; drafted 2-65, never inducted; brothers-in-law *Andrew and *Henry Myers served Co. I, 17th W. Va. Inf. (USA). Tenant; $0/102; b. Hardy Co., W. Va. 1838; m. Martha Myers 1857; moved to Taylor Co., W. Va. after war where living 1880. Son of Philip and Mary Ann (Hetzel) Miller, b. Va., settled Barbour 1840's; grandparents natives of Va.

MINARD, William
Drafted into Co. E, 17th W. Va. Inf. 2-24-65; disch. 6-30-65; brothers Henry and John served Co. I, 17th W. Va. Inf. (USA). Farm laborer; $0/50 (parents); b. Fayette Co., Pa. 1846; came to Barbour during the war with wife Margaret; (divorced in 1870's); moved to Taylor Co., W. Va. after war; returned to Barbour 1880's where listed Union veterans 1890. Son of Jacob and Ruth Minard; father b. Pa., settled Preston Co., W. Va. 1850's.

MINEAR, John
Enl. Co. F, 3rd W. Va. Inf. 6-21-61; wd. left arm Second Bull Run 8-29-62; re-enlisted 1-27-64, serving Co. D, 6th W. Va. Cav. upon consolidation of regiment with 5th W. Va. Cav.; hospitalized 5-65; disch. 8-9-65. Farmer; $560/150 (mother); b. Barbour 1840; Methodist-Episcopal Church; m. 1) Sarah Jane Isner; 2) Rebecca Shephard 1880; moved to Randolph Co., W. Va. after war, then to Lewis Co., W. Va. where listed Union veterans 1890. Son of Adam and Fanny (Mitchell) Minear; father b. Tucker Co., W. Va.; grandson of Adam and Elisabeth (Cobb) Minear; grandfather b. Bucks Co., Pa.; great-grandson of John Minear, immigrant from Belgium, settled Tucker Co. 1780's.

MINEAR, Adam
Enl. Co. F, 3rd W. Va. Inf. 6-25-61; re-enlisted 1-28-64, serving Co. D, 6th W. Va Cav. upon consolidation of regiment with 5th W. Va. Cav.; des. Fort Leavenworth, Kan. 7-15-65. Farmer; $560/150 (mother); b. Barbour 1842, brother of John; Methodist-Episcopal Church; m. Elisabeth Jane Proudfoot 1865; NFR.

MINEAR, Francis Marion
Enl. Co. I, 6th W. Va. Inf. 1-11-63; disch. 6-10-65. Farmer; $560/150 (mother); b. Barbour 1844, brother of John; Methodist-Episcopal Church; m. Ella Luckey; moved to Harrison Co., W. Va. after war where d. 1891.

MITCHELL, Hezekiah
Enl. Barbour Home Guard 10-19-64 for one year; brother-in-law *John McVicker Unionist. Farmer; $400/151; b. Hampshire Co., W. Va. 1810; m. Margaret Farrence 1830; living Barbour 1870. Son of Solomon and Elisabeth (Thompson) Mitchell; father b. N.J., settled Barbour 1840's.

MITCHELL, Ezekiel
Enl. Co. F, 3rd W. Va. Inf. 2-16-63; served Co. D, 6th W. Va. Cav. upon consolidation of regiment with 5th W. Va. Cav.; des. Fort Leavenworth, Kan. 7-15-65. Farmer; $400/151 (parents); b. Hampshire Co., W. Va. 1843, son of

Hezekiah and Margaret (Farrence) Mitchell; m. Sarah E. Ludwig 1869; moved to Jackson Co., W. Va. 1870 where living 1880.

MITCHELL, Aaron
Enl. Co. F, 15th W. Va. Inf. 8-23-62; disch. for disability 2-26-63; drafted 2-65, never inducted; father-in-law *Josiah Hawkins Unionist; brother-in-law *Leroy Hawkins served Co. N, 6th W. Va. Inf. (USA). Farmer; $400/140 (mother); b. Barbour 1841; m. Tamara Hawkins 1862; moved to Ritchie Co., W. Va. 1880's where listed Union veterans 1890. Son of John and Cassa (McDonald) Mitchell; grandson of Solomon and Elisabeth (Thompson) Mitchell.

MITCHELL, John W.
Enl. Co. I, 6th W. Va. Inf. 1-11-63; disch. 6-10-65. Farmer; $400/140 (mother); b. Barbour 1847, brother of Aaron; moved to Randolph Co., W. Va. after war.

MITCHELL, Robert
Elec. Overseer of Poor 1863; son-in-law *Isaac Talbott served Co. E, 62nd Va. Mtd. Inf. (CSA). Farmer; $7,580/200; b. Hampshire Co., W. Va. 1801; m. Sarah Keller 1821; d. Barbour 1870. Son of John and Mary Mitchell; father b. N.J., settled Barbour 1806.

MITCHELL, Josiah
Enl. Co. F, 15th W. Va. Inf. 8-23-62; disch. 6-14-65; brother-in-law *Cyrus Robinson served same company. Farmer; $7,580/200 (parents); b. Barbour 1839, son of Robert and Sarah (Keller) Mitchell; m. Mary Robinson 1859; listed Barbour Union veterans 1890.

MITCHELL, Middleton
Enl. Co. F, 15th W. Va. Inf. 8-23-62; wd. left arm; disch. 6-14-65; brothers-in-law *Archibald and *John England served Confederate Army. Farmer; $7,580/200 (parents); b. Barbour 1844, brother of Josiah; United Brethren Chruch; m. Doris England 1864; listed Barbour Union veterans 1890.

MOATS, John Huffman
Enl. Co. K, 15th W. Va. Inf. 2-22-64; listed sick Winchester, Va. 11-64; disch. 6-14-65; brother-in-law *Hamilton Isner served Co. F, 15th W. Va. Inf. (USA). Farmer; $500/50 (parents); b. Pa. 1832; German Baptist; came to Barbour 1850's; m. Elisabeth Firth 1856; listed Barbour Union veterans 1890. Son of Jacob and Elisabeth (Henderson-Gray) Moats; father German Baptist minister; grandson of Tevault and Hannah (McDonald) Moats, settled Barbour 1818.

MOATS, James
Enl. Co. F, 3rd W. Va. Inf. 6-25-61; disch. 8-15-64; re-enlisted as substitute Co. E, 7th W. Va. Inf. 3-29-65; disch. 7-1-65. Farmer; $500/50 (parents); b. Pa. 1840, brother of John H.; German Baptist; m. Delila Cole 1865; listed Barbour Union veterans 1890.

MOATS, John A.
Enl. Co. F, 15th W. Va. Inf. 8-23-62; disch. 6-14-65. Farmer; $500/220 (parents); b. Barbour 1834; United Brethren Church; m. Elisabeth Gainer 1866; listed Barbour Union veterans 1890. Son of Isaac and Susan (Gower) Moats, b. Pa.; grandson of Tevault and Hannah (McDonald) Moats.

MOATS, Eli
Enl. Co. F, 15th W. Va. Inf. 8-23-62; d. Winchester, Va. 10-1-64. Farmer; $500/220 (parents); b. Barbour 1838, brother of John A.; United Brethren Church.

MOATS, Moses
Enl. Co. F, 15th W. Va. Inf. 8-23-62; right leg shot off Winchester 9-19-64; disch. 6-14-65. Farmer; $500/220 (parents); b. Barbour 1839, brother of John A.; United Brethren Church; m. Malinda Streets 1871; listed Barbour Union veterans 1890; d. Barbour 1908.

MOATS, Samuel
Enl. Co. I, 6th W. Va. Inf. 11-19-61; disch. 11-25-64. Farmer; $500/220 (parents); b. Barbour 1840, brother of John A.; United Brethren Church; m. Virginia England 1866; listed Barbour Union veterans 1890.

MOATS, Sanford Huff
Enl. Barbour Home Guards 1-15-64 for one year; drafted into Co. C, 7th W. Va. Inf. 4-7-65; disch. 7-1-65. Farmer; $500/220 (parents); b. Barbour 1843, brother of John A.; United Brethren Church; m. 1) Lucy England 1866; 2) Lory L. Duckworth 1874; listed Barbour Union veterans 1890.

MONTGOMERY, Michael
Drafted Co. I, 17th W. Va. Inf. 2-16-65; des. from Grafton hospital 6-30-65; father arrested as secessionist sympathizer. $300/140 (parents); b. Barbour 1839; Methodist-Protestant Church; m. Mary Kelley 1860; moved to Preston Co., W. Va. after war. Son of *John and Nancy (Edwards) Montgomery; father b. Barbour; grandson of John Montgomery, b. Md., settled Barbour.

MONTGOMERY, Adam
Enl. Co. H, 7th W. Va. Inf. 9-19-61; wd. Antietam 9-17-62 and disch. for disability; brother-in-law *Thomas Digman served Co. K, 31st Va. Inf. (CSA). $300/140 (parents); b. Barbour 1843, brother of Michael; Methodist-Protestant Church; Democrat; m. Susan Digman 1863; moved to Preston Co., W. Va. 1870's where d. 1889.

MONTGOMERY, James Asberry
Enl. Co. H, 7th W. Va. Inf. 9-2-62; KIA Antietam 9-17-62. Farmer; $300/290 (parents); b. Barbour 1841. Son of Asberry and Anna (Hardin) Montgomery; parents b.; grandson of John Montgomery.

MOODY, John W.
Enl. Bat. E, 1st W. Va. Art. 8-12-62; disch. 6-30-65; brother Richard served Co. E, 3rd W. Va. Inf. (USA), d. Andersonville; brother Jonathon served Co. K, 3rd W. Va. Cav. (USA); brother-in-law Peter Tenny served Bat. E, 1st W. Va. Art. (USA). Tenant; $0/49; b. Va. 1837; m. Julia Ann Campbell 1857; moved to Gilmer Co., W. Va. after war where listed Union veterans 1890. Son of Wilton and Peachy Moody, b. Va.

MOORE, William Randolph
Enl. Co. H, 10th W. Va. Inf. 6-1-62; prom. to cpl. 11-29-62; disch. 6-25-65; brothers-in-law *William and *Jaspar Kelley served in same company. Farmer; $400/160; b. Barbour 1824; Baptist; Republican; m. 1) Catherine Price; 2) Lucinda Kelley 1855; listed Barbour Union veterans 1890. Son of Samuel and Elisabeth (Wright) Moore; father b. Barbour; grandson of Daniel and Deborah (Poling) Moore, b. Allegany Co., Md., settled Barbour.

MOORE, Silas R.
Enl. Co. H, 10th W. Va. Inf. 6-1-62; wd. in head 1864; disch. 8-9-65. Farmer; $400/160 (parents); b. Barbour 1842, son of William and Catherine (Price) Moore; Baptist; m. Nancy England 1864; listed Barbour Union veterans 1890.

MOORE, Isaiah
Enl. Co. H, 10th W. Va. Inf. 6-1-62; disch. 6-25-65. Tenant; $0/58 (mother); b. Barbour 1845, brother of William; Baptist; m. Martha England 1867; listed Barbour Union veterans 1890.

MOORE, Otho
Enl. Co. K, 15th W. Va. Inf. 1-18-64; shot in leg Cedar Creek 10-19-64; disch. 6-14-65. Farmer; $800/55 (parents); b. Barbour 1843; m. Melvina Price 1866;

listed Barbour Union veterans 1890. Son of Daniel and Jane (Booth) Moore, b. Barbour; grandparents b. Md.

MOORE, Daniel C.
Enl. Co. F, 15th W. Va. Inf. 9-10-62; disch. for disability 2-26-63; drafted 3-65, never inducted. Tenant; $0/34; b. Barbour 1828; m. Martha Jane Philips; living Barbour 1880. Son of William and Catherine (Burton) Moore; grandson of Daniel and Deborah (Poling) Moore, b. Md.

MOORE, Eli M.
Enl. Co. D, 17th W. Va. Inf. 3-2-65; disch. 6-30-65; brothers *Jesse and *Granville served Co. K, 31st Va. Inf. (CSA). Tenant; $0/95 (mother); b. Randolph Co., W. Va. 1842; m. Tabitha Wright Moore 1864; living Barbour 1880. Son of William and Sarah (Bennett) Moore; parents and grandparents b. Va.

MOORE, Lee McNeal
Enl. Co. C, 4th W. Va. Cav. 7-27-63; disch. 3-9-64; re-enlisted Co. K, 17th W. Va. Inf. 2-18-65; prom. to cpl.; disch. 6-30-65; brother-in-law *Jesse Cole served Co. C, 4th W. Va. Cav. (USA). Farmer; $400/150 (mother); b. Md. 1836; came to Barbour during war; m. Hannah Cole 1865; listed Barbour Union veterans 1890. Son of John and Mary Moore; father b. Pa.

MOSS, James A.
Co. B, 133rd W. Va. Militia, called into service 9-63 for three months. Farmer; $0/175; b. Va. 1816; married Martha _____; living Barbour 1880. Parents b. Va.

MUSGRAVE, John Calvin
Enl. Co. F, 12th W. Va. Inf. 9-10-62; disch. 6-16-65; brother Job served same company; brother Eli served Co. D, 179th Ohio Inf. Farmer; $1,200/271; b. Marion Co.., W. Va.1836; came to Barbour 1850's; m. Mary Linn 1859; moved to Tyler Co., W. Va. after war, then to Marion Co. where listed Union veterans 1890. Son of Zebulon and Elisabeth (McGinty) Musgrave; father b. Hardy Co., W. Va.; grandson of Job and Isabel (Watts) Musgrave; grandfather b. Pa., settled Hardy Co., then Marion Co.

MYERS, Martin
Union meeting held at his shop 5-61; elec. Justice of the Peace 1861; Chairman, Union Party County Committee 1863; County Supervisor of Elections 1863;

Delegate Union Party Convention Parkersburg 1863 and Grafton 1864; brother Josiah served Co. E, 62nd Va. Mtd. Inf. (CSA), captured with two of his sons and d. in prison. Shoemaker; $2,080/140; b. Pa. 1798; Lutheran; m. Sarah _____; d. Barbour 1860's.

MYERS, David Melancthon
Elec. to House of Delegates 1861; Delegate Second Wheeling Convention 6-61; elec. Circuit Court Clerk 1861 and 1863; Committee on Recruitment 8-62; Delegate Union Party Conventions Parkersburg 1863 and Grafton 1864; Deputy Court Reporter 1864. Shoemaker; $50/196; b. Barbour 1822. Son of Martin and Sarah Myers; Lutheran; m. Elisabeth _____; d. Barbour 1866.

MYERS, Louis A.
Com. Lt., Co. B, 3rd W. Va. Inf. 8-5-61; prom. to Capt. 11-9-62; disch. 8-16-64; Delegate Union Party Convention Grafton 1864. Shoemaker; $2,080/140 (parents); b. Barbour 1841, brother of David M.; Lutheran; m. Edith _____; moved to Wetzel Co., W. Va. after war where d. 1870's; widow listed Wetzel Co. Union veterans 1890.

MYERS, Andrew Jackson
Enl. Co. I, 6th W. Va. Inf. 11-19-61; prom. to cpl.; wd. left hand; disch. 11-25-64. Farmer; $200/60 (parents); b. Barbour 1840; Methodist-Protestant Church; moved to Taylor Co., W. Va. after war where listed Union veterans 1890. Son of Benjamin and Elisabeth (Annon) Myers and nephew of Martin Myers; parents b. Pa., settled Barbour 1834.

MYERS, Henry C.
Enl. Barbour Home Guard 10-1-63 for one year; enl. Co. I, 17th W. Va. Inf. 2-15-65; disch. 6-30-65. Farmer; $200/160 (parents); b. Barbour 1846, brother of Andrew; Methodist-Protestant Church; m. Mary E. Glotfelty 1868; living Barbour 1880.

NESTOR, James L.
Com. Lt., 139th W. Va. Mil. 8-16-62; prom. to Col. 9-20-62; never called into service; elec. Justice of the Peace 1863; District Committee Union Party 1863 and 1864. Farmer; $300/145; b. Barbour 1828; m. Hannah Skidmore; living Barbour 1880. Son of George and Amelia (Poling) Nestor, b. Md.; grandson of Jacob and Mary (Durr) Nestor, immigrants from Germany, settled Frederick Co., Md., then Barbour.

NESTOR, Andrew M.
Appointed U. S. Postmaster Nestorville 11-21-61; enl. Barbour Home Guards

10-1-63; re-enlisted 9-15-64; prom. to sgt.; Delegate Union Party Convention Grafton 1864; KIA Holsberry Farm, Barbour Co. 4-24-65; brothers-in-law *Michael and *Elias Haller served same company. Farmer; $600/133; b. Barbour 1834, brother of James; Methodist-Protestant Church; m. Margaret Vannoy 1856; widow listed Barbour Union veterans 1890.

NESTOR, George H.
Enl. Barbour Home Guard 11-10-63 for one year; prom. to sgt.; drafted 3-65, never inducted. Blacksmith; $0/196; b. Barbour 1831; Methodist-Protestant Church; m. Julie Ann Ogden 1857; listed Barbour Union veterans 1890. Son of Jacob and Nancy (Hoffman) Nestor, b. Barbour; grandson of George and Amelia (Poling) Nestor.

NESTOR, Francis Marion
Enl. Barbour Home Guard 10-15-64; disch. 5-30-65; drafted 3-65, never inducted; brother-in-law *Jacob Bennett served Co. K, 31st Va. Inf. (CSA). Farmer; $1,600/332 (parents); b. Barbour 1838, brother of George; Methodist-Protestant Church; m. Melvina Bennett 1864; living Barbour 1880.

NESTOR, Jonas J.
Enl. Barbour Home Guard 10-15-64; disch. 5-30-65. Farmer; $1,600/332 (parents); b. Barbour 1841, brother of George; Methodist-Protestant Church; m. Martha Boehm 1865; living Barbour 1880.

NESTOR, Sanford
Enl. Barbour Home Guard 11-10-63; re-enlisted 9-15-64; disch. 2-12-65; "His discipline was such as to be uncontrollable in a service of this kind;" brother-in-law *Jacob Bennett served Co. K, 31st Va. Inf. (CSA). Farmer; $1,600/332 (parents); b. Barbour 1846, brother of George; Methodist-Protestant Church; m. Amanda Bennett 1864; moved to Taylor Co., W. Va. 1880's where listed Union veterans 1890.

NESTOR, Abraham
Enl. Barbour Home Guard 11-10-63; re-enlisted 9-15-64; disch. 5-30-65. Miller; $75/75 (parents); b. Barbour 1843; Methodist-Protestant Church; m. 1) Mary A. Poling 1867; 2) Almeda Shaffer; living Barbour 1890. Son of William and Elisabeth (Harsh) Nestor; grandson of George and Amelia (Poling) Nestor.

NESTOR, William G.
Enl. Barbour Home Guard 9-1-63; re-enlisted 9-15-64; prom. to sgt; disch. 5-30-65; brothers-in-law *Robert Hoffman and *Samuel Harsh served same company;

brother-in-law *Henry Lohr served Co. K, 31st Va. Inf. (CSA) and Co. H, 10th W. Va. Inf. (USA). Farmer; $0/71; b. Barbour 1825; Methodist-Protestant Church; m. Sarah Lohr 1857; living Barbour 1880. Son of Jonas and Elisabeth (Holsberry) Nestor; grandson of George and Amelia (Poling) Nestor.

NEWCOMB, John A.
Enl. Co. B, 15th W. Va. Inf. 9-1-62; disch. 6-14-65. Tenant; $0/534; b. Frederick Co., Va. 1821; came to Barbour 1850's with wife Alcinda; moved to Marshall Co., W. Va. after war. Son of Leroy and Sarah (Epler) Newcomb, b. Va.

NEWCOMB, Leroy Manley
Enl. Co. F, 15th W. Va. Inf. 8-22-62; wd. left arm; disch. 6-14-65. Tenant; $0/64; b. Frederick Co., Va. 1831, half brother of John A.; Methodist-Episcopal Church; came to Barbour 1850's with wife Catherine; moved to Taylor Co, W. Va. after war where listed Union veterans 1890. Son of Leroy and Rebecca (Kline) Newcomb, b. Va.

NIKERK, Michael
Sympathizer. Teamster; $0/370; b. Washington Co., Md. 1811; United Brethren Church; came to Barbour 1850's with wife Nancy; d. Barbour 1863.

NUTTER, Anthony H.
Enl. Co. H, 10th W. Va. Inf. 5-8-62; POW Cedar Creek 10-19-64; believed to have d. in prison. Farmer; $1,000/267 (parents); b. Barbour 1843; Baptist; m. Mary Shaw. Son of George and Sarah (Coburn) Nutter, b. Barbour; grandson of Christopher and Rebecca (Morehead) Nutter; great-grandson of Thomas and Sarah (Godwin) Nutter, settled Harrison Co., W. Va. from Del. 1770's.

O'BRIEN, Emmett Jones
Refused commission as general in Confederate Army 1861; Delegate to Constitutional Convention 11-61; District Committee Union Party 1863 and 1864; elec. State Senator 1865; drafted 2-65, never mustered. Merchant and pre-war General, Virginia Militia; $8,050/440; b. Randolph Co., W. Va. 1819; Methodist-Episcopal Church; Democrat; m. Martha Hall 1854; moved to Lewis Co., W. Va. 1870 where d. 1888. Son of Daniel and Hannah (Norris) O'Brien; father immigrate from County Claire, Ireland, settled Md. 1796, then Randolph Co. 1804.

OGDEN, Joshua C.
Enl. Co. C, 4th W. Va. Cav. 7-27-63; disch. 3-9-64; re-enlisted Co. F, 17th W. Va. Inf. 9-29-64; disch. 6-30-65. Farmer; $1,000/266 (parents); b. Barbour or

Harrison Co., W. Va. 1833; m. Drusilla A. Cool 1865; moved to Upshur Co., W. Va. 1880's where listed Union veterans 1890; d. 1922. Son of Nathan and Jane (Duncan) Ogden; father b. Md.; grandson of Thomas and Elisabeth (Moore) Ogden, b. Md., settled Harrison Co.

O'NEAL, Bartholomew
Sympathizer; drafted 2-65, never inducted; brother-in-law *William Shaw Unionist. Farmer; $2,000/290; b. Barbour 1827; Democrat; m. Rebecca Baker; living Barbour 1880. Son of David and Jane O'Neal, b. Md.; grandson of Daniel O'Neal, immigrant from County Claire, Ireland, settled Md., then Barbour.

O'NEAL, Samuel
Sympathizer; brother-in-law *Solomon Alexander Confederate sympathizer. Farmer; $2,000/282; b. Barbour 1818; Methodist-Episcopal Church; Democrat; m. Mary Crites 1844; d. Barbour 1899. Son of John and Abigail (Anglin) O'Neal; father b. Washington Co., Md.; grandson of Daniel O'Neal.

O'NEAL, Lemuel
Sympathizer. Farmer; $5,500/892; b. Barbour 1820, brother of Samuel; Methodist-Episcopal Church; Democrat; m. Jemima _____; d. Barbour 1895.

O'NEAL, Thomas
Sympathizer. Farmer; $900/167; b. Barbour 1823, brother of Samuel; Methodist-Episcopal Church; Democrat; m. 1) Elisabeth Wells; 2) Nancy Jones 1857; moved to Kan. after war.

OSBURN, Zarah
Enl. Co. I, 6th W. Va. Inf. 1-11-63; disch. 6-30-65. Tenant; $0/120 (mother); b. Barbour 1839; m. Amanda B. _____; listed Barbour Union veterans 1890; d. Barbour 1893. Son of Thomas and Eliza Osburn; grandson of Zarah and Mary (Dimphar) Osburn, settled Barbour from Rockingham Co., Va. 1790's.

OSBURN, John L.
Enl. Co. I, 6th W. Va. Inf. 1-11-63; disch. 6-30-65. Tenant; $0/120 (mother); b. Barbour 1843, brother of Zarah; m. Mary _____; moved to Doddridge Co., W. Va. after war, then Taylor Co., W. Va. where d.1880's; widow listed listed Taylor Co. Union veterans 1890.

OSBURN, James H.
Enl. Barbour Home Guard 1-15-64; disch. 10-9-64 to enlist in U.S. Army, but rejected as unfit for service. Farm laborer; $0/0; b. Barbour 1848, brother of Zarah; m. Keturah _____; moved to Taylor Co., W. Va. after war where listed Union veterans 1890.

PAINTER, Eli
Com. Lt., 169th W. Va. Militia 8-16-62; never called into service; enl. Co. F, 15th W. Va. Inf. 8-23-62; prom. to sgt.; disch. 6-14-65; brother-in-law *Caleb Cress Unionist. Farmer; $1850/780; b. Shenandoah Co., Va. 1821; came to Barbour 1850's; Republican; m. Rebecca Wayne; moved to Upshur Co., W. Va. after war where listed Union veterans 1890. Son of John and Eve (Weaver) Painter, b. Shenandoah Co., moved to Hampshire Co., W. Va. 1840's, then Barbour; grandson of George Painter; great-grandson of John Painter, immigrant from Germany.

PARKS, Granville
Com. Lt., 169th W. Va. Mil. 12-14-64, never called into service; arrested for secessionist sympathies; letters filed by citizens of county attesting to his disloyalty; brother-in-law Peter Hardman served Co. B, 3rd W. Va. Inf. (USA). Farmer, $3,185/2,450 (parents); b. Harrison Co., W. Va. 1841; Methodist-Episcopal Church, joined Southern Methodists after war; Democrat; m. Barbara Susan Hardman 1862; came to Barbour 1863 where d. 1922. Son of Noah and Rachel (Willet) Parks; father b. Harrison Co.; grandfather b. Del.

PARSONS, Edwin
Sympathizer; with *Spencer Dayton organized pro-Union mass meeting White Oak 1-15-63; drafted 3-65, never inducted; father Delegate Second Wheeling Convention; brother James Delegate Constitutional Convention; brother Edgar served Co. E, 25th Va. Inf. (CSA); brother-in-law *William Elliott Confederate sympathizer; brother-in-law Morgan Kittle served Co. A, 18th Va. Cav. (CSA). Physician; $400/175; b. Tucker Co., W. Va. 1825; Democrat; m. Dama Rebecca Kittle 1858; came to Barbour that year where living 1880. Son of Solomon and Hannah (Parsons) Parsons; father b. Tucker Co.; grandson of James and Rebecca (Simps) Parsons; grandfather immigrant from England, settled Hardy Co., W. Va.

PAUGH, James H.
Enl. Co. H, 10th W. Va. Inf. 11-15-62; wd. Droop Mountain 11-3-63; father-in-law *Abraham Furr and brother-in-law *Francis Furr served same company. Farm laborer; $0/0; b. Barbour 1840; m. 1) Mary Furr 1862; 2) Lucinda J. Knabenshoe 1868; moved to Gilmer Co., W. Va. 1870's where listed Union veterans 1890. Son of Jeremiah and Mary Ann (Martin) Paugh; grandson of Joseph and Jane Paugh, b. N.J., settled Barbour.

PAUGH, John Draper Camden
Enl. Co. A, 1st W. Va. Cav. As substitute 3-3-65; disch. 7-8-65. Farmer; $5,600/780 (parents); b. Barbour 1846; m. Nancy Young; moved to Upshur Co., W. Va. 1880's where listed Union veterans 1890; d. 1901. Son of Daniel and Margaret (Benson) Paugh; grandson of Joseph and Jane Paugh.

PAYNE, Nathan
Elec. County Treasurer 1865; father Confederate sympathizer; brother-in-law *William Price Unionist. Miller; $600/144; b. Barbour 1825; moved to Ohio 1840's where m. Julie Sherman 1847; returned to Barbour same year; Republican; living Barbour 1880. Son of *John and Margaret (Bennett) Payne; parents b. Barbour; grandson of Henry and Elisabeth (Smith) Payne, b. Va., settled Barbour.

PAYNE, Julia Ann (Sherman)
Sympathizer; brother-in-law *Stingley Shaffer Unionist. $600/144; b. Union Co., Ohio 1825, wife of Nathan Payne; living Barbour 1880. Daughter of Israel and Dorothy Sherman; father b. N.Y., settled Ohio.

PAYNE, William
Com. Capt., 169th W. Va. Mil.; never called into service; Delegate Union Party Convention Grafton 1864; Inspector of Elections 1865; drafted 2-65, never mustered; claim for war-time services in 169th Militia rejected 1902. Farmer; $0/150 (parents); b. Barbour 1828, brother of Nathan; m. Mary Shaffer Sanders (widow of *David Sanders) 1864; living Barbour 1880.

PAYNE, James R.
Enl. Co. N, 6th W. Va. Inf. 10-5-64; disch. 6-15-65. Farmer; $0/150 (parents); b. Barbour 1840, brother of Nathan; m. Julia Catherine Hooker 1861; listed Barbour Union veterans 1890.

PAYNE, Francis E.
Sympathizer; brother-in-law *Andrew Simon Unionist; brother-in-law *Allen Simon listed Barbour Light Horse. Farmer; $1,300/565; b. Loudoun Co., Va. 1832; moved to Frederick Co., Va., then Taylor Co., W. Va., then Barbour 1850's where m. Virginia Simon 1855; Methodist-Episcopal Church, joined Southern Methodists after war; Democrat; living Barbour 1880. Son of Travis and Mary (Wise) Payne, b. Loudoun Co.; grandfather immigrant from England.

PEPPER, James B.
Enl. Co. C, 4th W. Va. Cav. 7-14-63; disch. 3-9-64; re-enlisted Co. F, 17th W. Va. Inf. 3-1-65; disch. 6-30-65. Farmer; $2,000/720 (parents); b. Barbour 1845;

m. 1) ___; 2) Francis Mason 1892; moved to Harrison Co., W. Va. after war where listed Union veterans 1890. Son of Johnson and Roanna (Bailey) Pepper; father b. Harrison Co.; grandson of William and Nancy (Johnson) Pepper; grandfather b. Sussex Co., Del., settled Harrison Co.

PETERSON, Samuel T.
Enl. Co. B, 2nd W. Va. Inf. 5-26-61; des. Washington, D.C. 9-1-62; NFR. Coal miner; $0/0; b. Va. 1839; came to Barbour 1850's.

PHELPS, George Austin
Com. Lt., 139th W. Va. Mil. 8-16-62; never called into service; enl. Co. F, 15th W. Va. Inf. 8-23-62; prom. to cpl.; wd. left leg; disch. 6-14-65. Farmer; $2,000/700; b. Md. 1839; came to Barbour 1850's; m. 1) Sarah H. Bowman 1866; 2) Catherine Boyles 1873; listed Barbour Union veterans 1890. Son of Waldo and Catherine (Hainel) Phelps.

PHILIPS, Richard
Elec. Justice of the Peace 1861; brother-in-law *Jacob Bennett Unionist. Farmer; $1800/840; b. Barbour 1811; m. Mary Ryan 1839; living Barbour 1880. Son of John and Bethiah (Wells) Philips; grandson of Thomas and Susanna (Kittle) Philips, settled Barbour from Loudoun Co., Va. 1780's; great-grandson of Jonathon and Hepzibah (Parker) Philips; Jonathon son of emigrant from England to Va. 1630's.

PHILIPS, Simon
Elec. Constable 1863 and 1864; brother *Obediah and brother-in-law *William Fitzwater served 62nd Va. Mtd. Inf. (CSA); brother-in-law *Jacob Philips Confederate sympathizer, killed during war. Farmer; $0/50; b. Barbour 1824; m. Susannah Fitzwater 1843; moved to Roane Co., W. Va. 1850's; returned to Barbour during war; moved to Randolph Co., W. Va. after the war where living 1880. Son of Joseph and Mary (Harris) Philips; grandson of John and Bethiel (Wells) Philips.

PHILIPS, Granville
Enl. Co. E, 62nd Va. Mtd. Inf. (CSA) 8-26-62; des. 11-4-62; enl. Co. N, 6th W. Va. Inf. 10-15-64; disch. 6-30-65; brother-in-law *Isaac Philips served Co. A, 1st W. Va. Cav. (USA). Tenant; $0/228 (parents); b. Barbour 1843; Baptist; Republican; m. Julia Ann Shireman Isner (widow of *Henry Isner) 1865; listed Barbour Union veterans 1890. Son of George and Nancy (McKinney) Philips; grandson of Isaac and Elisabeth (Kittle) Philips; great-grandson of Thomas and Susanna (Kittle) Philips.

PHILIPS, Asa
Wagoner, U.S. Army; POW Moorefield 1-2-63; enl. Co. I, 17th W. Va. Inf. 2-14-65; disch. 6-30-65; brother *Bennett served Co. K, 31st Va. Inf. (CSA); sister-in-law *Osa Philips Confederate sympathizer; son-in-law *Haymond Gainer served Co. E, 62nd Va. Mtd. Inf. (CSA). Tenant; $0/123; b. Barbour 1818; m. 1) Mary Philips 1846; 2) Ida ____; moved to Preston Co., W. Va. after war where d. 1880's; widow listed Preston Co. Union veterans 1890. Son of Jacob and Sarah (Bennett) Philips; grandson of Isaac and Elisabeth (Kittle) Philips.

PHILIPS, Isaac N.
Enl. Co. A, 1st W. Va. Cav. 7-18-64; wd. in hand; disch. 2-23-65; father *Jesse and brother *Jesse served Co. H, 62nd Va. Mtd. Inf. (CSA); brother-in-law *Granville Philips served Co. E, 62nd Va. Mtd. Inf. (CSA) and Co. N, 6th W. Va. Inf. (USA). Farm laborer; $0/4 (parents); b. Barbour 1842; Methodist-Protestant Church; m. Almira Philips 1860; listed Tucker Co., W. Va. Union veterans 1890. Son of Jesse and Mary (Wilt) Philips; grandson of Jesse and Margaret (Kittle) Philips; great-grandson of Henry and Lydia (Harris) Philips; great-great grandson of Thomas and Susannah (Kittle) Philips.

PHILIPS, John E.
Enl. Co. H, 62nd Va. Mtd. Inf. (CSA) 6-1-62; des. 10-23-62; enl. Co. A, 1st W. Va. Cav. 3-10-63; disch. 7-8-65; father served same company in 62nd. Farm laborer; $0/4 (parents); b. Barbour 1843, brother of Issac; m. Rebecca Cross; moved to Upshur Co., W. Va. after war where listed Union veterans 1890; d. 1924.

PICKENS, George T.
Elec. County Supervisor 1865; son-in-law *Levi Johnson Unionist. Farmer; $4,000/1,225; b. Barbour 1820; Methodist-Protestant Church; m. Elisabeth Reger; moved to Ill. after war where living 1880. Son of John and Agnes Pickens; father b. Highland Co., Va., settled Barbour; grandson of Alexander and Sarah Pickens, b. Bath Co., Va.

PITTMAN, George L.
Enl. Co. B, 10th W. Va. Inf. 8-16-62; never mustered into service; elec. Overseer of Poor 1863; drafted 3-65, never inducted; father-in-law *Henson Stout Unionist. Farmer; $1,000/380 (parents); b. Barbour 1849; Methodist-Episcopal Church; m. 1) Elisabeth Stout; 2) Nancy A. Stout 1865; listed Barbour Union veterans 1890. Son of Isaac and Elisabeth (Goldsberry) Pittman; father b. Barbour; grandson of Joel and Sarah (Currence) Pittman; grandfather pioneer Methodist minister, settled Barbour from Hanover Co., Va. 1803.

PITTMAN, Hiram C.
Com. Lt., 139th W. Va. Mil. 8-16-62; never called into service; District Committee Union Party 1863; family tradition has him in army and wounded 1863, but no record found; son filed pension claim for his service in 169th W. Va. Mil., rejected 1902. Farmer; $900/242; b. Barbour 1825; Methodist-Episcopal Church; m. Melissa Ann Wilson 1848; d. Barbour 1878. Son of Joel and Sarah (Currence) Pittman.

PITTMAN, Emmett A.
Teamster, U. S. Army. Teamster; $900/242 (parents); b. Barbour 1849, son of Hiram and Melissa Ann (Wilson) Pittman; Methodist-Episcopal Church; m. Lassy A. Jones 1873; living Barbour 1880.

PITZER, James H.
Enl. Barbour Home Guard 11-23-64; disch. 5-30-65; brothers-in-law *Asa Squires and *Joseph and *Cornelius Bowman served Union Army. Farmer; $300/150; b. Marion Co., W. Va. 1835; m. Lydia Bowman 1855; living Barbour 1870. Son of Price and Frances (Poling) Pitzer; parents b. Marion Co., settled Barbour 1840's; grandson of John and Elisabeth (Price) Pitzer; grandfather b. Loudoun Co., Va., settled Marion Co.; great-grandson of John and Elisabeth (Kisner) Pitzer, immigrants from Germany.

PITZER, Jaspar
Enl. Barbour Home Guard 11-23-64; disch. 5-30-65. Farmer; $650/190 (parents); b. Marion Co., W. Va. 1839, brother of James; moved to Mo. after war where m. Rebecca Carlisle 1868.

POE, Philip F.
Com. Lt., Co. E, 11th W. Va. Inf. 8-28-62; dismissed from the service; NFR. Farmer; $0/47; b. Va. 1828; m. Lydia Martin 1844.

POLING, Benjamin N.
Enl. Co. K, 6th W. Va. Inf. 8-26-62; disch. 6-30-65. Farmer; $350/162; b. Barbour 1845; Republican; moved to Jackson Co., W. Va. after war where m. Jane Rhoads 1872; listed Jackson Co. Union veterans 1890. Son of Wilson and Matilda (Rohrbaugh) Poling; father b. Barbour; grandson of Martin and Mary (Wilson) Poling; grandfather b. Md., settled Barbour; great-grandson of Roger and Margaret (Black) Poling.

POLING, Harvey
Com. Lt., 139th W. Va. Mil. 8-16-62; never called into service; brother Newton Capt., Co. K, 11th W. Va. Inf. (USA). $1,800/461; b. Barbour 1820; United

Brethren Church; m. Mary Emeline Markeley 1847; d. Barbour 1886. Son of Martin and Mary (Wilson) Poling.

POLING, Alfred John
Enl. Co. K, 6th W. Va. Inf. 8-20-62; disch. 6-30-65; claim for war-time services in 169th Mil. rejected 1902. Farmer; $5,000/366 (parents); b. Barbour 1846, half-brother of Harvey; United Brethren Church; m. Mary Elisabeth Lockney 1866; listed Barbour Union veterans 1890; d. Barbour 1911. Son of Martin and Ruth (Rohrbaugh) Poling.

POLING, Peter M.
Enl. Bat. K, 2nd Pa. Art. 1-29-62; transf. to Co. I, 21st Vet. Res. Corps 12-29-63; disch. 2-12-65. Farmer; $300/89 (parents); b. Barbour 1837; m. Emily Hershman Robinson 1868; moved to Preston Co., W. Va. 1870's where listed Union veterans 1890. Son of Benjamin and Jane (Moats) Poling; father b. Barbour; grandparents b. Md.

POLING, George T.
Enl. Co. B, 15th Ohio Inf. 2-27-64; transf. to Vet. Res. Corps 11-14-64; disch. 12-9-65. $0/50 (parents); b. Barbour 1845; m. Mary Ann Bolinger 1867; listed Barbour Union veterans 1890. Son of Isaac and Eleanor (Goff) Poling; grandson of Jonas and Rachel (Pitzer-Dawson) Poling; grandfather b. Md.; great-grandson of Martin Poling, b. Md., settled Barbour.

POST, Isaac W.
Sympathizer; brother Stephen Unionist; brother-in-law Lafayette Hinkle served Co. B, 133rd W. Va. Mil.; brother-in-law *William Hall served Co. D, 20th Va. Cav. (CSA). Farmer; $4,000/1,408; b. Barbour 1829; Baptist; Republican; m. Elisabeth Hall 1856; living Barbour 1880. Son of George and Comfort (Simon) Post, b. Harrison Co., W. Va.; grandson of Abraham and Christina Post, b. Hardy Co., W. Va., settled Upshur Co., W. Va.

POSTEN, David M.
Enl. Co. C, 4th W. Va. Cav. 8-26-63; disch. 3-9-64. Farmer; $0/14; b. Preston Co., W. Va. 1847; came to Barbour 1850's with wife Susan; moved to Taylor Co., W. Va. 1870's, then to Neb. where listed Union veterans 1890. Son of Wilson and Mary (Rodeheaver) Posten; grandson of James Posten, b. Va., settled Preston Co. from Hampshire Co., Va.

PRICE, William
Com. Capt., 139th W. Va. Mil. 8-16-62; prom. to Lt-Col. 9-20-62; never called into service; District Committee Union Party 1863; arrested 7-2-63; imprisoned

Richmond; released 3-64; elec. Justice of the Peace 1864 and 1865; father-in-law *John Payne Confederate sympathizer; brothers-in-law *Nathan, *William and *James Payne Unionists. Farmer; $800/455; b. Preston Co., W. Va. 1824; m. Bethany Payne 1845; moved to Calhoun Co., W. Va. 1880's. Son of James A. and Jemima (England) Price; grandson of William and Mary (Butler Lewis) Price; grandfather b. Allegany Co., Md., settled Preston Co.

PRICE, William George Washington
Com. Capt., 139th W. Va. Mil. 8-16-62, never called into service; enl. Co. F, 15th W. Va. Inf. 8-27-62; prom. to Lt. 6-20-64; report by brigade commander on Cedar Creek stated: "Lt. G. W. Price of Co. F went as far to the rear as Kernstown when he concluded to return and joined the command on the night of the 19th after the command had encamped for the night;" dismissed from the service 11-25-64; elec. Clerk County Court 1865; brother *Albert served Co. D, 20th Va. Cav. (CSA); sister *Amanda (Price) Murphy secessionist; brother-in-law *Herbert Murphy served 25th Va. Inf. (CSA); brother-in-law *Levi Cross served Co. F, 15th W. Va. Inf. (USA). Farmer; $250/320; b. Barbour 1828; Methodist-Episcopal Church; Republican; m. Elisabeth England 1848; listed Barbour Union veterans 1890; d. 1914. Son of William and Ann (Poling) Price; b. Md.

PRICE, Isaac
Elec. Constable 1862; com. Lt., 139th W. Va. Mil. 8-16-62, never called into service; enl. Co. F, 15th W. Va. Inf. 8-27-62; wd. in hand Lynchburg 6-18-64; wd. in hand Winchester 9-19-64; wd. in leg and lost both arms Hobbs Hill 10-13-64, earning him nickname "No Arms." Farmer; $1,000/48; b. Barbour 1827, brother of William G. W.; Methodist-Episcopal Church; Republican; m. 1) Mary Elisabeth Stonestreet 1846; 2) Elisabeth England Kinney 1867; listed Barbour Union veterans 1890.

PRICE, Lewis
Enl. Co. H, 10th W. Va. Inf. 6-15-62; listed sick 6-65. Farmer; $1,000/48 (parents); b. Barbour 1847, son of Isaac and Mary (Stonestreet) Price; Methodist-Episcopal Church; m. Mary E. Brown; listed Barbour Union veterans 1890; d. Barbour 1927.

PRINGLE, Jacob
Enl. Co. F, 11th W. Va. Inf. 9-1-62; wd. in right arm; disch. 5-29-65; brother-in-law John Reed served in same company; brothers-in-law *Nathaniel and *Daniel Reed listed Barbour Light Horse. Tenant; $0/50; b. Harrison Co., W. Va. 1832; Methodist-Episcopal Church; came to Barbour 1850's where m. Margaret Reed

1854; moved to Roane Co., W. Va. where listed Union Veterans 1890. Son of Isaac and Ester (Rogers) Pringle; grandson of William and Nellie (Rollins) Pringle; great-grandson of Samuel and Charity (Cutwright) Pringle; Samuel first settler of Upshur Co., W. Va. 1760's.

PROUDFOOT, John H.
Delegate Union Party Convention Grafton 1864; drafted 2-65, never inducted; claim for war-time service in 169th Mil. rejected 1902. Farmer; $15,000/2,268; b. Barbour 1822; Baptist; m. Sarah A. Modisett 1847; living Barbour 1899. Son of Alexander and Elisabeth (Cole) Proudfoot; father b. Fauquier Co., Va.; grandson of John and Leah (Hitt) Proudfoot; grandfather immigrant from Scotland to Fauquier Co., settled Barbour 1803.

PROUDFOOT, James R.
Elec. Justice of the Peace 1860, continued to serve during war. Farmer; $1,220/162; b. Barbour 1828; Methodist-Episcopal Church; Republican; m. Mary Ann Mouser 1854; living Barbour 1899. Son of William and Jane (Robinson) Proudfoot; grandson of John and Leah (Hitt) Proudfoot.

PROUDFOOT, Edward J.
Sympathizer. $1,800/307; b. Barbour 1828, brother of James; Methodist-Episcopal Church; Republican; m. 1) Elisabeth Stark 1857; 2) Nancy Vivian Blake 1871; living Barbour 1880.

RADABAUGH, Simon Peter
Cpl., Co. B, 133rd W. Va. Mil., called into service 9-63; brothers-in-law *John Cooper and *Benjamin Radabaugh listed Barbour Light Horse; sister-in-law *Margaret Reed Confederate sympathizer. Tenant; $0/2,600; born Upshur Co., W. Va. 1833; Methodist Episcopal Church; m. 1) Lucinda Reed 1855; 2) Sarah M. Vance; moved to Braxton Co., W. Va. 1878. Son of George and Sarah (Heavener) Radabaugh; grandson of Adam and Catherine (Simmons) Radabaugh; parents and grandparents b. Va.

RAMSEY, John Morgan
Sympathizer, assisting post-war Board of Registration; drafted 3-65, never inducted; father-in-law *John Coontz Confederate sympathizer; brother-in-law *Jesse Schoonover served Co. A, 11th W. Va. Inf. (USA); brother-in-law *William Coontz Confederate sympathizer. Farmer; $800/337; born Fayette Co., Pa. 1836; m. Eliza Coontz 1858; d. Barbour 1914. Son of James and Mary (McClarney) Ramsey, b. Fayette Co., Pa.. settled Barbour 1840's; grandson of William and Sarah (Butler) Ramsey.

RAMSEY, William Hudson
Enl. Co. H, 10th W. Va. Inf. 5-8-62; prom. to sgt.; reduced to ranks at own request 12-6-62; disch. 5-7-65. Farmer; $2,500/80 (mother); b. Fayette Co., Pa. 1840, brother of John M.; Republican; moved to Pleasants Co., W. Va. where listed Union veterans 1890; d. Harrison Co., W. Va. 1931.

RANDALL, Malsias
Enl. Co. H, 12th W. Va. Inf. 8-27-62; wd. in left hand; disch. 6-16-65. Farmer; $200/220; b. Harrison Co., W. Va. 1822; Methodist-Episcopal Church; came to Barbour 1850's with wife Ellen; returned to Harrison Co. after war where listed Union veterans 1890. Son of Abner and Lydia Randall; grandson of James and Elisabeth (Jones) Randall; grandfather b. Kent Co., Md., settled Harrison Co.

RANKIN, Charles Mercer
Enl. Co. H, 7th W. Va. Inf. 9-2-61; prom. to sgt.; KIA Antietam 9-17-62.; brother-in-law *Lafayette Gall served Co. D, 20th Va. Cav. (CSA). Tenant; $1,000/887; b. Augusta Co., Va. 1831; Methodist-Episcopal Church; came to Barbour 1850's with parents and wife Suffrah. Son of Armstrong and Amelia Rankin; father b. Augusta Co.; grandfather b. Pa., settled Augusta Co.

REED, John W.
Enl. Co. H, 10th W. Va. Inf. 8-5-63; wd. both legs Kernstown 7-24-64 and disch. Farmer; $2,000/227 (mother); b. Barbour 1841; m. Mary M. Rosenbarger 1871; moved to Doddridge Co., W. Va. 1870's where listed Union veterans 1890. Son of Jonathon and Mahala (Costolow) Reed; father b. Loudoun Co., Va.; grandson of Peter and Sarah Reed, settled Barbour. Andrew Reed, 17th century resident of Westmoreland Co., Va. earliest known ancestor of Reeds of Barbour; his descendants moved to Prince William and Loudoun Cos., Va. from where settled Barbour late 18th century.

REED, Amaziah
Enl. Co. K, 6th W. Va. Inf. 10-2-62; disch. 6-30-65; brother-in-law *Jesse Leeson served Co. F, 15th W. Va. Inf. (USA). Tenant; $0/40 (parents); b. Barbour 1843; Methodist-Episcopal Church; m. Matilda _____; moved to Ritchie Co., W. Va. after war, then Wood Co., W. Va. where listed Union veterans 1890. Son of John and Martha (Thompson) Reed.

REED, Allen
Enl. Co. B, 7th W. Va. Inf. as substitute 3-20-65; disch. 7-1-65; NFR. Farmer; $600/75 (mother); b. Barbour 1846. Son of Stephen and Edith Reed; grandson of Ashabel and Louvina (Peppers) Reed; great-grandson of Jonathon and Sarah Reed.

REED, Alexander D.
Enl. Co. A, 46th Btln. Va. Cav. (CSA) 7-11-63; des. same day; drafted into Co. F, 7th W. Va. Inf. 3-15-65; disch. 7-1-65. Farmer; $600/75 (mother); b. Barbour 1839; m. 1) Muhilda _____; 2) Lucy Spencer 1878; moved to Ritchie Co., W. Va. after war; listed Harrison Co., W. Va. Union veterans 1890 as living Barbour. Son of William and Mary (Adams) Reed.

REEVES, Josiah Washington
Elec. Constable 1864. Tailor and Methodist-Protestant minister; $1,500/310; b. Md. 1811; m. Nancy Kemper Moore 1828; came to Barbour from Culpepper Co., Va. 1845; d. Md. 1889. Son of Thomas Washington Reeves.

REYNOLDS, Minor S.
Elec. Constable 1861; District Committee Union Party 1863; brothers-in-law *Elijah and William McIntosh served Co. H, 12th W. Va. Inf. Blacksmith; $1,380/385; b. Ireland 1828; Methodist-Episcopal Church; settled Taylor Co., W. Va. where m. Matilda McIntosh; came to Barbour 1850's; d. Barbour 1869. Son of James and Mariah Reynolds.

ROBERTS, William H.
Sympathizer. Farmer; $600/345; b. Lichfield Co., Conn. 1806; came to Barbour 1850's from Ohio with wife Ophia; d. Barbour 1870's.

ROBERTS, Albert D.
Enl. Co. K, 6th W. Va. Inf. 10-1-62; disch. 6-30-65. Farmer; $600/345 (parents); b. Lichfield Co., Conn. 1841, son of William and Ophia Roberts; m. Clarinda J. Wolf 1868; living Barbour 1870.

ROBINSON, John
District Committee Union Party 1863; brother-in-law *Jacob Woodford Confederate sympathizer. Tenant; $160/322; b. N.J. 1793; Methodist-Episcopal Church; m. Mary Proudfoot 1811; d. Barbour 1865. Son of James and Elisabeth (Davis) Robinson, b. N.J., settled Barbour 1796.

ROBINSON, William
Sympathizer; forced to flee county during Jones-Imboden Raid. Shoemaker; $1,000/1,020; b. Barbour 1827, son of John and Mary (Proudfoot) Robinson; Methodist-Episcopal Church; Democrat; m. Mary Sayre 1850; d. Taylor Co., W. Va. 1896.

ROBINSON, Cyrus Vance
Enl. Co. F, 15th W. Va. Inf. 8-26-62; disch. 6-14-65; father-in-law *Joshua Glascock Unionist; brother-in-law *Josiah Mitchell served same company. Farmer; $0/421; b. Barbour 1838; Methodist-Episcopal Church; Democrat; m. Sarah L. Glascock 1862; listed Barbour Union veterans 1890. Son of Elias and Rebecca (Moran) Robinson; father b. Barbour; grandson of John and Mary (Proudfoot) Robinson.

ROBINSON, James Perry
Elec. Justice of the Peace 1863; son *Smith served Co. A, 25th Va. Inf. and Co. D, 19th Va. Cav. (CSA). Merchant; $0/62; b. Barbour 1812, brother of John; m. Lydia ____; living Barbour 1880.

ROBINSON, Thomas B.
Enl. Co. B, 4th W. Va. Cav. 7-27-63; prom. to cpl.; disch. 3-9-64; re-enlisted Co. C, 17th W. Va. Inf. 9-22-64; disch. 6-30-65. $0/62 (parents); b. Barbour 1844, son of James and Lydia Robinson; m. Sally Barbee 1869; listed Barbour Union veterans 1890.

ROBINSON, Simon M.
Enl. Co. C, 17th W. Va. Inf. 9-22-64; disch. 6-30-65. $0/62 (parents); b. Barbour 1847, brother of Thomas; m. 1) Rebecca Duckworth 1867; 2) Jerusha ____; listed Barbour Union veterans 1890.

ROGERS, Arnold
Elec. Justice of the Peace 1861 and 1863; brother Benjamin served Co. B, 9th W. Va. Inf. (USA). Farmer; $3,000/577; b. Preston Co., W. Va. 1792; Methodist-Episcopal Church; m. 1) Mary Rogers 1815; 2) Cynthia ____; d. Barbour 1870's. Family said to have lived in Va. since 17th century.

ROGERS, Martin Van Buren
Enl. Bat. G, 1st W. Va. Art. 10-23-63; transf. to Bat. C 6-8-64; d. of cholera Parkersburg, W. Va. 7-24-64. Farmer; $3,000/755 (parents); b. Barbour 1846, son of Arnold and Cynthia Rogers; Methodist-Episcopal Church.

ROGERS, Nathan
Enl. Co. F, 15th W. Va. Inf. 9-5-64; disch. 6-14-65. Tenant; $0/150 (parents); b. Barbour 1844; m. Martha Hawkins 1865; moved to Braxton Co., W. Va. after war. Son of Frances and Lydia Rogers; parents and grandparents b. Va.

ROGERS, James D.
Drafted Co. G, 7th W. Va. Inf. 3-23-65; disch. 7-1-65. Tenant; $0/150 (parents);

b. Barbour 1846, brother of Nathan; moved to Taylor Co., W. Va. after the war; widow listed Taylor Co. Union veterans 1890.

ROGERS, Leeper
Com. Lt., 169th W. Va. Mil.; never called into service; elec. Constable 1865; drafted 2-65, never inducted. Farmer; $1,500/636 (parents); b. Monroe Co., Ohio 1838; Methodist-Episcopal Church; m. Margaret R. ____; living Barbour 1880. Son of Jacob and Sarah (Baker) Rogers; father b. Lewis Co.,W. Va., moved to Ohio where married; returned to Barbour 1840's.

ROHR, Lewis H.
Elec. Constable 1865; brother Henry served Co. C, 21st W. Va. Mil., called into service 10-64; brother-in-law *Samuel Welch served Co. H, 10th W. Va. Inf. (USA), brothers-in-law *Benjamin and *John Welch Confederate sympathizers. $0/212; b. Harrison Co., W. Va. 1821; m. Rebecca Jane Welch; moved to Ritchie Co., W. Va. after war, then Roane Co., W. Va. 1871 where d. 1882. Son of James and Jane (Cather) Rohr; father b. Fayette Co., Pa.; grandson of John and Susannah Rohr; grandfather b. N.J., settled Harrison Co. 1796.

ROHRBAUGH, Anthony S.
Elec. Justice of the Peace 1861. Farmer; $7,400/740; b. Barbour 1819; Methodist-Episcopal Church; m. 1) Millie Hoff 1840; 2) Clarissa Johnson Morrison 1844; d. Barbour 1877. Son of John and Nancy Rohrbaugh; father b. Hardy Co., W. Va.; grandson of John and Elisabeth (Harnes) Rohrbaugh, immigrants from Germany, settled Hardy Co. from Pa.

ROLLINS, Isaac
Enl. Co. H, 10th W. Va. Inf. 5-9-62; prom. to Lt.; dismissed from the service 8-1-64; com. Lt., 169th W. Va. Militia 11-5-64; never called into service; NFR. Shoemaker; $0/275; b. Upshur Co., W. Va. 1826; United Brethren Church; m. Rachel Wamsley 1857; came to Barbour 1858. Son of Barney and Catherine (Wetherholt) Rollins; father b. Culpepper Co., Va.; grandson of Moses and Mary (Smith) Rollins, b. Culpepper Co., settled Upshur Co.

ROSENBARGER, Bartholomew
Com. Lt., 139th W. Va. Mil. 8-16-62; prom. to Capt., 10-20-62; never called into service; elec. Cconstable 1864. Farmer; $900/316; b. Jefferson Co., W. Va. 1825; Baptist; came to Barbour 1849 where m. Margaret Amanda Wilson; moved to Mo. 1865 where d. 1904. Son of David and Elisabeth (Shaull) Rosenbarger; grandson of John and Barbara (Pugh) Rosenbarger; grandfather b. Pa., settled Jefferson Co.; great-grandson of Erasmus Rosenbarger, immigrant from Germany.

RUSSMISELL, Peter
Elec. Constable 1865. Farmer; $2,500/532; b. Augusta Co., Va. 1817; moved to Upshur Co., W. Va. where m. Cecilia Eagle 1846; moved to Barbour 1850's; living Barbour 1880. Son of Adam and Sarah (Sherman) Russmisell; father b. Pa.

SAFFLE, Elias
Enl. Co. F, 3rd W. Va. Cav. 4-3-65; disch. 6-30-65. Tenant; $0/50; b. Pa. 1834; m. Emily Montgomery; moved to Taylor Co., W. Va. 1880's where listed Union veterans 1890. Son of Joseph and Arena Saffle, b. Pa, settled Barbour.

SAFFLE, Corbin
Enl. Co. C, 4th W. Va. Cav. 7-27-63; disch. 3-9-64; re-enlisted Co. B, 17th W. Va. Inf. 9-2-64; disch. 6-30-65. Farmer; $800/432 (parents); b. Pa. 1840, brother of Elias; m. Sarah Chipps 1865; moved to Braxton Co., W. Va. after war where listed Union veterans 1890.

SANDERS, David William
Enl. Co. H, 10th W. Va. Inf. 11-15-62; KIA Droop Mountain 11-6-63; brother-in-law *Draper Shaffer served same company. Farmer; $1,000/379; b. Preston Co., W. Va. 1832; Lutheran; came to Barbour 1850's where m. Mary Shaffer 1857. Son of Alexander and Susanna (Spessart) Sanders; father b. Frederick Co., Md.; grandson of Hiram and Sarah (Shaffer Crider) Sanders.

SAYERS, Enoch
Elec. Justice of the Peace 1861; District Committee Union Party 1863; drafted 2-65, never inducted; brother-in-law *Jesse Cole served Co. C, 4th W. Va. Cav. (USA). Farmer; $2,540/737; b. Barbour 1825; Methodist-Episcopal Church; m. Elisabeth Felton 1851; moved to Iowa after war where d. 1901. Son of Solomon and Mary Ann (Ball) Sayers; father b. Barbour; grandson of Jedediah and Elisabeth (Weaver) Sayers, b. Pa., settled Barbour; great-grandson of David and Hannah (Frazier) Sayers.

SCHOONOVER, Jesse B.
Enl. Co. A, 11th W. Va. Inf. 6-9-61; disch. for disability 3-20-62; NFR; brother-in-law *William Ramsey served Co. H, 10th W. Va. Inf. (USA). Farmer; $0/164; b. Barbour 1841; m. Emaline Ramsey 1859. Son of John and Margaret (Sherman) Schoonover; father b. Barbour; grandson of Thomas and Basheba (Nutter) Schoonover, b. Randolph Co., W. Va.

SCOTT, William Sanford
Elec. County Supervisor 1865; brother Amos arrested 6-61, escaped and later served Co. E, 15th W. Va. Inf. (USA); brother Newton served Co. B, 4th W. Va. Cav. (USA); father-in-law *Henry Martin Unionist. Farmer; $1,100/444; b. Rockingham Co., Va. 1830; came to Barbour 1850's; m. Barbara Martin; Methodist-Episcopal Church; d. Barbour 1907. Son of William and Sophia (Head) Scott, b. Rockingham Co., settled Preston Co., W. Va. 1835; grandson of Thomas Scott, immigrant from Scotland, settled Rockingham Co.

SEARS, James Sassan
Enl. Bat. H, 1st W. Va. Art. 8-23-64; disch. 7-11-65; in addition to brothers listed below, brother John served Hardy Co. Home Guards and 2nd Md. Inf. (USA); brother *Alexander served Co. E, 62nd Va. Mtd. Inf. (CSA). Farmer; $500/127; born Hardy Co., W. Va. 1821; came to Barbour 1850's with wife Louisa; moved to Roane Co., W. Va. after war where living 1880. Son of John and Ruth (Orrihood) Sears; father b. Pa., settled Barbour 1850's; grandson of John Sears.

SEARS, Israel
Enl. Co. C, 6th W. Va. Cav. 10-1-64; disch. 2-5-65; drafted immediately after, but not inducted; brother-in-law *Alpheus Zinn Unionist; sister-in-law *Lucinda (Gawthorpe) Zinn Confederate sympathizer; brother-in-law Thomas Gawthorpe served 133rd W. Va. Mil., POW 9-63; brother-in-law James Gawthorpe served Co. A, 20th Va. Cav. (CSA). Farm servant; $0/0; b. Hardy Co., W. Va. 1836, brother of James; m. 1) Harriet Gawthorpe 1860; 2) Alcinda E. Board 1867; moved to Ill. after war where living 1880.

SEARS, Abel
Enl. Co. K, 6th W. Va. Inf. 10-1-62; disch. 6-30-65; NFR. Farm servant; $0/327 (father); b. Hardy Co., W. Va. 1844, brother of James.

SEVIER, William H.
Enl. Co. D, 4th Pa. Cav. 2-9-65; disch. 7-1-65. Farmer; $0/30; born Preston Co., W. Va. 1843; came to Barbour 1850's; m. Margaret Ann Virginia Demoss 1867; moved to Taylor Co., W. Va. after war where d. 1880's; widow listed Taylor Co. Union veterans 1890. Son of Bartholomew and Hulda (Hileman) Sevier; father b. Preston Co.; grandson of Bartholomew and Margaret Sevier, b. Va., settled Preston Co.

SHAFFER, John Peter
Teamster, Union Army; brother-in-law *William Janes served Barbour Home Guard. Farmer; $1,000/278; b. Barbour 1844; German Baptist Church; m. Elisabeth Janes; d. Barbour 1912. Son of Daniel and Elisabeth (Boyles) Shaffer; father b. Barbour; grandson of John Peter and Mary (Nestor) Shaffer; grandfather b. Germany; great-grandson of John Peter and Elisabeth Shaffer, immigrants from Germany, settled Preston Co., W. Va. 1790's.

SHAFFER, George W.
Enl. Co. H, 10th W. Va. Inf. 11-15-62; discharge date unknown. Farmer; $0/158; b. Preston Co., W. Va. 1836; came to Barbour 1850's with wife Delila; moved to Calhoun Co., W. Va. after war where d. 1918. Son of Elisha and Mary (Seypole) Shaffer; father b. Washington Co., Md.; grandson of Benjamin and Susan (Weishar) Shaffer, b. Md.

SHAFFER, Benjamin Franklin
Com. Lt., 139th W. Va. Mil. 8-16-62; never called into service; elec. County Supervisor 1865; drafted 3-65, never inducted; brother-in-law *David Sanders served Co. H, 10th W. Va. Inf. (USA). Farmer; $0/143; b. Preston Co., W. Va. 1829; m. Jemima Morgan; living Barbour 1880. Son of Henry and Malinda (Johnson) Shaffer; father b. Washington Co., Md.; grandson of Benjamin and Susan (Weishar) Shaffer.

SHAFFER, Balliard
Elec. Overseer of the Poor 1865; claim for war-time service in 169th Mil. rejected 1902; father-in-law *John Payne Confederate sympathizer; brothers-in-law *William Price, *Nathan, *James and *William Payne Unionists. Farmer; $0/110; b. Barbour 1830, brother of Benjamin; m. 1) Elisabeth Payne 1856; 2) Mary Payne 1892; d. Randolph Co., W. Va.

SHAFFER, Stingley
Elec. Overseer of the Poor 1865; drafted 3-65; never inducted; claim for war-time service in 169th Mil. rejected 1902; sister-in-law *Julie Ann (Sherman) Payne Unionist. Farmer; $0/111; b. Barbour 1835, brother of Benjamin; m. Elisabeth C. Sherman 1858; d. Barbour 1919.

SHAFFER, John R.
Enl. Co. F, 6th W. Va. Inf. 9-3-64; disch. 6-30-65; Farmer; $3,500/407 (parents); b. Barbour 1837, brother of Benjamin; m. Susan ____; moved to Preston Co., W. Va. 1880's where listed Union veterans 1890.

SHAFFER, Draper C.
Enl. Co. H, 10th W. Va. Inf. 3-20-62; prom. to sgt. 5-9-62; disch. 5-7-65. Farmer; $3,500/407 (parents); b. Barbour 1838, brother of Benjamin; m. Samantha Payne 1865; moved to Preston Co., W. Va. after war where listed Union veterans 1890.

SHANABARGER, Christopher Columbus
Com. Capt., 139th W. Va. Mil. 8-16-62; never called into service; enl. Co. F, 15th W. Va. Inf. 9-10-62; wd. in wrist Berryville 9-3-64; disch. 6-14-65; brother-in-law *Holsberry Stalnaker Unionist. Farmer; $2,400/700; b. Fayette Co., Pa. 1824; Methodist-Episcopal Church; m. 1) Mary Janes; 2) Tabitha Stalnaker 1858; d. Barbour 1868. Son of James and Sophia Shanabarger, settled Barbour 1857 from Allegany Co., Md.

SHANABARGER, Samuel
Enl. Co. I, 6th W. Va. Inf. 9-27-61; transf. to Bat. F, 1st W. Va. Art. 7-9-62; POW Martinsburg, W. Va. 7-1-63, held Richmond Prison; exch. 11-63; disch. Farmer; $2,400/700 (parents); b. Allegany Co., Md. 1843, son of Christopher and Mary (Janes) Shanabarger; Methodist-Episcopal Church; m. Catherine Haller 1868; post-war Methodist minister, later joined United Brethren Church; moved to Upshur Co., W. Va. 1870's where listed Union veterans 1890.

SHARPES, James W.
Enl. Co. F, 17th W. Va. Inf. 2-16-65; wd. left leg; disch. 6-30-65; brother *Minor served Co. D, 20th Va. Cav. (CSA). Farmer; $3,000/719; born Taylor Co., W. Va. 1843; m. Sarah ____; moved to Upshur Co., W. Va. after war, then Preston Co., W. Va. 1870's, returning to Upshur Co. after 1880 where listed Union veterans 1890; d. 1909. Son of William and Matilda (Bailey) Sharpes; father b. Preston Co.; grandson of Jesse and Sarah (Neptune) Sharpes; grandfather b. Md.; great-grandson of immigrant from Wales.

SHAW, John
Enl. Co. E, 3rd W. Va. Cav. 10-20-62; disch. 6-30-65; Farmer; $0/266; b. Barbour 1825; m. Malinda ____; moved to Ill. 1870's; d. 1898. Son of Larkin and Sarah (O'Neal) Shaw; father b. Harrison Co., W. Va.; grandson of Charles and Catherine (Jett) Shaw, settled Harrison from Fauquier Co., Va.

SHAW, Hezekiah
Listed Barbour Light Horse; enl. Co. C, 4th W. Va. Cav. 7-27-63; disch. 3-9-64. Farmer; $1,200/875 (mother); b. Barbour 1838, brother of John; m. Rebecca

Johnson; moved to Mo. after war, returned to Taylor Co., W. Va. 1870's where living 1880; widow listed Barbour Union veterans 1890.

SHAW, William H.
Enl. Co. F, 17th W. Va. Inf. 9-24-64; disch. 6-30-65. Farmer; $1,200/875 (mother); b. Barbour 1843, brother of John; m. Amelia M. Auvil 1866; moved to Tucker Co., W. Va. after war where d. 1870's.

SHAW, William J.
Sympathizer and abolitionist; brother-in-law *Bartholomew O'Neal Unionist. Farmer; $1,000/220; pre-war Sheriff and Justice of the Peace; b. Preston Co., W. Va. 1793; Methodist-Episcopal Church; Democrat; m. Edith O'Neal; d. Barbour 1876. Son of William and Sarah (Shaw) Shaw; father immigrant from Ireland.

SHAW, Samuel
Sympathizer; appointed U.S. Postmaster Coveton; drafted 3-65, never inducted; father-in-law *John Shroyer Unionist; brother-in-law *Lewis Shroyer served Co. C, 4th W. Va. Cav. (USA). Farmer; $12,000/1,383; b. Allegany Co., Md. 1828; Methodist-Episcopal Church; m. Elisabeth Hannah Shroyer 1864; d. Barbour 1901. Son of Joseph and Frances (Smar) Shaw, b. Allegany Co., Md.; grandson of Joseph Shaw, Methodist minister, immigrant from England.

SHAW, Benjamin D.
Enl. Barbour Home Guard. Farmer; $12,000/1,383 (parents); b. Allegany Co., Md. 1844, brother of Samuel; Methodist-Episcopal Church; came to Barbour 1856; d. Barbour 1899.

SHINGLETON, Anderson
Enl. Co. F, 15th W. Va. Inf. 8-26-62; wd. in shoulder Hobb's Hill 10-13-64; disch. 6-14-65; three brothers in Union army. Tenant; $0/30; b. Harrison Co., W. Va.1818; Methodist-Episcopal Church; m. Hannah Grey; came to Barbour 1859; moved to Taylor Co., W. Va. after war; returned to Barbour 1880's where listed Union veterans 1890; d. 1891. Son of John and Polly (Humphries) Shingleton; father b. Culpepper Co., Va.; grandson of William and Levina Shingleton; grandfather immigrant from England, settled Culpepper Co., then Harrison Co., then Pleasants Co., W. Va.

SHINGLETON, Abraham
Enl. Co. F, 15th W. Va. Inf. 8-23-62; wd. in knee Cedar Creek 10-19-64; disch. 6-14-65. Tenant; $0/30 (parents); b. Harrison Co., W. Va. 1844, son of Anderson and Hannah (Grey) Shingleton; Methodist-Episcopal Church; m. Sarah Ingram 1873; listed Barbour Union veterans 1890.

SHOCKEY, Ira
Enl. Home Guard, Washington Co. Ohio; drafted 3-65; claim for war-time service in 169th Mil. rejected 1902. Farmer; $1,300/446 (parents); b. Washington Co., Ohio 1843; Methodist-Protestant Church; came to Barbour 1855; m. Melissa Newlon 1865; moved to Randolph Co., W. Va. 1870's where living 1899. Son of Jacob and Minerva (Haines) Shockey; father b. Ohio; grandson of Abraham and Margaret Shockey, b. Pa.

SHOCKEY, Francis
Enl. as substitute Co. G, 7th W. Va. Inf. 3-14-65; disch. 7-1-65. Farmer; $1,300/446 (parents); b. Washington Co. Ohio 1845, brother of Ira; Methodist-Protestant Chruch; m. Susan V. Newlon 1868; living Barbour 1880.

SHOEMAKER, Joseph
Enl. Co. H, 10th W. Va. Inf. 6-17-62; arrested 6-10-63 for murder of *Jacob Philips; tried and aquitted 1865. Tenant; $0/53; b. Va. 1816; m. Sarah Ann _____; moved to Marion Co., W. Va. after war where listed Union veterans 1890. Son of George and Margaret Shoemaker; parents b. Va.

SHOEMAKER, John W.
Enl. Co. H, 10th W. Va. Inf. 11-15-62; disch. 6-26-65; NFR. Tenant; $0/53 (parents); b. Barbour 1845, son of Joseph and Sarah Ann Shoemaker.

SHOMO, John Madison
Enl. Co. F, 15th W. Va. Inf. 8-23-62; disch. 6-14-65; brother-in-law *James Harris served Barbour Home Guard. Blacksmith; $200/266; b. Shenandoah Co., Va. 1826; Methodist-Episcopal Church; came to Barbour 1830's; m. Sarah A. Williams 1849; d. Barbour 1880's; widow listed Barbour Union veterans 1890. Son of Daniel and Dianna (Reamer) Shomo; father b. Pa.; grandson of Anthony and Elisabeth Shomo, settled Shenandoah Co.

SHOMO, Daniel Joseph
Blacksmith, Union Army. $700/220; b. Shenandoah Co., Va. 1830, brother of John; Methodist-Episcopal Church; m. Sophia Hays 1851; d. Barbour 1893.

SHOWALTER, William Ulysses
Elec. County Supervisor 1865; drafted 3-65, never inducted. $1,100/375; b. Fayette Co., Pa. 1822; Methodist-Episcopal Church; came to Barbour 1850's; m. Sarah E. Woodyard 1850; d. Barbour 1900. Son of Henry and Mary (Billhimer) Showalter, b. Rockingham Co., Va. settled Pa.

SHROYER, John M.
Elec. Justice of the Peace 1860, continued to served during war; appointed U. S. Postmaster Coveton 4-22-62; killed by Confederate raiders 1-17-65; son-in-law *Samuel Shaw Unionist. Farmer; $9,300/1,240; b. Taylor Co., W. Va. 1811; Methodist-Episcopal Church; Republican; m. Elisabeth Gawthorpe 1836; came to Barbour 1840's. Son of Lewis and Elisabeth (Baker) Shroyer; parents settled Taylor Co. from Md.

SHROYER, Lewis Melvin
Enl. Co. C, 4th W. Va. Cav. 7-27-63; disch. 3-9-64; appointed U. S. Postmaster Coveton 2-6-65. Farmer; $9,300/1,240 (parents); b. Taylor Co., W. Va. 1842, son of John M. and Elisabeth (Gawthorpe) Shroyer; Methodist-Episcopal Church; m. Henrietta _____; returned to Taylor Co. after war where listed Union veterans 1890.

SHURTLIFF, Aaron
Enl. Co. A, 10th W. Va. Inf. 3-13-62; disch. 3-12-65. Farm laborer; $N/G; b. Barbour 1846; Presyterian; m. Margaret _____; moved to Kan. after war where living 1880. Son of Oliver and Nancy (Trader) Shurtliff; father b. Mass.; grandson of James and Dorcas (Lyon) Shurtiff.

SHURTLIFF, Marcellus Clay
Enl. Co. B, 17th W. Va. Inf. 9-2-64; disch. 6-30-65. Farm laborer; $N/G; b. Barbour 1847, brother of Aaron; Presbyterian; m. Eliza Philips 1869; NFR.

SHUTTLESWORTH, John H.
Delegate First and Second Wheeling Conventions; com. Lt., 3rd W. Va. Inf. 8-5-61, serving as quartermaster; commended for bravery Second Bull Run; disch. 1864; elec. House of Delegates 1864; brother Benjamin Delegate First and Second Wheeling Conventions; brother Notley Capt. Co. B, 3rd W. Va. Inf. Farmer; $11,000/3,265; b. Harrison Co., W. Va. 1817; Methodist-Episcopal Church; m. Louisa J. Martin 1840; came to Barbour 1850's; moved to Ritchie Co., W. Va. after war, then returned to Harrison Co. where d. 1880's; widow listed Harrison Co. Union veterans 1890. Son of Notley and Frances (Ferguson) Shuttlesworth, b. Monongalia Co., W. Va.; grandson of Philip Shuttlesworth, b. Pa., settled Monongalia Co.

SIGLEY, George W.
Enl. Co. H, 10th W. Va. Inf. 5-8-62; wd. Kernstown 7-24-64; d. 8-13-64. Farmer; $0/100 (parents); b. Harrison Co., W. Va. 1844; came to Barbour during war. Son of John and Mary (Morris) Sigley, b. Harrison Co.; grandfather b. Pa.

SIMON, Abraham
President, pro-secessionist meeting Stewart's Run, Barbour 2-61; enl. Co. H, 10th W. Va. Inf. 11-8-62; dismissed from service by general court martial 1863; District Committee Union Party 1864; brother-in-law *William Ward Unionist; brother-in-law Simon Roberts served Co. K, 10th W. Va. Inf. (USA). Farmer; $5,000/557; b. Hardy Co., W. Va. 1806; Baptist, joined Methodist-Episcopal Church after war; Republican; m. Jemima Roberts 1833; d. Barbour 1880's. Son of Jacob and Mary (Stump) Simon; grandson of Benjamin and Elisabeth (Stump) Simon, b. Hardy Co., settled Barbour; great-grandson of George and Mary Simon.

SIMON, Moses
Com. Capt., 169th W. Va. Mil. 8-16-62; prom. to Lt.-Col. 9-20-62; never called into service. Farmer; $0/327; b. Barbour 1834, son of Abraham and Jemima (Roberts) Simon; Baptist; m. Mary Ann Thompson; moved to Upshur Co., W. Va. after war where d. 1920.

SIMON, Michael
Com. Capt., 169th W. Va. Mil. 8-16-62; prom. to Col. 9-20-62; never called into service; elec. Constable 1865. Farmer; $5,000/911; b. Hardy Co., W. Va. 1821, brother of Abraham; United Brethren Church; m. Catherine George 1845; living Barbour 1880.

SIMON, Branson R.
Elec. Constable 1862; drafted 2-65, never inducted; claim for war-time service in 169th Mil. rejected 1902. $5,000/1,132; b. Hardy Co., W. Va. 1828, brother of Abraham; United Brethren Church; m. 1) Elisabeth Ann Matheny 1856; 2) Ellen Hickman 1872; living Barbour 1880.

SIMON, Benjamin
Com. Major, 169th W. Va. Mil. 8-22-62; never called into service; elec. Constable 1863; drafted 2-65, never inducted; brother-in-law *William Malcomb Unionist. Farmer; $0/327; b. Barbour 1836; m. Edith Malcomb 1857; living Barbour 1880. Son of Jacob and Margaret Simon; father b. Hardy Co., W. Va.; grandson of Jacob and Sarah (Stump) Simon; great-grandson of Benjamin and Elisabeth (Stump) Simon.

SIMON, Alfred E.
Enl. Co. H, 10th W. Va. Inf. 5-8-62; wd. both legs Winchester 9-19-64; disch. 5-14-65. $N/G; born Barbour 1844; m. Susan Bean 1866; moved to Mineral Co., W. Va. after war where listed Union veterans 1890. Son of Simon and Sarah Simon; grandson of Jacob and Sarah (Stump) Simon.

SIMON, Andrew
Com. Capt., 169th W. Va. Mil. 12-14-64; never called into service; brother *Allen listed Barbour Light Horse; brother-in-law *Francis Payne Unionist. Farmer; $6,000/2,208 (parents); b. Barbour 1844; Baptist; m. Ella Syrena McClaskey 1871; living Barbour 1880. Son of Abram and Mary (Yeager) Simon; father b. Hampshire Co., W. Va.; grandson of Benjamin and Elisabeth (Stump) Simon.

SIMON, Joseph B. A.
Com. Lt., 169th W. Va. Mil. 12-14-64; never called into service. Farmer; $8,000/1,586 (parents); b. Barbour 1844; m. 1) Minerva McCoy 1865; 2) Garnetta Russel 1883. Son of Anthony and Minerva (Corder) Simon; father b. Hampshire Co., W. Va.; grandson of Benjamin and Elisabeth (Stump) Simon.

SINER, John
Enl. Co. K, 45th U. S. Colored Infantry 8-6-64; disch. 11-5-65; NFR. Slave; $0/0; born Va.

SIPE, Noah Isaac
Enl. Co. C, 4th W. Va. Cav. 7-27-63; disch. 3-9-64; re-enlisted Bat. H, 1st W. Va. Art. 3-24-64; POW New Creek 11-28-64; brother-in-law *James W. George served Co. F, 15th W. Va. Inf. (USA). Farmer; $400/309 (parents); b. Barbour 1836; m. Nancy Warner 1868; moved to Kan. 1870's, then to Ok. where d. 1926. Son of Jacob and Delila (Zirkle) Sipe; parents b. Rockingham Co., Va., settled Barbour 1815; grandfather b. Pa., settled Rockingham Co.

SIPE, John J.
Enl. Co. F, 15th W. Va. Inf. 8-27-62; wd. in shoulder Petersburg 4-2-65; disch. 6-14-65. Tenant; $0/40; b. Barbour 1842, brother of Noah; m. 1) Alinda _____; 2) Cassandra Weaver 1860; listed Barbour Union veterans 1890.

SIPE, David T.
Enl. Co. A, 6th W. Va. Inf. 11-5-61; re-enlisted 1-15-64; prom. to sgt.; disch. 6-30-65. Farmer; $400/309 (parents); b. Barbour 1842, brother of Noah; m. Julie Ann Baker 1866; listed Barbour Union veterans 1890.

SKIDMORE, Elihu
Enl. Co. F, 15th W. Va. Inf. 9-10-62; wd. in heel Winchester 9-19-64; disch. 6-14-65. Farmer; $649/140; b. Randolph Co., W. Va. 1820; Methodist-Episcopal Church; m. Harriet Wright Cottrail 1846; listed Barbour Union veterans 1890; d. 1900. Son of John and Juda (Pittman) Skidmore; grandson of Thomas and Eleanor (Ingram) Skidmore, settled Randolph Co., from Fauquier Co., Va. 1780's.

SKIDMORE, George
Delegate Union Party Convention Grafton 1864; drafted 2-65, never inducted. $900/277; b. Barbour 1825; Methodist-Episcopal Church; Republican; m. Tabitha Ward 1849; d. Barbour 1883.

SKIDMORE, Hiram
Enl. Co. I, 3rd W. Va. Cav. 11-14-63; disch. 6-30-65. Farmer; $1,988/421; b. Barbour 1821; Methodist-Protestant Church; m. 1) Penelope ____; 2) Martha Rice 1876; moved to Lewis Co., W. Va. 1870's where living 1880. Son of Thomas and Mary (Kittle) Skidmore.

SMITH, John W.
Enl. Co. G, 3rd W. Va. Inf. 6-27-61; prom. to cpl; wd. left leg Rocky Gap 8-26-63; disch. 8-12-64. Farmer; $600/103 (parents); b. Page Co., Va. 1839; came to Barbour 1850's; m. Louvina Ward 1874; living Barbour 1880. Son of Michael and Susan Smith, b. Pa.

SMITH, Solomon
Elec. Constable 1864; drafted 3-65, never inducted; brother-in-law *Gideon Harris served Co. K, 31st Va. Inf. (CSA). Farmer; $600/455; b. Barbour 1827; m. Ingaby Harris; living Barbour 1880. Son of Jacob and Nancy (Philips) Smith, b. Barbour; grandson of William and Barbara (Springston) Smith, settled Barbour from Va.

SMITH, Moses
Enl. Co. F, 15th W. Va. Inf. 9-15-62; des. Cedar Creek 10-19-64; father-in-law *William Coontz Confederate sympathizer; brothers-in-law *John and *James Coontz served Confederate army. Farmer; $0/190 (parents); b. Barbour 1843; m. Barbara Ellen Coontz 1864; moved to Doddridge Co., W. Va. 1880's where listed Union veterans 1890. Son of Alpheus and Ann (Glascock) Smith; grandson of William and Barbara (Springston) Smith.

SNODGRASS, Francis C.
Elec. Constable 1863; step-brothers *Joseph, *Noah and *Emery McCauley Unionists; brothers-in-law *James and *Jaspar Pitzer served Barbour Home Guard. $2,000/205; b. Marion Co., W. Va. 1837; Methodist-Episcopal Church; Democrat; m. Elisabeth E. Mouser 1860; living Barbour 1880. Son of Francis and Mary Snodgrass; father b. Marion Co.; grandson of Francis and Rebecca Snodgrass; grandfather said to have immigrated from England.

SQUIRES, Asa
Enl. Barbour Home Guard 11-23-64; disch. 5-30-65; drafted 3-65, never inducted. Farmer; $600/240; b. Barbour 1837; Methodist-Episcopal Church; m. 1) Sarah Jane Pitzer; 1854 2) Rebecca Queen 1874; d. Barbour 1914. Son of John and Mary (Fortney) Squires; father b. Preston Co., W. Va.; grandson of Nehemiah and Sarah (Poling) Squires; grandfather settled Preston Co. from Fauquier Co., Va.

STALNAKER, Holsberry
Elec. Justice of the Peace 1865; drafted 3-65, never inducted; brother-in-law *Christopher Shanabarger served Co. F, 15th W. Va. Inf. (USA); brother-in-law *Nestor Hardin Unionist. Farmer; $3,300/720; b. Barbour 1828; Methodist-Episcopal Church, joined Southern Methodists after war; m. Caroline M. Parsons; living Barbour 1880. Son of Andrew and Rachel (Holsberry) Stalnaker; father b. Barbour; grandson of William and Margaret (McHenry) Stalnaker; great-grandson of Jacob and Elisabeth (Truby) Stalnaker, b. Va., settled Randolph Co., W. Va. 1780's.

STANSBERRY, Augustus J.
Enl. Co. F, 15th W. Va. Inf. 8-23-62; des. Camp Wiley, W. Va. 10-8-62. Farmer; $1,500/589 (parents); b. Monongalia Co., W. Va. 1844; Methodist-Protestant Church; m. Mary Ann Boyles 1864; listed Barbour Union veterans 1890; d. Barbour 1928. Son of Josiah and Sarah (Pride) Stansberry; father b. Monongalia Co.; grandson of Francis Stansberry, b. Va., settled Monongalia Co.

STANSBERRY, Francis Marion
Enl. Co. N, 6th W. Va. Inf. 10-31-61; re-enlisted 2-26-64; disch. 6-30-65. Farmer; $1,500/589 (parents); b. Monongalia Co., W. Va. 1838, brother of Augustus; Methodist-Protestant Church; m. Harriet Ann Schoonover 1864; living Barbour 1880.

STEERMAN, Augustus J.
Com. Lt., 139th W. Va. Mil. 8-16-62; never called into service. Farmer; $750/617 (parents); b. Barbour 1837; m. 1) Millara A. Thorn 1870; 2) Olive E. Evick 1874; moved to Randolph Co., W. Va. after war where living 1880. Son of Hiram and Jane Steerman; parents and grandparents b. Va.

STEMPLE, Christopher Columbus
Enl. Co. F, 15th W. Va. Inf. 8-23-62; wd. in side Winchester 9-19-64; disch. 6-14-65. Farmer; $500/210; b. Barbour 1842; Methodist-Episcopal Church; m. Sophrona Baker 1869; listed Barbour Union veterans 1890 . Son of John and

Julianne (Hovatter) Stemple; father b. Preston Co., W. Va. came to Barbour 1840's; grandson of Adam and Mary (Hebb) Stemple; great-grandson of Gottfried and Margaret (Boyles) Stemple, immigrants from Germany, settled Md., then Preston Co. 1780's.

STEVENS, Barnaster P.
Sympathizer; "A good and remarkably shrewd Union man;" assisted scouts reconnoitering Confederates positions Laurel Hill, Barbour 7-61. Farmer; $4,500/643; b. Loudoun Co., Va. 1796; m. 1) Lucinda Philips 1825; 2) Elisabeth Carnes 1835; came to Barbour 1840's where d. 1863.

STEVENS, Elisabeth (Carnes)
Sympathizer. $4,500/643; b. Va. 1806, wife of Barnaster; d. 1870's.

STEVENS, John W.
Enl. Co. H, 7th W. Va. Inf. 9-2-61; disch. 9-2-64. Farmer; $4,500/643; b. Marion Co., W. Va. 1843, son of Barnaster and Elisabeth (Carnes) Stevens; m. Louisa Lane 1867; living Barbour 1880.

STEVENS, David E.
Enl. Co. C, 4th W. Va. Cav. 7-27-63; disch. 3-9-64; step-brother *Isaiah Kelley served Co. H, 10th W. Va. Inf. (USA). Farmer; $950/408 (brother); b. Taylor Co., W. Va. 1845; m. Jane Goff; moved to Calhoun Co., W. Va. 1869 where listed Union veterans 1890. Son of Nimrod and Nancy Stevens; father b. Marion Co., W. Va.; grandson of William and Susanna (Gandy) Stevens; great-grandson of John and Nancy (Whitford) Stevens; great-grandfather b. New England, settled Loudoun Co., Va., then Marion Co. 1805.

STEWART, Robert B.
Delegate Union Party Convention Grafton 1864. Farmer; $4,500/643; b. Highland Co., Va. 1805; came to Barbour 1835; Republican; m. Harriet McClung; living Barbour 1880. Son of Edward and Mary (Callahan) Stewart; grandson of William and Margaret (Ushur) Stewart; grandfather immigrant from from Scotland, settled Highland Co.

STEWART, Felix G.
Listed Barbour Light Horse; listed Barbour Union veterans 1890 as "U. S. Service;" brother-in-law *Milton Reed listed Barbour Light Horse. Farmer; $6,500/1,275 (parents); b. Bath Co., Va. 1836; Baptist; came to Barbour 1837; Republican; m. Ingaby Nutter 1874; d. Barbour 1892. Son of John and Elsie (Stewart) Stewart; parents b. Highland Co., Va.; grandson of Edward and (Callahan) Stewart.

STICKLE, John H.
Enl. Co. B, 6th W. Va. Inf. 9-26-64; disch. 6-30-65; brother-in-law *Robert R. Talbott Confederate sympathizer. Tenant; $0/293 (parents); b. Barbour 1837; Methodist-Protestant Church; m. 1) Fannie Crutcher 1867; 2) Martha M. Stout; 3) Clara Knisely 1893; moved to Doddridge Co., W. Va. after war where listed Union veterans 1890; d. Doddridge Co. 1932. Son of George and Sarah (Downs) Stickle, b. Va., settled Barbour from Loudoun Co., Va. 1820's.

STOCKWELL, Henry H.
Enl. Co. B, 3rd W. Va. Cav. 3-3-64; POW Blacksburg, Va. 5-13-64; d. of scurvey Andersonville 11-64; brother Abraham served Home Guard, Taylor Co.; brothers *Issac and *William served Confederate army. Farmer; $0/95 (parents); b. Barbour or Taylor Co., W. Va. 1846. Son of Joseph and Rachel Stockwell, b. Va.; grandson of John Stockwell, settled Taylor Co. from Pa.

STOUT, Leonard
Elec. Justice of the Peace 1862; brother-in-law *Henson Hoff Unionist; son-in-law *Elias Channell served Co. K, 6th W. Va. Inf. (USA). Miller; $0/80; b. Hampshire Co., W. Va. 1800; m. Rachel Hoff 1819; d. Barbour 1870's. Son of St. Leger and Ann (Bucklew) Stout; father b. N.J., settled Barbour early 1800's; grandson of St. Leger and Susanna (Simpson) Stout, b. N.J.

STOUT, Henson L.
Elec. Constable 1861; enl. Co. K, 6th W. Va. Inf. 10-1-62; disch. 6-30-65; son-in-law *George Pittman served Co. B, 10th W. Va. Inf. (USA). $1,100/361; b. Barbour 1827, son of Leonard and Rachel (Hoff) Stout; Methodist-Episcopal Church; Republican; m. Mary J. Swearington 1845; living Barbour 1880.

STRADER, Aaron
Enl. Bat. E, 1st W. Va. Art. 8-1-62; injured by horse; disch. 6-28-65; brother Granville served Co. I, 3rd W. Va. Cav. (USA); father-in-law *William Ward and brother-in-law Alva Teter Unionists. Tenant; $0/322; b. Upshur Co., W. Va. 1838; Methodist-Episcopal Church; Republican; m. Priscilla Ward 1857; listed Barbour Union veterans 1890; returned to Upshur Co. where d. 1913. Son of Michael and Eva (Radabaugh) Strader; father b. of Hardy Co, W. Va.; grandson of John and Mary (Post) Strader, settled Upshur Co. 1820.

STREETS, William
Enl. Co. F, 15th W. Va. Inf. 8-23-62; disch. 6-14-65. Farmer; $520/202 (parents); b. Barbour 1838; Methodist-Protestant Church; m. Sarah A. Firth 1860; moved to Preston Co., W. Va. 1880's where listed Union veterans 1890.

Son of Samuel and Susan (Haller) Streets; grandson of Brooks and Margaret (McDonald) Streets, b. Allegany Co., Md., settled Barbour.

STREETS, Melker J.
Enl. Co. F, 15th W.Va. Inf. 8-27-62; KIA Snickers Ferry 7-18-64. Farmer; $520/202 (parents); b. Barbour 1843, brother of William; Methodist-Protestant Church.

STURM, Henry Jr.
Elec. Justice of the Peace 1863; arrested for secessionist activities 2-24-64 and sent to Camp Chase, Ohio; brother *Michael Confederate sympathizer. Farmer; $0/231; b. Barbour 1830; m. Jane Ryan; d. Barbour 1919. Son of Nicolas and Ann (McClaskey) Sturm; father b. Barbour; grandson of Nicolas and Elisabeth (Gainer) Sturm; grandfather b. Berkeley Co., W. Va. settled Barbour 1800; great-grandson of John and Magdelena (Dellinger) Sturm, immigrants from Germany, settled Md., then Va.

SUDDARTH, Josiah
Enl. Co. H, 10th W. Va. Inf. 5-8-62; d. of disease 5-14-62. Apprentice shoemaker; $0/0; b. Albemarle Co., W. Va. 1837; came to Barbour 1850's. Son of Joseph and Mary Suddarth; grandson of James Suddarth, b. Va.

SWARTZ, Jacob Markwood
Enl. Co. K, 6th W. Va. Inf. 8-8-62; disch. 6-30-65; brother-in-law *William Anglin served Co. L, 6th W. Va. Inf. (USA). Blacksmith; $500/170 (parents); b. Pendleton Co., W. Va. 1842; United Brethren Church; came to Barbour 1851; m. Anne E. Fletcher 1870; moved to Kan. after war; returned to Harrison Co., W. Va. where listed Union veterans 1890. Son of Jacob and Rebecca (Cummins) Swartz, b. Rockingham Co., Va.; grandson of Samuel and Mary (Guile) Swartz; grandfather b. Pa., settled Rockingham Co.

SWARTZ, John W.
Enl. Co. K, 6th W. Va. Inf. 9-7-64; disch. 6-30-65. $500/170 (parents); b. Pendleton Co., W. Va. 1846, brother of Jacob; United Brethren Church; m. Rebecca Divers 1868; moved to Harrison Co., W. Va. 1870's, then to Kan. 1880's.

SWECKER, Noah
Drafted Co. M, 3rd W. Va. Cav. 4-8-65; disch. 6-30-65. Farmer; $700/286 (parents); b. Lewis Co., W. Va. 1846; Methodist-Episcopal Church; d. Barbour 1865. Son of Absalom and Hannah Swecker; parents and grandparents b. Va.

SWICK, James J.
Sympathizer, assisting post-war Board of Registration; brother-in-law *Alexander Greathouse served Co. D, 20th Va. Cav. (CSA); brother-in-law *John Heatherly listed Barbour Light Horse. Farmer; $N/G; b. Barbour 1840; m. Juditha Greathouse 1865; living Barbour 1880. Son of Edward and Phoebe Swick; parents b. Va.; grandson of Anthony and Martha Swick; grandparents b. Loudoun Co., Va., settled Barbour 1826.

TAFT, Nathan Harmon
Arrested 5-61; freed after Battle of Philippi; elec. to House of Delegates 6-61; Delegate Second Wheeling Convention 6-61; elec. Prosecuting Attorney 9-61; appointed Adjutant, 139th W. Va. Militia 7-28-62; Committee on Recruitments 8-62; Co. D, 133rd W. Va. Militia, called into service 9-63; Delegate for Upshur Co., W. Va. Union Party Convention Parkersburg 1863; mother-in-law *Elisabeth Jarvis Confederate sympathizer; brothers-in-law *William Jarvis and *Isaac Strickler served Confederate army. Attorney; $250/80; b. N.Y. 1820; came to Barbour 1848; Democrat; m. Sarah Ellen Jarvis 1849; moved to Upshur Co. 1863; d. Lewis Co., W. Va. 1867.

TALBOTT, Elam Dowden
Sympathizer; brother *Robert Confederate sympathizer; father-in-law *Daniel Capito Unionist; sister-in-law *Helen Capito Confederate sympathizer; brothers-in-law John and Christian Capito served 17th W. Va. Inf. (USA). Physician and slave owner; $11,240/3,178; b. Barbour 1810; Baptist; Democrat; m. Julia Capito 1850; d. 1881. Son of Richard and Margaret (Dowden) Talbott; father b. Fauquier Co., Va., settled Barbour 1780; grandson of William and Elisabeth (Cottrill) Talbott; William immigrant from England.

TALLMAN, John Boone
Enl. Co. A, 6th W. Va. Inf. 11-5-61; disch. 5-18-64; described by comrad as one "who knew and performed every duty of a soldier without a murmer. He was not learned, did not know what fear meant." Farmer; $1,200/207 (mother); b. Pocahontas Co., W. Va. 1841; Methodist-Episcopal Church; came to Barbour 1849; moved to Mo. 1880's. Son of James and Mary (Poage) Tallman, b. Pocahontas Co.; grandson of James and Nancy (Crawford) Tallman, b. Pa., settled Pocahontas Co., then Ky.; great-grandson of Benjamin and Dinah (Boone) Tallman.

TALLMAN, Robert Logan
Enl. Co. H, 10th W. Va. Inf. 6-1-62; listed sick Frederick, Md. 9-64; disch. 6-26-65. Farmer; $1,200/207 (mother); b. Pocahontas Co., W. Va. 1846, half-brother

of John; Methodist-Episcopal Church; m. Harriet Louvenia Blake 1873; listed Barbour Union veterans 1890. Son of James and Mary (Logan) Tallman.

TEETS, Daniel
Elec. Overseer of Poor 1863; drafted 2-65, never inducted; claim for war-time service in 169th Mil. rejected 1902. Farmer; $1,500/500; b. Barbour or Preston Co., W. Va. 1823; m. Lavilla ____; living Barbour 1880. Son of Anthony Teets, b. Preston Co., settled Barbour; grandson of Michael Teets, immigrant from Germany, settled Preston Co.

TETER, Joseph Sr.
Attended "Shoe Shop" meeting at Martin's store 5-61; brother *Jacob Confederate sympathizer. Farmer; $6,000/1,138; b. Pendleton Co. W. Va., 1796; Methodist-Episcopal Church; came to Barbour 1798; m. 1) Catherine Harner 1816; 2) Mary Mitchell McCann 1824; d. Barbour 1881. Son of Jacob and Elisabeth (Holden) Teter; father b. Pa.; grandson of George and Mary Ann Margaret (Hinkle) Teter.

TETER, Joseph Jr.
District Committee Union Party 1863; elec. House of Delegates 1863; elec. County Supervisor 1863, 1864 and 1865; Delegate Union Party Convention Grafton 1864. Farmer; $6,375/1,559; b. Barbour 1828, son of Joseph and Mary (McCann) Teter; Methodist-Protestant Church; Republican; moved to Ohio where m. Arinda Fawcett 1856; returned to Barbour 1850's; d. 1898.

TETER, Jesse
Committee on Recruitment 8-62; com. Col., 139th W. Va. Mil. 11-22-62, never called into service; Medical Board, Grafton Army Hospital; Superintendant of Elections 2-63; District Committee Union Party 1863; elec. Township Commissioner 1863; Delegate Union Party Convention Grafton 1864; father arrested and sent to Camp Chase; son *Worthington listed Barbour Light Horse; brothers-in-law*George and *William Philips served Confederate army; brother-in-law *David Foy Unionist; brothers-in-law *Josiah Wilson, *Fenelon Howes and *Charles Groves served Co. F, 15th W. Va. Inf. (USA). Farmer; $1,800/695; b. Barbour 1823; Methodist-Episcopal Church; Republican; m. Elisabeth Philips 1849; d. Barbour 1901. Son of *Jacob and Mary (Coberly) Teter; grandson of Jacob and Elisabeth (Holden) Teter.

TETER, James
Listed Barbour Light Horse; arrested and sent to Camp Chase, Ohio 4-29-63; transf. to Fort Delaware 7-14-63; released; enl. Co. F, 15th W. Va. Inf. 4-16-64;

listed sick 11-64; disch. 6-14-65. Farmer; $1,500/618; b. Barbour 1825, brother of Jesse; Methodist-Episcopal Church; m. Rebecca Yeager 1848; moved to Ok. 1870's where living 1880.

TETER, Oliver
Enl. Co. F, 15th W. Va. Inf. 8-27-62; disch. for disability 9-15-64; brother-in-law *George Arbogast served same company. Tenant; $0/85; b. Barbour 1827, brother of Jesse; Methodist-Episcopal Church; m. Elisabeth Arbogast 1855; listed Barbour Union veterans 1890.

TETER, Abel
Enl. Co. F, 15th W. Va. Inf. 8-27-62; disch. for disability 2-26-65; brother-in-law *Adam Ware served same company. Farmer; $2,500/409; b. Barbour 1839, brother of Jesse; Methodist-Episcopal Church; m. 1) Harriet Ware 1862; 2) Anna M. Rosenbarger 1883; listed Barbour Union veterans 1890; d. Barbour 1897.

THOMASSON, Richard S.
Enl. Co. H, 10th W. Va. Inf. 5-8-62; rejected as physically unfit by mustering officer 11-15-62. $2,140/8,200 (mother); b. Louisa Co., Va. 1839; came to Barbour 1860; m. Elisabeth Ellyson 1860; four of wife's brothers served CSA; d. Barbour 1870's. Son of Martha Thomasson, b. Louisa Co.; grandson of George and Diana Thomasson; great-grandson of George Thomasson, b. Mass.

THOMPSON, Commodore Perry
Com. Capt., 169th W. Va. Mil. 11-5-64; never called into service; brother *George Capt. Co. H, 31st Va. Inf. (CSA); brothers-in-law *John and *James Woodford Unionists. $3,000/411 (mother); b. Barbour 1842; Baptist; m. Harriet Eliza Bosworth 1867; d. Barbour 1916. Son of Hezekiah and Sarah (Logan) Thompson; father b. Hampshire Co., W. Va.; grandson of William and Elisabeth Thompson, b. Fauquier Co., Va.

THOMPSON, John Bunyon
Com. Capt., 169th W. Va. Mil. 8-16-62; never called into service; enl. Co. F, 15th W. Va. Inf. 9-10-62; disch. 6-14-65. Blacksmith; $0/130; b. Upshur Co., W. Va. 1831; came to Barbour 1839; Republican; m. Sarah Ann Jones; moved to Taylor Co., W. Va. 1870's, to Wetzel Co., W. Va. 1880's where listed Union veterans 1890. Son of David and Mary Ellen (Wyatt Collett) Thompson; father b. Green Co., Va.; grandson of Jacob and Mildred (Raines) Thompson; great-grandson of David Thompson, b. Pendleton Co., W. Va.

THORN, Robert Graham
Enl. Co. H, 10th W. Va. Inf. 11-15-62; disch. 8-9-65; brother-in-law *John W. Coontz served Co. D, 20th Va. Cav. (CSA). Farmer; $300/231 (parents); b. Barbour 1845; Methodist-Episcopal Church; m. Catherine Columbia Corley 1868; moved to Randolph Co., W. Va. after war where living 1880. Son of Jacob and Eve (Coontz) Thorn; parents b. Barbour; grandson of John and Judith (Yeager) Thorn, b. Pa.

THORN, George W.
Enl. Co. F, 15th W. Va. Inf. 9-1-62; wd. in hand Petersburg 4-2-65; disch. 6-14-65. Farmer; $1,500/597 (parents); b. Barbour 1840; Methodist-Episcopal Church; m. Phebe Swick 1868; d. Barbour 1880's; widow listed Barbour Union veterans 1890. Son of John and Judith (Yeager) Thorn.

TRACY, John S.
Enl. Co. G, 3rd W. Va. Inf. 6-27-61; prom. to cpl.; wd. Second Bull Run 8-29-62; d. New York 9-62; brother William served in same company, d. during war. Miller; $0/0; b. Fauquier Co., Va. 1840; came to Barbour 1850's. Son of James and Maria (Porter) Tracy, b. Va., settled Harrison Co., W. Va. 1850's from Clarke Co., Va.

TRAYHERN, James
Elec. Sheriff 1861; arrested 1-3-61 and imprisoned Richmond; released 1-64; District Committee Union Party 1864; brother-in-law *Fielding Harvey Lt., 139th W. Va. Militia. Merchant; $450/4,650; b. Loudoun Co., Va. 1816; Republican; m. Francis Ann Overfield 1844; d. 1875. Son of Israel and Sarah Trayhern; father settled Barbour from Loudoun Co. 1840's; grandson of James and Dinah (Gregg) Trayhern; great-grandson of William and Rebecca Trayhern, b. Ann Arundel Co., Md., settled Loudoun Co. 1760's.

TRAYHERN, John F.
Enl. Co. C, 4th W. Va. Cav. 7-27-63; disch. 3-9-64. $N/G; b. Barbour 1846, son of James and Francis (Overfield) Trayhern; m. Serena ____; listed Barbour Union veterans 1890.

TRIMBLE, William C.
District Committee Union Party 1863 and 1864; elec. County Supervisor 1863, 1864 and 1865; brother *Andrew Confederate sympathizer. Farmer; $5,080/120; b. Highland Co., Va. 1816; Republican; m. Elisabeth Samples; came to Barbour 1833; d. Barbour 1877. Son of John and Sarah (Waybright) Trimble; grandson of James and Susan (Shanaberry) Trimble; grandfather immigrant from Scotland.

TUTT, Edwin C.
Attended "Shoe Shop" meeting Martin's store 5-61. Mechanic; $800/123; b. Hardy Co., W. Va. 1825; came to Barbour 1840's; m. Elisabeth ____; moved to Kan. 1868. Son of James and Lucinda (Fink) Tutt, b. Culpepper Co., Va. where family dates back to mid-eighteenth century.

VALENTINE, Francis D.
Enl. Co. C, 4th W. Va. Cav. 7-27-63; disch. 3-9-64; father served Co. E, 14th Va. Cav. (CSA), taken prisoner and joined U. S. Navy; brother William served Co. G, 14th W. Va. Inf. (USA). Farmer; $500/250; b. Randolph Co., W. Va. 1831; m. Ellen V. ____; listed Barbour Union veterans 1890. Son of Henry and Matilda (Toothman) Valentine; father b. Md.; grandson of Isaac Valentine.

VANSCOY, Adam
Enl. Co. E, 3rd W. Va. Cav. 10-20-62; POW Covington, W. Va. 12-19-63; d. of chronic diarrhea Andersonville Prison 5-16-64; brother-in-law *David Waggoner served Co. H, 31st Va. Inf. (CSA). Tenant; $0/70; b. Randolph Co., W. Va. 1835; Methodist-Episcopal Church; m. Susan Waggoner 1863. Son of Jonas and Lydia (Hornbeck) Vanscoy; father b. Randolph Co.; grandson of Aaron and Jean (Taffle) Vanscoy; grandfather b. Vt., settled Pendleton Co., W. Va. then Randolph Co.

VANSCOY, Daniel
Enl. Co. E, 3rd W. Va. Cav. 9-15-62; disch. 6-6-65; brother-in-law *Henson Yoke Lt., Co. H, 62nd Va. Mtd. Inf. (CSA); brothers-in-law William, Isaac and John Yoke served Union Army. $300/80 (parents); b. Barbour or Randolph Co. W. Va. 1836, brother of Adam; Methodist-Episcopal Church; m. Rachel Yoke; moved to Harrison Co., W. Va. after the war, then Doddridge Co., W. Va. 1880's where listed Union veterans 1890; d. 1928.

VANSCOY, Jesse
Enl. Co. F, 3rd W. Va. Inf. 6-25-61; wd. Second Bull Run 8-29-62; disch. 8-15-64; brother-in-law Jacob Currence served Co. F, 31st Va. Inf. (CSA). $300/80 (parents); b. Barbour 1839, brother of Adam; Methodist-Episcopal Church; m. Catherine Currence 1864; moved to Doddridge Co., W. Va. after war where listed Union veterans 1890.

VANSCOY, Abel
Enl. Co. F, 3rd W. Va. Inf. 6-25-61; wd. right leg Second Bull Run 8-29-62; disch. for disability 11-26-62; re-enlisted Co. F, 17th W. Va. Inf. 9-5-64; disch. 6-30-65. $300/80 (parents); b. Barbour 1843, brother of Adam; Methodist-

Episcopal Church; m. 1) Mary C. Mathews 1879; 2) Elisabeth Ann ____ ; moved to Harrison Co., W. Va. after the war, then Doddridge Co., W. Va. 1880's where listed Union veterans 1890.

VISQUESNAY, Charles Emile
Sympathizer. Blacksmith; $400/213; b. France 1824; Methodist-Episcopal Church; Republican; came to Barbour from Augusta Co., W. Va. 1840's; m. Mary A. Row; d. Barbour 1896. Son of Charles and Haselle Visquesnay, immigrants from France, settled Barbour.

WAGGONER, William
Enl. Barbour Home Guard 9-1-63 for one year; prom. to sgt. $300/240; b. Preston Co., W. Va. 1822; came to Barbour 1840's; m. Edith Boyles; moved to Upshur Co., W. Va. where died 1897. Son of John George and Susan (Bishop) Waggoner, b. Md.

WALLACE, Richard M.
Enl. Co. H, 12th W. Va. Inf. 9-10-62; prom. to sgt.; detailed for recruiting duty 12-63; appointed regimental chaplain 8-19-64; disch. 6-16-65. Methodist-Episcopal minister; $151/200; b. Fayette Co., Pa. 1815; moved to Harrison Co., W. Va. where m. Mary Manser; came to Barbour 1850's; returned to Harrison Co. after war where d. 1880's; widow listed Harrison Co. Union veterans 1890.

WALLACE, John F.
Enl. Co. H, 31st Va. Inf. (CSA); des.10-63; enl. Bat. H, 1st W. Va. Art. 1-4-64 for six months; d. of disease Wheeling 4-10-64. $151/200 (parents); b. Harrison Co., W. Va. 1847, son of Richard M. and Mary (Manser) Wallace; Methodist-Episcopal Church.

WALTER, William
Elec. Township Commissioner 1864. Cabinet maker; $2,500/950; b. Barbour 1806; Methodist-Episcopal Church; m. Evaline Baker 1842; d. Barbour 1878. Son of Simon and Marie (Lowery) Walter, b. Md., settled Barbour 1790's.

WARD, James Henry
Delegate Union Party Convention Parkersburg 1863; brother Aquilla Unionist; brother *McKinsey Confederate sympathizer; son-in-law *William George Unionist; son-in-law William Wood served Union Army. $12,000/2,133; b. Upshur Co., W. Va. 1798; Methodist-Protestant Church; Republican; m. 1) Barbara Radabaugh 1824; 2) Laura Woodford; d. Barbour 1885. Son of Job and Tabitha (Cummins) Ward; father b. Pa.; grandson of Joshua Ward, immigrant from Ireland.

WARD, Aquilla Jr.
Elec. Justice of the Peace 1863. Farmer; $12,000/2,133 (parents); b. Upshur Co., W. Va. 1826, son of James and Barbara (Radabaugh) Ward; Methodist-Protestant Church; m. Comfort Cooper; d. Barbour 1909.

WARD, Johnson
Elec. Justice of the Peace 1861; elec. Township Commissioner 1863; brother-in-law *Jacob Reger served Co. H, 62nd Va. Mtd. Inf. (CSA). Methodist-Protestant minister; $2,500/200; b. Upshur Co., W. Va. 1804, brother of James; m. Martha Reger 1833; moved to Lewis Co., W. Va. after the war where d. 1888.

WARD, Abraham R.
Elec. Constable 1862. Farmer; $440/249; b. Upshur Co., W. Va. 1837, son of Johnson and Martha (Reger) Ward; Methodist-Protestant Church; m. Barbara Cool 1858; moved to Harrison Co., W. Va. after war where living 1880.

WARD, William
Delegate Union Party Convention Grafton 1864; claim for war-time service in 169th Mil. rejected 1902; brothers-in-law *Abraham, *Michael and *Branson Simon Unionists; son-in-law *Aaron Strader served Bat. E, 1st W. Va. Art. (USA). Farmer; $4,000/683; b. Upshur Co., W. Va. 1821; Methodist-Episcopal Church; Republican; m. Mahala Simon 1840; living Barbour 1870. Son of John and Nancy (Osborn) Ward.

WARDER, Noah E.
Elec. Constable 1862; District Committee Union Party 1863; Delegate Union Party Convention Grafton 1864; brother Thornberg served Co. K, 17th W. Va. Inf. (USA). $2,200/300; b. Taylor Co., W. Va. 1839; moved to Ind. after war. Son of James and Nancy (Powell) Warder; father b. Taylor Co.; grandson of Henry and Nancy (Ford) Warder; grandfather b. Md.

WARE, Adam W.
Enl. Co. F, 15th W. Va. Inf. 8-23-62; disch. 6-14-65; brother-in-law *Abel Teter served same company. Farmer; $2,000/326; b. Barbour 1843; m. Elisabeth _____; listed Barbour Union veterans 1890. Son of Benona and Matilda (Wooten) Ware; father b. Randolph Co., W. Va.; grandson of Richard and Matilda Ware; grandfather b. Md., settled Randolph Co., then Barbour 1834.

WATKINS, Almancer Grant
Enl. Co. F, 15th W. Va. Inf. 8-27-62; prom. to cpl.; KIA Hobbs Hill 10-13-64

brother-in-law *Benjamin Ekis Co. K, 6th W. Va. Inf. Tenant; $0/80; b. Monongalia Co., W. Va. 1826; came to Barbour 1850's; m. Mary Hardin.

WAUGH, Jacob
Elec. Constable 1863; drafted 3-65, never inducted. Farmer; $1,500/636; b. Pocahontas Co., W. Va. 1821; Methodist-Episcopal Church; Republican; m. Sarah Ann Grey; came to Barbour 1850's; moved to Upshur Co., W. Va. after war where d. 1882. Son of Samuel and Ann (McGuire) Waugh; father b. Pocahontas Co.; grandson of James and Mary Waugh; grandfather immigrant from Scotland.

WEAVER, Francis Marion
Enl. Barbour Home Guard 9-1-63; "left company in consequence of being dismounted;" NFR. Tenant; $0/60; b. Barbour 1834; Methodist-Episcopal Church; m. Eliza _____. Son of Daniel and Mary (Mitchell) Weaver; father b. Bucks Co., Pa.; grandson of Henry and Abigail (Griggs) Weaver, settled Barbour from Monongalia Co., W. Va.

WEAVER, William S.
Enl. Barbour Home Guard 11-1-63 for one year; prom. to sgt.; brothers-in-law *Edward, *Noah and *Emery McCauley Unionists. $50/155 (mother); b. Barbour 1838, brother of Francis; Methodist-Episcopal Church; m. Alcinda McCauley 1865; living Barbour 1880.

WEAVER, Henry
Drafted Co. K, 17th W. Va. Inf. 2-15-65; disch. 6-30-65; son-in-law John McVicker served Union army. Tenant; $0/105; b. Barbour 1830; Methodist-Episcopal Church; m. 1) Elisabeth Mitchell; 2) Emily Murphy 1870; listed Barbour Union veterans 1890. Son of John and Martha (Keller) Weaver; father b. Pa.; grandson of Henry and Abigail (Griggs) Weaver.

WEAVER, Elam
Drafted Co. K, 17th W. Va. Inf. 2-1-65; disch. 6-30-65; brother-in-law *Enoch Haddix served Co. C, 17th W. Va. Inf. (USA). Tenant; $150/150; b. Barbour 1840, brother of Henry; Methodist-Episcopal Church; m. Lucinda Haddix 1858; moved to Ritchie Co., W. Va. 1870's where listed Union veterans 1890.

WEAVER, Henry S.
Enl. Co. F, 15th W. Va. Inf. 8-23-62; wd. Lynchburg 6-18-64; disch. 6-14-65; brother George served Co. C, 1st W. Va. Cav. (USA). Farmer; $2,000/390 (parents); b. Barbour 1824; m. Mary J. McVicker; moved to Taylor Co, W. Va.

1870's where d. 1880's; widow listed Taylor Co. Union veterans 1890. Son of Uriah and Margaret (Duckworth) Weaver; grandson of Henry and Abigail (Griggs) Weaver.

WEAVER, Augustus John Smith
Enl. Co. F, 15th W. Va. Inf. 8-23-62; wd. left leg Lynchburg 6-18-64; disch. 6-14-65; brother-in-law Aaron McDaniel served Co. H, 12th W. Va. Inf. (USA). Farmer; $2,000/390 (parents); b. Barbour 1841, brother of Henry S.; m. Evaline McDaniel 1863; listed Barbour Union veterans 1890; d. 1922.

WEESE, Nimrod
Enl. Co. H, 10th W. Va. Inf. 6-15-62; wd. in stomach Droop Mountain 11-6-63; disch. 8-20-65; brother-in-law *Alfred Yeager served Barbour Home Guard (USA). $1,000/565 (parents); b. Randolph Co., W. Va. 1840; m. Lucy Thorn 1867; listed Barbour Union veterans 1890. Son of John and Hannah (Weese) Weese; descendant of Jacob Weese, b. Va., settled Randolph Co. 1770's.

WELCH, Samuel O.
Enl. Co. H, 10th W. Va. Inf. 10-13-62; wd. left leg Winchester 9-19-64 and disch.; brother *John listed Barbour Light Horse; brother *Benjamin Confederate sympathizer, arrested and d. in prison; brother-in-law *Henry Rohr Unionist; brother-in-law John Houston served Co. A, 14th W. Va. Inf. (USA); brother-in-law *William Callahan Confederate sympathizer. Farmer; $9,000/1,505 (parents); b. Barbour 1848; Methodist-Protestant Church; listed Barbour Union veterans 1890; d. Barbour 1885. Son of Samuel and Margaret (Ratliff) Welch; grandson of Isaac Welch, b. Va., settled Barbour.

WENTZ, James Wilson
Enl. Home Guard, Upshur Co. 1-1-64 for one year; father abolitionist; brothers William, Henry, David and John served U.S. Army; brother-in-law *David Harris served Co. H, 31st Va. Inf. (CSA); Tenant; $0/128; b. Rockbridge Co., Va. 1838; Methodist-Episcopal Church; m. Lucy Catherine Harris 1858; living Barbour 1880. Son of John and Margaret (Cox) Wentz; father b. Rockbridge Co., settled Barbour 1840's; grandson of William and Mary (Dietrick) Wentz; grandfather immigrant from Germany, settled Rockbridge Co. from Md.

WHEELER, Abraham
Enl. Co. H, 10th W. Va. Inf. 5-8-62; disch. 5-8-65; son-in-law Elias Barker served Co. B, 6th W. Va. Inf. (USA). Farmer; $0/247; b. Preston Co., W. Va. 1813; Methodist-Episcopal Church; m. 1) Elisabeth White; 2) Susanna Jones Starker 1876 (widow of *Adam Starker, CSA); moved to Upshur Co., W. Va.

1880's. Son of John and Catherine (Gower) Wheeler; father settled Preston Co. from Lancaster Co., Pa.; grandson of immigrant from England.

WHEELER, William S.
Enl. Co. H, 10th W. Va. Inf. 5-8-62; wd. Winchester 9-19-64; disch. 5-7-65. Farmer; $0/247 (parents); b. Barbour Co. 1842, son of Abraham and Elisabeth (White) Wheeler; Methodist-Episcopal Church; m. Olive E. Morrison 1870; moved to Taylor Co., W. Va. 1870's where listed Union veterans 1890.

WHITE, Norman B.
Sympathizer. Merchant; $0/205; b. Allegany Co., Md. 1829; Methodist-Protestant Church; Republican; m. Caroline Blower 1857; moved to Upshur Co., W. Va. after 1880 where d. 1919. Son of Abraham and Amelia (White) White, b. Md., settled Barbour 1834.

WHITE, John J.
Enl. Co. E, 3rd W. Va. Inf. 7-5-61; wd. McDowell 5-8-62; d. 5-12-62. Farmer; $1,200/300 (parents); b. Md. 1843. Son of Levi and Jane White, b. Md.

WHITE, William P.
Enl. Co. A, 1st W. Va. Cav. 3-3-65; disch. 7-8-65; NFR; brother-in-law Branson Simon served Co. B, 10th W. Va. Inf. (USA). Farmer; $3,000/405 (parents); b. Va. 1839; Methodist-Protestant Church; m. Sarah D. Simon 1853. Son of Joseph and Elisabeth (Roberts) White; father b. Md.; grandson of Adam and Margaret White.

WILLIAMS, Thomas
Elec. Constable 1865. $N/G; b. N.Y. 1819; came to Barbour 1850's; moved to Tucker Co., W. Va. 1879 where living 1884.

WILLIAMS, Isaac
Enl. Co. H, 10th W. Va. Inf. 5-1-62; POW Cedar Creek 10-19-64; disch. 5-8-65. Farmer; $0/90 (parents); b. Bath Co., Va. 1837; m. Lucinda Davis Queen 1866; moved to Gilmer Co., W. Va. where listed Union veterans 1890; d. 1905. Son of Salem and Sarah (Willet) Williams; father b. Md., settled Barbour 1830's.

WILLIAMS, Andrew Jackson
Enl. Co. F, 1st W. Va. Inf. 5-21-61; disch. 8-21-61; re-enlisted Bat. H, 1st W. Va. Art. 8-12-63; disch. 4-15-64; re-enlisted Co. E, 6th W. Va. Inf. 8-20-64; disch. 6-30-65. Tenant; $70/232; b. Bath Co., Va. 1838, brother of Isaac; m. Julianna Row; moved to Preston Co., W. Va. 1880's where listed Union veterans 1890; d. 1898.

WILLIAMS, Noah
Enl. Co. H, 10th W. Va. Inf. 5-8-62; wd. right leg Winchester 9-19-64; disch. 5-7-65. Farmer; $0/90 (parents); b. Bath Co., W. Va. 1844, brother of Isaac; m. Mary E. Hershman 1865; moved to Harrison Co., W. Va. 1870's where listed Union veterans 1890.

WILLIAMSON, Nathan
Enl. Co. F, 15th W. Va. Inf. 8-27-62; wd. Lynchburg 6-18-64; wd. in foot Winchester 9-19-64; wd. in arm Petersburg 4-2-65; disch. 5-15-65. Farmer; $1,000/506 (parents); b. Taylor Co., W. Va. 1842; United Brethren Church; m. Sarah Lawley 1866; listed Barbour Union veterans 1890. Son of John and Rebecca (Rector) Williamson; parents and grandparents b. Va.

WILLIAMSON, Lemuel
Enl. Co. K, 6th W. Va. Inf. 10-5-64; disch. 6-30-65. Farmer; $1,000/506 (parents); b. Taylor Co., W. Va. 1847, brother of Nathan; United Brethren Church; m. Adaline E. Swick 1871; moved to Upshur Co., W. Va. 1877 where living 1880.

WILMOTH, John Kittle
Enl. Co. F, 15th W. Va. Inf. 8-23-62; disch. 6-14-65. Farmer; $106/278; b. Randolph Co., W. Va. 1827; came to Barbour 1850's where m. Delila Carr 1858; listed Barbour Union veterans 1890. Son of John and Ann (Kittle) Wilmoth; grandson of Nicolas and Sidney (Currence) Wilmoth; great-grandson of Thomas and Nancy Wilmoth, settled Randolph Co. 1770's.

WILMOTH, General Marion
Enl. Co. H, 10th W. Va. Inf. 5-8-62; prom. to cpl. 11-29-62; disch. 5-7-65. Farmer; $300/45 (parents); b. Randolph Co., W. Va. 1840; m. Prudence Hooker 1867; listed Harrison Co. Union veterans 1890 as living Barbour. Son of Noah and Mary (Philips) Wilmoth; grandson of Jonathon and Margaret Wilmoth; great-grandson of Thomas and Nancy Wilmoth.

WILMOTH, Allen Vanscoy
District Committee Union Party 1863; elec. Justice of the Peace 1863; Delegate Union Party Convention Grafton 1864. Farmer; $150/95; b. Randolph Co., W. Va. 1830; United Brethren Church; m. Hester Ann Thompson 1852; d. Barbour 1903. Son of Absalom and Rebecca (Vanscoy) Wilmoth; grandson of Thomas and Amy (Schoonover) Wilmoth; great-grandson of Thomas and Nancy Wilmoth.

WILSON, Lewis
Elec. County Court Clerk 1861-1865; County Committee Union Party 1863. Miller; $5,000/325; b. Barbour 1818; family moved to Ohio 1820's, returning to Barbour 1830's; m. Ann M. Keys 1844; Republican; living Barbour 1899. Son of William and Jane (Booth) Wilson; father b. Hardy Co., W. Va.; grandson of William and Elisabeth (Friend) Wilson; great-grandson of William and Elisabeth (Black) Wilson, immigrants from Ireland to Hardy Co. 1715.

WILSON, Elisabeth
Sympathizer; described by Union troops occupying Philippi as "a real favorite among the officers." $5,000/325 (parents); b. Barbour 1842, daughter of Lewis and Ann (Keys) Wilson; m. *James E. Hall 1869; living Barbour 1880.

WILSON, Alpheus P.
Delegate Union Party Convention Parkersburg 1863; elec. Justice of the Peace 1863; brother-in-law *John R. Thompson Confederate sympathizer. Farm laborer; $320/160; b. Guersey Co., Ohio 1825, brother of Lewis; came to Barbour 1850's; m. 1) Mary McVicker 1847; 2) Jane R. Thompson 1856; moved to Taylor Co., W. Va. after war; returned to Barbour 1870's where living 1880.

WILSON, Daniel
Enl. Co. B, 2nd W. Va. Inf. 5-21-61; prom. to Lt.; prom. to Capt. 5-20-62; resigned commission for health reasons 4-23-63; regimental historian described him as "A devoted friend of the Union, never flinching from any duty, no matter how arduous or hazardous." Doctor; $0/200; b. Guersey Co., Ohio 1834, brother of Lewis; m. 1) Naomi Reger 1847; 2) Mary ____; moved to Mich. 1870's where d. 1878.

WILSON, James Lewis
Enl. Co. B, 2nd W. Va. Inf. 7-5-63; served as drummer; transf. to Co. K upon organization of 5th W. Va. Cav.; POW New Creek 4-4-64; disch. 12-4-65. $0/200 (parents); b. Barbour 1848, son of Daniel and Naomi (Reger) Wilson; appointed to West Point after war, serving with 4th U. S. Art. after graduation; m. Camilla Zantzinger 1876; d. 1902.

WILSON, Thomas Devault
Assisted Federal scouts 7-61; drafted 3-65, never inducted; brother-in-law Samuel Nestor served Co. B, 11th W. Va. Inf. (USA); brothers-in-law *William Fitzwater and George Nestor served Co. E, 62nd Va. Mtd. Inf. (CSA). Farmer; $600/306; b. Randolph Co., W. Va. 1820; m. Margaret Nestor; moved to Tucker Co., W. Va. 1870's where living 1884. Son of Thomas and Elisabeth (Moats) Wilson; parents b. Md.

WILSON, Thomas Marion
Enl. Co. D, 3rd W. Va. Inf. 6-29-63; wd. left hand Rocky Gap 8-26-63; POW New Creek 4-4-64; d. Richmond Prison 4-2-65. Farmer; $600/306 (parents); b. Barbour or Randolph Co., W. Va. 1842, son of Thomas D. and Margaret (Nestor) Wilson.

WILSON, Andrew Jackson
U. S. Army, unit unknown. Farmer; $600/306 (parents); b. Barbour or Randolph Co. W. Va. 1843, brother of Thomas; m. Anisi ____; moved to Randolph Co. 1870's where living 1880.

WILSON, William P.
Elec. Constable 1865. Farmer; $2,100/747; b. Md. 1811; German Baptist Church; m. Eliza A. Simmons; came to Barbour 1840's; living Barbour 1880.

WILSON, John H.
Elec. Constable 1861; enl. Co. F, 15th W. Va. Inf. 8-23-62; prom. to cpl.; disch. 6-14-65; NFR. Farmer; $2,100/747 (parents); b. Allegany Co., Md. 1834, son of William P. and Eliza (Simmons) Wilson; German Baptist Church.

WILSON, Josiah
Enl. Co. F, 15th W. Va. Inf. 8-23-62; disch. 6-14-65; brothers-in-law *James, *Abel and *Oliver Teter served same company; father-in-law *Jacob Teter Confederate sympathizer. Farmer; $2,100/747 (parents); b. Allegany Co., Md. 1838, brother of John H.; German Baptist Church; m. Elisabeth Teter 1862; post-war minister United Brethren Church; listed Barbour Union veterans 1890.

WILSON, Solomon Thomas
Teamster, Union Army; drafted 2-65, never inducted. Teamster; $2,100/747 (parents); b. Allegany Co., Md. 1842, brother of John H.; German Baptist Church; Republican; m. Elisabeth Ware 1867; d. Barbour 1922.

WILSON, Alpheus P.
Enl. Bat. F, 1st W. Va. Art. 10-31-61; no record of discharge. Farmer; $2,100/747 (parents); b. Allegany Co., Md. 1844, brother of John H.; German Baptist Church; m. Rachel H. Wilmoth 1869; living Barbour 1880.

WILSON, Daniel B.
Sympathizer. Tenant; $0/120; b. Allegany Co., Md. 1834; m. Christina Gainer 1866; living Barbour 1880. Son of John and Hannah (Townsend) Wilson.

WINANS, Simon
Enl. Co. F, 15th W. Va. Inf. 8-22-62; wd. right shoulder Hobb's Hill 10-13-64; disch. 5-15-65; brothers-in-law *Henry and *George Markely served Co. N, 6th W. Va. Inf. (USA). Farmer; $300/55; b. Lewis Co., W. Va. 1833; Methodist-Episcopal Church; Republican; m. 1) Elisabeth Teets 1856; 2) Evaline Markeley 1859; listed Barbour Union veterans 1890; living Barbour 1899. Son of Benjamin and Catherine (Simon) Winans; parents b. Va.; grandfather b. N.J.

WINANS, Enos
Enl. Co. H, 7th W. Va. Inf. 9-2-61; wd. Robinsons Cross Roads 11-27-63; POW Spotsylvania 5-5-64; d. Andersonville Prison 11-4-64. Farmer; $900/665 (mother); b. Lewis Co., W. Va. 1836, brother of Simon; Methodist-Episcopal Church.

WOOD, Thomas
Sympathizer; known to Union troops passing home as gracious host; with wife kept notebook of soldiers who visited them which by 1862 included several hundred signatures; son-in-law *William Lantz served Co. D, 20th Va. Cav. (CSA); NFR. Baptist minister; $3,500/833; b. N.Y. 1813; m. Elisabeth Glascock.

WOOD, Elisabeth (Glascock)
Sympathizer, wife of Thomas Wood; brothers *John and *Joshua Glascock Unionists; NFR. $3,500/833; b. Barbour 1818; Baptist. Daughter of William and Alsie (Cole) Glascock.

WOOD, William Spencer
Enl. Co. F, 3rd W. Va. Inf. 10-24-63; served Co. B, 6th W. Va. Cav. upon consolidation of regiment with 5th W. Va. Cav.; disch. 5-22-66. Farmer; $3,500/833 (parents); b. Barbour 1839, son of Thomas and Elisabeth (Glascock) Wood; Baptist; m. Phoebe Strader 1875; living Barbour 1880.

WOODFORD, Robinson
Elec. Constable 1865; father Confederate sympathizer; brother *John served Co. H, 31st Va. Inf. (CSA); brother *Benjamin served Co. E, 62nd Va. Mtd. Inf. (CSA). Farmer; $10,000/9,154 (parents); b. Barbour 1829; Baptist; m. Mary Woodford 1847; moved to Gilmer Co., W. Va. after war where living 1880. Son of *Jacob and Mary (Robinson) Woodford; parents b. Barbour; grandson of William and Hannah (Moss) Woodford, b. Va., settled Barbour from Highland Co. 1804; great-grandson of William Woodford of Alexandria, Va.

WOODFORD, James Manville
Com. Lt., 169th W. Va. Mil. 11-5-64, never called into service; brother-in-law *Commodore Thompson served same regiment; brother-in-law *George Thompson Capt., Co. H, 31st Va. Inf. (CSA). Farmer and slave owner; $10,000/9,154 (parents); b. Barbour 1836, brother of Robinson; Baptist; m. Elisabeth Thompson 1859; living Barbour 1880.

WOODFORD, John Harvey
President Unionist rally Philippi 8-62; Delegate Union Party Convention Grafton 1864; com. Lt, 169th W. Va. Mil. 4-29-65; never called into service; father Confederate sympathizer; brother-in-law *George Thompson served Co. H, 31st Va. Inf. (CSA); brother-in-law *Robert Talbott Confederate sympathizer; brother-in-law *Commodore Thompson Unionist. Farmer and slave owner; $5,000/7,105; b. Barbour 1829; Baptist; Democrat; m. Ingabie Thompson 1850; d. Barbour 1894. Son of *John Howe and Nancy (Minear) Woodford; father b. Rockingham Co. Va.; grandson of William and Hannah (Moss) Woodford.

WOODFORD, Asa Wesley
Sympathizer; helped raise 10th W. Va. Inf. Farmer; $54,000/23,000 (parents); b. Barbour 1833, brother of John; Baptist; Democrat; m. 1) Rebecca Cather 1855; 2) Sarah Cather 1895; moved to Ritchie Co., W. Va., then to Lewis Co., W. Va. 1870's where living 1899.

WOODFORD, John Wesley
Com. Lt., 169th W. Va. Mil. 11-5-64; never called into service; father-in-law *John R. Williamson Confederate sympathizer. Farmer; $5,000/1,697 (parents); b. Barbour 1842; Baptist; m. Colombia Williamson 1864; living Barbour 1880. Son of William and Sarah (Jackson) Woodford; parents slave owners; grandson of William and Hannah (Moss) Woodford.

WOOTERS, William W. A.
Enl. Co. H, 10th W. Va. Inf. 5-8-62; prom. to sgt.; POW 1864; disch. 8-20-65. Tailor; $120/27; b. Va. 1820; came to Barbour 1840's where m. Lydia Coffman; listed Barbour Union veterans 1890. Parents b. Va.

WRIGHT, Willis
Elec. Justice of the Peace 1863; brother-in-law *David Cleavenger served Co. H, 62nd Va. Mtd. Inf. (CSA). Farmer; $2,500/1,268; b. Ohio 1809; m. Edith Chrislip 1834; living Barbour 1880. Son of Joshua Wright, b. Va., settled Barbour, then Ohio, returning to Barbour; grandparents said to be immigrants from England.

WRIGHT, Lloyd
Enl. Co. F, 3rd W. Va. Inf. 6-25-61; re-enlisted 2-29-64, serving Co. D, 6th W. Va. Cav. upon consolidation of regiment with 5th W.Va. Cav.; prom. to sgt. 3-1-66; disch. 5-22-66. Farmer; $2,000/374 (parents); b. Barbour 1840; m. 1) Sarah _____; 2) Missouri Fittro 1878; listed Barbour Union veterans 1890. Son of Thompson and Irene (Adams) Wright; father b. Ohio; grandson of Joshua Wright.

WRIGHT, Arnold
Elec. Justice of the Peace 1861 and 1863; District Committee Union Party 1864. Farmer; $300/80 (mother); b. Randolph Co., W. Va. 1821; Republican; m. Elisabeth Hays; living Barbour 1880. Son of Jacob and Catherine Wright; grandson of William Wright, settled Randolph Co.

WRIGHT, William J.
Enl. Co. F, 15th W. Va. Inf. 8-27-62; right thumb shot off; disch. 6-14-65; brothers-in-law Valentine, Cain and Lafayette Hinkle served Union Army. $400/65; b. Randolph Co., W. Va. 1834, brother of Arnold; m. Sarah A. Hinkle 1861; listed Barbour Union veterans 1890.

WRIGHT, John W.
Enl. Co. H, 10th W. Va. Inf. 6-12-62; disch. 6-26-65. $300/65 (mother); b. Randolph Co., W. Va. 1847, brother of Arnold; m. Martha E. Yoke 1866; listed Barbour Union veterans 1890.

WRIGHT, John W.
Enl. Co. B, 2nd W. Va. Inf. 5-20-61; disch. 6-14-64; brother *Richard served Co. C, 19th Va. Cav. (CSA). Farmer; $800/242 (parents); b. Rockbridge Co., Va. 1836; m. Martha E. Fitzpatrick 1860; listed Barbour Union veterans 1890. Son of William and Angeline Wright, b. Va., settled Barbour 1840's, then Gilmer Co., W. Va. during the war; grandparents b. Va.

WRIGHTSMAN, Jesse L.
Enl. Barbour Home Guard 9-1-63; disch. for disability 4-5-64, suffering from typhoid fever. Farmer; $500/414; b. Botetourt Co., Va. 1822; Baptist; came to Barbour from Roane Co., W. Va. 1840's; m. Mary Ann Stemple 1846; living Barbour 1880. Son of John and Susanna (Kinsey) Wrightsman; grandson of John and Mary (Colton) Wrightsman; grandfather immigrant from Germany, settled Botetourt Co.

YEAGER, Alfred
Enl. Barbour Home Guard 10-1-63; "left company 8-64 in consequence of being dismounted;" drafted 3-65, never inducted; brother-in-law *Nimrod Weese served Co. H, 10th W. Va. Inf. (USA). Tenant; $0/50 (parents); b. Barbour 1840; United Brethren Church; m. 1) Catherine Ann Weese 1863; 2) Martha Digman 1869; moved to Calhoun Co., W. Va. where listed Union veterans 1890. Son of Absalom and Mary Ann (Coberly) Yeager, b. Barbour; grandson of George and Eve Yeager; grandfather b. Pa., settled Barbour from Pendleton Co., W. Va.

YEAGER, Daniel M.
Enl. Co. F, 15th W. Va. Inf. 8-26-62; disch. 6-14-65. Tenant; $0/50 (parents); b. Barbour 1845, brother of Alfred; United Brethren Church; m. Nancy George 1865; moved to Randolph Co., W. Va. 1870's where listed Union veterans 1890; living Randolph Co. 1899.

YEAGER, Isom
Enl. Co. H, 7th W. Va. Inf. 9-2-61; wd. and disch. for disability 1863; drafted 3-65, never inducted; NFR. Farmer; $0/253 (parents); b. Barbour 1828. Son of William and Elisabeth (Thorn) Yeager; grandson of George and Eve Yeager.

YEAGER, Jacob
Enl. Co. H, 10th W. Va. Inf. 11-12-62; d. of wounds Point of Rocks, Md. 3-30-65. Farmer; $0/253 (parents); b. Barbour 1831, brother of Isom; m. Cassandra Parsons 1852.

YEAGER, William
Enl. Co. F, 15th W. Va. Inf. 8-23-62; prom. to cpl.; wd. in shoulder Winchester 9-19-64; disch. 6-14-65; brother-in-law *George Arbogast served same company. Tenant; $0/253; b. Barbour 1834, brother of Isom; m. 1) Mary England 1854; 2) Martha Arbogast 1855; listed Barbour Union veterans 1890.

YEAGER, George M.
Listed Barbour Light Horse; elec. Justice of the Peace 1861; secretary, pro-Union mass meeting 8-62; Com. Capt., Barbour Home Guard 7-63; dismissed 8-63; Co. F, 133rd W. Va. Mil., called into service 9-63 for three months; Delegate Union Party Conventions Parkersburg 1863 and Grafton 1864; NFR. Farmer; $2,000/675; b. Barbour 1827; German Baptist; m. Margaret ____. Son of Jonathon and Elisabeth (Miller) Yeager; grandson of George and Eve Yeager.

YEAGER, Francis Marion
Enl. Co. H, 10th W. Va. Inf. 11-5-62; MIA Cedar Creek 10-19-64. Farmer; $200/80 (parents); b. Barbour 1843; Campbellite Church. Son of John and Anna (Trader) Yeager; grandson of George and Eve Yeager.

YEAGER, Isaac
Enl. Co. F, 17th W. Va. Inf. 9-5-64; disch. 6-30-65. $200/80 (parents); b. Barbour 1844, brother of Francis; Campbellite Church; m. Louise Bennett 1865; moved to Calhoun Co., W. Va. after war where listed Union veterans 1890.

ZINN, Alpheus
Attended "Shoe Shop" meeting at Myer's store 5-61; wife Confederate sympathizer; brother-in-law James Gawthorpe served Co. A, 20th Va. Cav. (CSA); brother-in-law Thomas Gawthorpe served 133rd W. Va. Mil. (USA). Farmer; $4,760/920; b. Barbour 1812; Baptist; m. 1) Mary Woodford 1845; 2) *Lucinda Gawthorpe 1854; d. Barbour 1875. Son of Peter and Catherine (Criss) Zinn; grandson of George and Mary (Saylor) Zinn, immigrants from Switzerland.

ZINN, David
Elec. Township Commissioner 1863; County Supervisor 1864; Delegate Union Party Convention Grafton 1864. Farmer; $13,000/540; b. Barbour 1820, brother of Alpheus; Baptist; Republican; m. 1) Louisa Coberly; 2) Lavinia Zinn; d. Barbour 1866.

ZINN, Peter
County Central Committee for vote on new constitution 2-63; County Supervisor of Elections 1863; appointed School Commissioner 1864; District Committee Union Party 1863 and 1864; elec. County Treasurer 1864; drafted 2-65, never inducted. $1,800/387; b. Barbour 1834; Methodist-Episcopal Church; m. Delila Anglin 1855; d. Barbour 1866. Son of Isaac and Elisabeth (Carlin) Zinn; grandson of Peter and Phoebe (Criss) Zinn.

ZIRKLE, Lewis
Elec. Constable 1865. Farmer; $3,000/250 (parents); b. Barbour 1837; United Brethren Church; m. 1) Clarissa Jane Reed 1856; 2) Mahala Summers 1898; moved to Upshur Co., W. Va. 1876 where d. 1917. Son of Daniel and Catherine (Bowman-Wilt) Zirkle, b. Rockingham Co., Va., settled Barbour 1836; grandson of Lewis and Mary (Coldwell) Zirkle; grandfather b. Pa.; great-grandson of Lewis and Eva Zirkle, immigrants from Germany.

ZIRKLE, Oliver S.
Enl. Barbour Home Guard 10-1-63; disch. for disability. Tenant; $0/75; b. Barbour 1839, brother of Jacob; United Brethren Church; m. Elisabeth Reed 1856; moved to Upshur Co., W. Va. 1876 where living 1926.

ZIRKLE, Jacob
Enl. Co. F, 15th W. Va. Inf. 8-23-62; wd. in shoulder Kernstown 7-24-64; disch. 6-14-65. Farmer; $3,000/250 (parents); b. Barbour 1841, half brother of Lewis; United Brethren Church; joined Methodist-Episcopal Church after war; m. Rebecca Sluss 1865; listed Barbour Union veterans 1890. Son of Daniel and Catherine (Degarmo) Zirkle.

CONFEDERATES

ALEXANDER, Solomon George
Served 169th Va. Mil., called out 5-61; claimed to have fired first shot of the Battle of Phillippi; brother-in-law Armistead Queen served Co. D, 20th Va. Cav. (CSA); brothers-in-law *Samuel, *Lemuel and *Thomas O'Neal Unionists. Joiner; $0/313; b. Augusta Co., Va. 1839; Methodist-Episcopal Church; came to Barbour 1840's; m. Mary O'Neal 1858; moved to Upshur Co., W. Va. after war where d. 1913. Son of John and Diannah (Alor) Alexander; father b. Augusta Co.; grandson of Simon and Sarah Alexander; grandfather immigrant from Scotland, settled Augusta Co.

ALFORD, Thomas
Enl. Co. K, 31st Va. Inf. 5-18-61; prom. to sgt.; POW Greenbrier 10-3-61; paroled; KIA Port Republic 6-8-62. Servant; $0/70 (parents); b. Augusta Co., Va. 1838. Son of James and Elisabeth Alford; parents b. Va., settled Barbour 1850's; grandfather immigrant from England

ALFORD, James Henry
Enl. Co. K, 31st Va. Inf. 5-18-61; POW Greenbrier 10-3-61; paroled; re-enlisted Co. D, 20th Va. Cav. 4-1-64; AWOL 7-64 to 10-64; paroled Staunton, Va. 5-12-65. Servant; $0/70 (parents); b. Augusta Co., Va. 1842, brother of Thomas; m. Mary Eliza Colebank 1867; moved to Randolph Co., W. Va. 1870's where living 1880.

ALFORD, John Calvin
Guerrilla; arrested 1-64; "A notorious guerrilla, and has been the terror of Barbour for many a day;" d. of disease Camp Chase, Ohio 3-7-64. Servant; $0/70 (parents); b. Augusta Co., Va. 1847, brother of Thomas.

ANDERSON, Thomas Jefferson
Enl. Co. D, 20th Va. Cav. 5-1-63; AWOL 7-64; arrested Clarksburg, W. Va. and released on oath 11-5-64; Farmer; $0/40; b. Loudoun Co., Va. 1814; m. Mary _____; moved to Harrison Co., W. Va. 1850's; came to Barbour during war; moved to Randolph Co., W. Va. 1870's where living 1880. Parents b. Va.

ANDERSON, George A.
Enl. Co. D, 20th Va. Cav. 10-4-63; des. 7-64; POW Clarksburg, W. Va. and released on oath 11-3-64; brother *James served Co. H, 10th W. Va. Inf. (USA). Farmer; $0/153 (parents); b. Loudoun Co., Va. 1844; came to Barbour 1850's; m. Sarah McCauley 1865; moved to Calhoun Co., W. Va. 1870's where living 1880.

Son of Eli and Sarah Francis (Stillings) Anderson; grandson of James and Sarah Anderson, b. Va.

ANDRICK, Henry
Sympathizer; home burned 1863. Farmer; $2,000/340; b. Shenandoah Co., Va. 1819; Presbyterian; m. Sarah Pfau; came to Barbour 1850's; d. Barbour 1895. Son of Joseph and Rebecca (Carsh) Andrick, b. Shenandoah Co.; grandson of George and Barbara (Foltz) Andrick.

ANDRICK, Christian Henry
Enl. Co. H, 31st Va. Inf. 5-14-61; POW Gettysburg; released; drafted 3-65, never inducted. Farmer; $2,000/340 (parents); b. Shenandoah Co., Va. 1847, son of Henry and Sarah (Pfau) Andrick; Presbyterian; m. Elisabeth Jones 1874; d. Barbour 1932.

ANGLIN, David
Sympathizer; arrested 1-13-63 as hostage for *James Trayhern; transf. to Camp Chase, Ohio 4-29-63; released 1-24-64. Tenant; $1,000/272; b. Barbour 1821; m. 1) Nancy Heatherly 1848; 2) Julia Reed 1875; d. Barbour 1870's. Son of William and Nancy (Cade) Anglin; grandson of William and Susanna Anglin, b. Bath Co., Va., settled Barbour 1780's.

ARMESY, Thomas B.
Enl. Co. C, 31st Va. Inf. 5-21-61; prom. to sgt.; elec. Lt. 5-1-62, but never commissioned; absent 8-31-62 due to "mental derangement;" com. Capt. Co. A, 33rd Btln. Va. Cav. 9-1-62, reorganized as 17th Va. Cav. 1-63; lost election for Lt. Col.; POW Harrison Co., W. Va. 4-18-63; exch. 8-29-64; POW 4-15-65; released on oath 7-7-65. Blacksmith; $100/310; b. Marion Co., W. Va. 1824; moved to Harrison Co. where m. Roanna Davis 1844; came to Barbour 1850's; moved to Ritchie Co., W. Va. after war, then to Upshur Co., W. Va. 1870's where living 1880. Parents b. Va.

ARMESY, John W.
Enl. Co. B, 17th Va. Cav. 8-25-62; transf. to Co. K 1863, assigned as teamster; sur. Appomattox 4-9-65. $100/310 (parents); b. Harrison Co., W. Va. 1845, son of Thomas and Roanna (Davis) Armesy; m. Adaline ____; moved to Harrison Co. after war where living 1880.

ARMSTRONG, George
Enl. Co. H, 31st Va. Inf. 5-14-61; transf. to 25th Va. Inf. 2-17-62 as assistant surgeon; wd. in hip McDowell 5-8-62; disch. as disabled 1-9-64 NFR; brother Edward served 25th and 31st Va. Inf.; father prominent secessionist leader.

Boarder; $0/0; b. Taylor Co., W. Va. 1835; came to Barbour 1850's. Son of Edward and Sophia (Rightmire) Armstong; father b. Harrison Co., W. Va.; grandson of Maxwell and Catherine (Davisson) Armstrong; grandfather settled Harrison Co. from Frederick Co., Va.

ARMSTRONG, Thomas Jefferson
Enl. Co. A, 20th Va. Cav. 5-10-63; des. 10-64 and sur. Philippi 10-12-64; gave oath and released 10-14-64. Tenant; $0/165 (parents); b. Barbour 1839; Methodist-Protestant Church; m. Lydia Adams 1866; living Barbour 1880. Son of _____ and Isabel Armstrong; parents b. Va.

AUVIL, Daniel M.
Pre-war Col., 169th Va. Mil., called out under his command 5-61; POW Philippi 6-3-61 and sent to Camp Chase, Ohio; released; refugee in Monterey, Va. during war. Attorney and County Prosecutor; $2,980/630; b. Barbour 1823; m. Eliza Keyser 1845; moved to McDowell Co., W. Va. after the war where d. 1893. Son of Lewis and Mary (Moats) Auvil; father b. Pa.; grandson of Daniel and Anna Margareta (Hochwaeter) Auvil, settled Barbour.

AUVIL, Henry D.
Sympathizer; indicted for treason 9-61; refugee in Monterey, Va.; brothers-in-law *Harrison and *Elliott Stalnaker served Co. E, 62nd Va. Mtd. Inf. (CSA). Attorney; $4,850/880; b. Barbour 1835, brother of Daniel; m. 1) Mary Stalnaker Howdershelt 1855; 2) Dorothy Edmonds 1871; moved to Pendleton Co., W. Va. after war where d. 1895.

BARNHOUSE, John W.
Enl. Co. K, 31st Va. Inf. 5-29-61; des. 7-61; re-enlisted Co. H, 62nd Va. Mtd. Inf. 8-1-62; transf. to McClanahan's Battery; des. Braxton Co., W. Va. 5-18-63; sur. and released on oath 6-3-63; NFR; five brothers of wife served CSA. Tenant; $0/24; b. Tucker Co., W. Va. 1844; came to Barbour 1850's; m. Sarah Cross 1859. Son of _____ and Mariah Barnhouse; grandson of George and Susanna (Pittman) Barnhouse; grandfather b. Hardy Co., W. Va., settled Tucker Co. 1790's.

BARRON, Henry
Enl. Co. H, 31st Va. Inf. 5-14-61; des. 7-61; arrested Philippi 10-61 by local constables and sent to Camp Chase, Ohio; released on oath 2-62. Hotel Keeper; $7,850/1,750; b. Frederick Co., Va. 1818; came to Barbour 1840's where m. Affie Dilworth 1844; living Barbour 1880. Son of Thomas and Fanny Barron; descendant of James and Hannah (Brown) Barron of Frederick Co.

BARTLETT, William E.
Listed Barbour Light House; com. Lt., 169th W. Va. Militia 8-16-62. Cf. Unionists.

BEAN, John
Enl. Co. D, 20th Va. Cav. 5-1-63; sur. Clarksburg, W. Va. and released on oath 3-18-65. Farmer; $4,600/917 (parents); b. Barbour 1833; m. Martha H. Hickman 1854; moved to Upshur Co., W Va. 1870's where living 1880. Son of Benjamin and Nancy (Queen) Bean, b. Va.

BEAN, Wesley
Enl. Co. D, 20th Va. Cav. 5-1-63; prom. to sgt.; demoted to ranks; 7-63; des. 1863; brothers-in-law *Nathaniel and *Elam Poling served CSA. Farmer; $4,600/917 (parents); b. Barbour 1844, brother of John; m. Virginia Poling 1863; living Barbour 1880.

BEERY, John H.
Enl. Co. H, 31st Va. Inf. 5-14-61; des. 7-61; re-enlisted Co. A, 26th Va. Cav. 6-10-63; POW 7-23-63. Bookkeeper; $0/0; b. Rockingham Co., Va. 1837; Mennonite; came to Barbour 1850's where m. Artissa F. Fair 1861; d. 1860's. Son of Henry and Lydia (Grove) Beery, b. Rockingham Co.; grandson of John and Barbara (Kagy) Beery, b. York Co. Pa., settled Rockingham Co.

BENNETT, Laban
Sympathizer; father Unionist. Farmer; $2,500/397; b. Barbour 1829; m. Sarah Keller 1847; d. Barbour 1863. Son of *Jacob and Sarah (Philips) Bennett. Cf. Unionists.

BENNETT, James Waldo
Sympathizer; hid Confederate soldiers on furlough; brother *Jacob Unionist. Farmer; $0/180; b. Barbour 1819; m. Mary Ann Fitzwater; d. Barbour 1894. Son of Jesse and Phoebe Bennett, b. Loudoun Co., Va., settled Barbour; grandson of Jacob and Sarah Bennett, b. Va.

BENNETT, Jesse T.
Enl. Co. K, 31st Va. Inf. 5-29-61; prom. to cpl.; KIA Port Republic 6-9-62. Farmer; $0/180; b. Barbour 1840, son of James and Mary Ann (Fitzwater) Bennett.

BENNETT, Jacob S.
Enl. Co. K, 31st Va. Inf. 5-29-61; indicted for treasons 9-20-61; prom. to orderly sgt.; disch. for disability 6-14-62; returned home where arrested; exch. 11-20-62;

d. during war; son-in-law *Valentine Poling served Co. E, 62nd Va. Mtd. Inf. (CSA); brother-in-law *Francis Nestor served Barbour Home Guard. Farmer; $1,500/100; b. Barbour 1814; m. Elisabeth Gainer 1833. Son of Asa and Rachel (Johnson) Bennett; grandson of Jacob and Sarah Bennett.

BENNETT, Jonathon P.
Enl. Co. K, 31st Va. Inf. 5-14-61; POW Fisher's Hill 9-23-64; released on oath 5-8-65. Farmer; $1,500/100 (parents); b. Barbour 1839; m. Malissa E. Sturm 1866; living Barbour 1880. Son of Jacob and Elisabeth (Gainer) Bennett.

BENNETT, Asa C.M.
Enl. Co. H, 31st Va. Inf. 8-62; des. after 10-63; drafted 3-65 but not inducted. Farmer; $1,500/100 (parents); b. Barbour 1842, brother of Jonathon; m. Lettice Ann Poling 1865; living Barbour 1880.

BENSON, William H.
Enl. Co. H, 31st Va. Inf. 5-14-61; POW Laurel Hill 7-61; released on oath; re-enlisted Co. D, 20th Va. Cav. 5-1-63; lost leg and POW Bulltown 10-13-63; brother-in-law *Wilson Paugh served Co. D, 20th Va. Cav. (CSA). Farmer; $0/95; b. Barbour 1839; Methodist-Protestant Church; m. 1) Olive Paugh 1860; 2) Nancy _____; moved to Harrison Co., W. Va. after war, then to Doddridge Co., W. Va. where living 1880. Son of Mathias and Roanna (Hickman) Benson; father b. Pendleton Co., W. Va.; grandson of William and Elisabeth (Trimble) Benson; William b. Highland Co., Va., settled Barbour 1833; great-grandson of Methias Benson, immigrant from Scotland.

BIBEY, William M.
Guerrilla; POW Barbour 1863 by Co. B, 2nd W. Va. Inf. $0/167; b. Bath Co., Va. 1838; Baptist; came to Barbour 1840's; m. Mary Jane Elisabeth Cade 1866; living Barbour 1880. Son of John and Mary Ann Elisabeth (Hooker) Bibey; father b. Amherst Co., Va. where family dates back to mid-18th Century.

BOEHM, John Samuel
Enl. Co. B, 11th Va. Cav. 3-10-62; AWOL 2-28-63; POW Philippi 4-26-63; exchanged 5-11-63; assigned to duty as blacksmith, Quartermaster Dept.; paroled Appomattox 4-9-65. Tenant; $0/115 (parents); b. Shenandoah Co., Va. 1841; came to Barbour 1850's; m. 1) Mary Peer 1871; 2) Catherine Copeland 1873; returned to Shenandoah Co. after war where d. 1921. Son of Jacob and Margaret (Orndorff) Boehm; grandson of Samuel and Anna (Stover) Boehm, b. Shenandoah Co.

BOEHM, Henry Harrison
Enl. Co. A, 46th Btln. Va. Cav. 7-10-63; des. next day. Tenant; $0/115 (parents); b. Shenandoah Co., Va. 1844, brother of John; m. Sarah J. Mouser 1866; d. Barbour 1881.

BOLTON, James Madison
Enl. Co. K, 31st Va. Inf. 5-18-61; des. 7-61; re-enlisted Co. E, 62nd Va. Mtd. Inf. 8-26-62; des. 12-4-62; returned voluntarily; POW near Gettysburg 7-5-63. Farmer; $300/100; b. Barbour 1837; Baptist; m. Drusilla England 1856; d. Barbour 1865. Son of James and Sarah (Jones) Bolton; father b. Pendleton Co., W. Va.; grandson of William Bolton; great-grandson of Jacob and Margaret Bolton, settled Pendleton Co. from Pa.

BOLYARD, Jacob
Sympathizer; arrested 1-13-63 as hostage for *James Trayhern; transf. to Camp Chase, Ohio 4-29-63; released 1-24-64; son-in-law *Adam Harsh served Co. K, 31st Va. Inf. Farmer; $1,500/447; b. Preston Co., W. Va. 1805; Methodist-Episcopal Church; settled Barbour where m. Sarah Poling 1825; d. Barbour 1880. Son of Stephen and Margaret (Wagoner) Bolyard; father b. Leigh Co., Pa., settled Preston Co. 1800; grandson of Joseph Bolyard, immigrant from Germany.

BONER, William J.
Enl. Co. H, 31st Va. Inf.; prom. to cpl.; wd. left leg Cold Harbor 6-27-64; listed sick Staunton Hospital 8-31-64; NFR. $4,150/6,478 (mother); b. Bath Co., Va. 1839. Son of William and Caroline (Corley) Boner; father b. Bath Co., came to Barbour 1850's; mother tavern keeper and slave owner; grandson of William and Hannah Boner; grandfather b. York Co., Pa., settled Bath Co.

BONER, John Allen
Enl. Co. E, 62nd Va. Mtd. Inf. 8-26-62; POW Fisher's Hill 9-23-64; exch. 3-17-65; paroled Clarksburg, W. Va. 4-24-65. $4,150/6,478 (mother); b. Bath Co., Va. 1842, brother of William; m. Martha Poe 1867; moved to Calhoun Co., W. Va. after war.

BONER, Sampson S.
Enl. Co. D, 20th Va. Cav. 4-1-64; wd. and POW Fisher's Hill 9-23-64; exch. 10-30-64; des. and sur. Beverly, W. Va. 12-17-64; released on oath 12-22-64. $4,150/6,478 (mother); b. Bath Co. 1848, brother of William; m. 1) Matilda ____; 2) Louisa ____; moved to Randolph Co., W. Va. 1880's where d. 1929.

BOOTH, Peyton Carr
Enl. Co. E, 62nd Va. Mtd. Inf.; wd. in knee and POW Barbour 5-11-63 by men of Co. B, 2nd W. Va. Inf.; d. in prison, Chester, Pa. 8-16-63. Farmer; $15,000/10,875; b. Barbour 1817; m. Harriet Philips. Son of Isaac Booth and Christine Carr; father b. Monongalia Co., W. Va.; grandson of Daniel and Jean (Houston) Booth; grandfather b. Monongalia Co. or Berkely Co., W. Va., settled Barbour 1780's; great-grandson of James and Nancy (Stalnaker) Booth, settled Monongalia Co. from Berkeley Co.

BOOTH, Isaac Newton
Enl. Co. G, 11th Va. Cav. 5-8-62; des. 12-26-62; killed Barbour 5-11-63 by men of Co. B, 2nd W. Va. Inf. $10,000/ 10,875 (parents); b. Barbour 1841, son of Peyton and Harriet (Philips) Booth.

BOOTH, William Nelson
Enl. Co. C, 46th Bttln. Va. Cav. (26th Va. Cav.) 4-23-63; des. 10-8-64; sur. Philippi 2-9-65 and sent to Wheeling Prison; released on oath 3-65; drafted 3-65, never inducted. $10,000/10,875 (parents); b. Barbour 1845, brother of Isaac; m. Roxia J. Bennett 1879; d. Barbour 1907.

BOWMAN, Henry Van Meter
Sympathizer; killed 1-5-63 by men of Co. A, 6th W. Va. Inf.; brother Samuel Confederate sympathizer; brother Adam Unionist; son-in-law Charles Ridgeway Capt., Co. B, 25th Va. Inf. (CSA). Miller; $4,000/814; b. Tucker Co., W. Va. 1810; Methodist-Episcopal Church; m. Margaret Wilmoth 1836; came to Barbour 1854. Son of Adam and Rachel (Van Meter) Bowman; father b. Hampshire Co., W. Va.; grandson of Martin and Elisabeth Bowman; descendant of George Bowman, settled South Branch in early 18th century.

BOWMAN, Adam Coleman
Enl. Co. K, 31st Va. Inf. 5-18-61; POW 7-61; paroled 3-12-62; returned to eastern Va. where served in Ordinance Department; enl. Fontaine's Regiment, Virginia State Line; com. Lt., Co. K, 19th Va. Cav.; prom. to Capt., Co. H; wd. twice; sur. 4-65. $4,000/814 (parents); b. Tucker Co. 1839, son of Henry and Margaret (Wilmoth) Bowman; Methodist-Episcopal Church, joined Southern Methodists after war; Democrat; m. Tracy J. Wilmoth 1874; d. Barbour 1909.

BRADFORD, Thomas Armistead
Secessionist candidate for Richmond Convention 1-61; enl. Co. H, 31st Va. Inf. 5-14-61; appointed Lt. 7-1-61; resigned commission 5-1-62 when lost election for company commander; re-enlisted Co. D, 20th Va. Cav. 3-1-64; detached

service in Ordinance Dept; paroled 5-11-65; brothers-in-law John and Squire Bosworth served 31st Va. Inf. (CSA). Attorney; $0/1,215; b. Orange Co., Va. 1825; Presbyterian; Democrat; came to Barbour 1856; m. Lucy Bosworth 1859; d. Barbour 1888. Son of Alexander and Hannah (Burton) Bradford; father b. Fauquier Co., Va., settled Orange Co.; grandson of Alexander and Jemima (Jones) Bradford, b. Fauquier Co.

BRYAN, John Washington
Enl. Co. K, 31st Va. Inf. 5-14-61; prom. to cpl.; elec. Lt. 5-1-62; wd. Belle Grove 7-19-64; d. 7-20-64; father-in-law *William Coffman and brothers-in-law *Benjamin, *John, *Elijah Coffman, *Lafayette Keller served Union army and Home Guard; brother-in-law *Joel Leyman Unionist. Apprentice blacksmith; $0/0; b. Hardy Co., W. Va. 1836; Methodist-Protestant Church; came to Barbour 1840's; m. Sarah Coffman 1857. Son of William and Barbara (Swisher) Bryan; father b. Hardy Co.; grandparents b. Va.

BURNER, Abraham Crogan
Listed Lt., Barbour Light Horse; enl. Co. H, 62nd Va. Mtd. Inf. 2-1-63; elec. Lt. 4-4-63; wd. Williamsport 7-7-63; d. Harrisonburg 7-23-63; brother George served Bat. E, 1st W. Va. Art. (USA) which also fought at Williamsport; brother-in-law *Martin Reger listed Barbour Light Horse; brother-in-law *James Hartman Confederate sympathizer; brother-in-law James Loudon served Co. A, 10th W. Va. Inf. (USA). Farmer; $16,070/3,888 (parents); b. Pendleton Co., W. Va. 1828; Methodist-Episcopal Church; came to Barbour 1829. Son of Jacob and Kesiah (Stump) Burner; grandson of Abraham and Mary (Hull) Burner, b. Pendleton Co.; great-grandson of Earhart Burner, immigrant from Germany.

BURNSIDES, John R.
Enl. Co. K, 31st Va. Inf. 5-18-61; des. 7-61. Blacksmith; $0/70; b. Va. 1833; came to Barbour 1850's with wife Sarah; moved to Taylor Co., W. Va. after war where living 1880; parents b. Va.

BUTCHER, Julia Ann (Rightmire)
Sympathizer; refugee at Staunton, Va. during war; sister *Elisabeth Jarvis and brothers-in-law Edward Armstrong and Eli Butcher Confederate sympathizers. Widow; $0/170; b. Barbour 1815; Baptist; m. Burrel B. Butcher 1834; moved to Ill. 1830's where husband died; returned to Barbour 1840's; moved to Morgan Co., W. Va. after war where living 1880. Daughter of John and Ann (Ashby) Rightmire, b. Va., settled Barbour 1790's; family dates back to early 18th century Va.

BUTCHER, Eli C.
Enl. Co. H, 62nd Va. Mtd. Inf. 2-27-63; des. Barbour 9-63. $0/170 (mother); b. Barbour 1838, son of Burrel and Julie Ann (Rightmire) Butcher; Baptist; m. Harriet ____; moved to Ritchie Co., W. Va. after war where living 1880. Father b. Barbour; grandson of Eli and Elisabeth (Hart) Butcher; grandfather b. Loudoun Co., Va.; great-grandson of Samuel Butcher, b. Loudoun Co., settled Randolph Co., W. Va., then Wood Co., W. Va.

CADE, Baylis
Enl. Co. H, 10th W. Va. Inf. (USA) 6-1-62; des. 8-22-62; enl. Co. G, 11th Va. Cav. 9-1-62; des.; re-enlisted Co. A, 20th Va. Cav. 1863; on roll to 10-64; father Union sympathizer; brother *William served Co. H, 10th W. Va. Inf. (USA). Cf. Unionists.

CALLAHAN, Charles S.
Listed Barbour Light Horse; enl. Co. E, 62nd Va. Mtd. Inf. 7-2-62; des.; drafted 2-65, never inducted; NFR; brothers-in-law *William and *John Daniels served Co. D, 20th Va. Cav. (CSA) . Farmer; $5,000/830 (parents); b. Barbour 1837; United Brethren Church; m. Margaret Daniels 1862. Son of John and Malinda (Chrislip) Callahan; grandson of William and Mary (Pickens) Callahan, b. Bath Co., Va., settled Barbour 1835.

CALLAHAN, Salathiel M.
Listed Barbour Light Horse; transf. to Co. H, 14th Va. Cav. 6-15-61; des. Petersburg 8-61; re-enlisted Co. D, 20th Va. Cav. 5-1-63; POW Highland Co., Va. 7-63; escaped from jail at Grafton, W. Va., retaken and sent to Camp Chase, Ohio, then Rock Island, Ill; exch. 2-22-65; listed sick Jackson Hospital, Va. Farmer; $5,000/830 (parents); b. Barbour 1839, brother of Charles; United Brethren Church; m. Virginia Lang 1867; moved to Tucker Co., W. Va. where d. 1884.

CALLAHAN, James D.
Listed Barbour Light Horse; transf. to Co. H, 31st Va. Inf. 7-2-61; prom. to sgt. 7-63; POW Spotsylvania 5-10-64; NFR. Farmer; $2,400/149; b. Barbour 1838; Methodist-Protestant Church. Son of William and Ann (Douglas) Callahan, b. Barbour; grandson of William and Mary (Pickens) Callahan.

CALLAHAN, William F.
Sympathizer; arrested and sent to Camp Chase, Ohio 4-29-63; transf. to Fort Delaware 7-14-64; brother-in-law *John Welch listed Barbour Light Horse; brother-in-law *Benjamin Welch Confederate sympathizer; brother-in-law

*Samuel Welch served Co. H, 10th W. Va. Inf. (USA). Farmer; $16,000/1,700 (grandparents); b. Barbour 1840, brother of James; Methodist-Protestant Church; m. Penelope Welch; living Barbour 1880.

CAMPBELL, George Washington
Sympathizer; arrested and sent to Camp Chase, Ohio; transf. to Fort Delaware 7-14-63; NFR. Farmer; $N/G; b. Barbour 1835, son of Thomas and Barbara Campbell, b. Va.

CAMPBELL, John H.
Enl. Co. H, 31st Va. Inf. 5-14-61; wd. 8-62; POW Fisher's Hill 9-23-64; reported as having joined U. S. Vols. Apprentice printer; $0/0; b. Barbour 1841, brother of George W.; m. Margaret F. ____; living Barbour 1880.

CAMPBELL, William F.
Enl. Co. H, 31st Va. Inf. 7-2-61; wd. left hand and POW Gettysburg 7-3-63; exch. 9-25-63; remained hospitalized until 11-64 when disch.; NFR. Tailer; $0/120 (parents); b. Pocahontas Co., W. Va. 1833; came to Barbour 1850's. Son of Harrison and Nancy (Miller) Campbell; father b. Rockingham Co., Va., settled Randolph Co., W. Va. 1840's, then Barbour 1850's; grandson of James and Amelia (Harrison) Campbell; grandfather immigrant from Ireland, settled Va.

CAMPBELL, James H.
Enl. Co. H, 31st Va. Inf. 5-14-61; POW Gettysburg 7-3-63; d. Point Lookout Prison 3-15-64. $0/120 (parents); born Pocahontas Co., W. Va. 1831, brother of William F.

CAMPBELL, Charles P.
Enl. Co. H, 31st Va. Inf. 2-17-63; des. or transf. to Co. E, 20th Va. Cav. 5-1-64; paroled Staunton, Va. 5-25-65; NFR. $0/120 (parents); b. Augusta Co., Va. 1845, brother of William F.

CANFIELD, Ahab
Enl. Co. E, 62nd Va. Mtd. Inf. 8-26-62; four brothers served in same company, three dying during war. Farm laborer; $0/115; b. Randolph Co. 1838; came to Barbour 1850's; m. Eleanor ____; living Barbour 1870. Son of David and Mary (Kelly) Canfield; father b. Randolph Co., moved to Gilmer Co., W. Va. after war; grandson of Titus and Phoebe (Buckbee) Canfield, b. N.Y.; great-grandson of Daniel and Elisabeth (Nettleton) Canfield, b. N.Y., settled Randolph Co. 1795.

CANFIELD, Israel
Enl. Co. H, 62nd Va. Mtd. Inf. 6-1-62; des. Randolph Co., W. Va. 8-63; arrested and sent to Camp Chase, Ohio; sent to Rock Island Prison, Ill. where enl. in Co. K, 2nd U. S. Vol. Inf. 10-22-64; stepbrothers *Loman and *George Hartsoc served U.S. Army. $0/0; b. Barbour 1846; m. Susanna McGinnis 1866; living Barbour 1880. Son of Uriah and Nancy (Schoonover) Canfield; parents b. Randolph Co.; grandson of Amos and Nancy (Schoonover); Amos b. N.Y.; great-grandson of Daniel and Elisabeth (Nettleton) Canfield.

CAPITO, Mary Helen
Sympathizer; arrested 7-62 for defacing flag of Co. K, 6th W. Va. Inf.; husband Confederate sympathizer; father Union sympathizer; brothers John and Christianserved 17th W. Va. Inf. (USA). $500/170 (parents); b. Barbour 1842; m. *John P. Thompson 1864; moved to Ohio after 1880. Daughter of *Daniel and Jerusha (Hart) Capito. Cf. Unionists.

CARLIN, Granville C.
Gave pro-secessionist speeches at mass meeting, Stewart's Run, Barbour Co. 2-61; Major, 169th Va. Mil., called out 5-61; com. Capt., Co. F, 1st Partisan Rangers; POW and wounded in right arm while escaping 9-62; resigned commission 12-20-62 under charges of incompetence; re-enlisted Co. C, 26th Va. Cav. 1-1-64; on roll to 10-31-64. Farmer; $2,975/849; b. Harrison Co., W. Va. 1836; came to Barbour 1840's; m. Susan Rider 1870; moved to Braxton Co., W. Va. 1870's where listed Civil War veterans 1890. Son of John and Sarah (Gall) Carlin; father b. Harrison Co.; grandson of John and Catherine (Reed) Carlin; grandfather b. Ohio Co., W. Va.; great-grandfather immigrant from Ireland.

CARTER, John F.
Enl. Co. E, 62nd Va. Mtd. Inf. 8-26-62; on rolls to 12-31-64; brother Isaac served Co. C, 133rd W. Va. Mil., POW by 20th Va. Cav.; brother Jaspar served Bat. E, 1st W. Va. Art. (USA). Farmer; $0/0; b. Hampshire Co., W. Va. 1828; m. Sarah Jane Strother 1855; moved to Harrison Co., W. Va. after war where d. 1892. Son of Albert and Mary (Thompson) Carter, b. Hampshire Co., settled Barbour 1840's, then Upshur Co., W. Va. 1850's.

CARTER, Charles Buck
Enl. Co. H, 31 Va. Inf. 5-14-61; des. 7-61; brother *David served Co. H, 7th W. Va. Inf. (USA). Farmer; $4,000/1,030 (mother); b. Page Co., Va. 1839; came to Barbour 1840's; m. Nancy Mustoe 1861; d. Barbour 1889. Son of Robert and Elisabeth (Coontz) Carter, b. Va.; grandson of Nathaniel Carter.

CARTER, Page D.
Enl. Co. D, 20th Va. Cav. 5-1-63; brothers *Henry and Thomas served Co. B, 10th W. Va. Inf. (USA); brother-in-law *David Waggoner served Co. H, 31st Va. Inf. Doctor; $500/255; b. Nelson Co., Va. 1824; Baptist; came to Barbour 1840's; m. Mary Ann Perry 1847; moved to Pocahontas Co., W. Va. after war where d. 1885. Son of Henry and Martha (Emerson) Carter. Cf. Unionists.

CHRISLIP, Peregrine
Listed Barbour Light Horse; later Union sympathizer. Cf. Unionists.

CHRISLIP, Ervin G.
Listed Barbour Light Horse; brother-in-law *Alpheus Corder listed Barbour Light Horse; brother-in-law *Andrew Daniels served Co. D, 20th Va. Cav. (CSA). Tenant; $0/165; b. Lewis Co., W. Va. 1835; Methodist-Episcopal Church; m. Mary Daniels 1856; d. Barbour 1919. Son of Abraham and Amanda (Britten) Chrislip; father b. Barbour; grandson of Jacob and Nancy (Singer) Chrislip, b. Pa.

CLEAVENGER, Benjamin
Listed Barbour Light Horse; later com. Lt., 169th W. Va. Mil.. Cf. Unionists.

CLEAVENGER, David C.
Enl. Co. H, 62nd Va. Mtd. Inf. 8-1-62; prom. to cpl. 4-5-63; POW Randolph Co., W. Va. 12-6-63; exch. 3-4-64; hospitalized Richmond 10-64; brother-in-law *Willis Wright Unionist; son-in-law *Lemuel Marks served Barbour Light Horse. Farmer; $3,000/575; b. Barbour 1811; Baptist; m. Jemima Wright 1837; moved to Gilmer Co., W. Va. 1870's where d. 1899. Son of Edward and Elisabeth (Knight) Cleavenger; father b. Frederick Co., Va.; grandson of Samuel and Margaret (Ramsey) Cleavenger, b. Frederick Co., settled Barbour 1802.

CLEAVENGER, John D.
Listed Barbour Light Horse. Farmer; $3,000/575 (parents); b. Barbour 1840, son of David and Jemima (Wright) Cleavenger; Baptist; m. Barbara Chrislip 1862; moved to Calhoun Co., W. Va. 1870's where living 1880.

CLEAVENGER, Samuel
Listed Barbour Light Horse; enl. Co. H, 62nd Va. Mtd. Inf. 8-1-62; disch. 4-10-65. Farmer; $3,000/575 (parents); b. Barbour 1842, brother of John D.; Baptist; m. Barbara ____; moved to Randolph Co., W. Va. 1870's, then to Ritchie Co., W. Va. where listed Civil War veterans 1890.

CLEAVENGER, Abraham
Enl. Co. H, 62nd Va. Mtd. Inf. 8-1-62; POW Randolph Co., W. Va. 12-6-63; took oath and released Fort Delaware 6-19-65. Farmer; $3,000/575 (parents); b. Barbour 1843, brother of John D.; Baptist; m. Elisabeth Nutter 1866; moved to Gilmer Co., W. Va. after war where living 1880.

COONTZ, John
Sympathizer; arrested 1-13-63 as hostage for *James Trayhern; released 1-24-64; son-in-law *Flavius Jones served Co. E, 62nd Va. Mtd. Inf. (CSA); son-in-law *John Ramsey Unionist. Farmer; $2,500/2,090; b. Barbour 1800; m. Delila England 1819; d. Barbour 1881. Son of Philip and Barbara (Barnhouse) Coontz; father b. Frederick Co., Md., settled Hardy Co., W. Va., then Barbour.

COONTZ, William
Sympathizer; killed in a fight with *William Ramsey 1863; son-in-law *Moses Smith served Co F, 15th W. Va. Inf. (USA). Farmer; $1,400/502; b. Barbour 1823, son of John and Delila (England) Coontz; m. Lucinda Ramsey 1840.

COONTZ, John William
Enl. Co. D, 62nd Va. Mtd. Inf.; POW Beverly, W. Va. 10-29-64; d. in prison 3-6-65; brother-in-law *Robert Thorn served Co. H, 10th W. Va. Inf. (USA). Farmer; $1,400/502 (parents); b. Barbour 1841, son of William and Lucinda (Ramsey) Coontz; m. Lucinda Thorn England 1860.

COONTZ, James W.
Enl. Co. E, 62nd Va. Mtd. Inf. 8-26-62; des. Hardy Co., W. Va. 11-3-62; re-enlisted Co. D, 20th Va. Cav. 4-1-64; POW Beverly, W. Va. 10-29-64; enl. Co. E, 5th U. S. Vols. 4-27-64. Farmer; $1,400/502 (parents); b. Barbour 1846, brother of John; m. Mary Jane Price 1869; living Barbour 1870.

COONTZ, James C.
Enl. Co. E, 62nd Va. Mtd. Inf. 8-26-62; des. Hardy Co., W. Va. 11-3-63; re-enlisted Co. D, 20th Va. Cav. 4-1-64; listed AWOL 10-64; surrendered Philippi 5-1-65; paroled 5-4-65. Farmer; $2,000/577 (parents); b. Barbour 1846; m. Prudence Harris 1866; living Barbour 1880. Son of Henry and Sarah (Ramsey) Coontz; father b. Barbour; grandson of John and Delila (England) Coontz.

COONTZ, John
Enl. Co. D, 20th Va. Cav. 4-1-64; POW Beverly, W. Va. 10-31-64 and sent to Camp Chase, Ohio; NFR. Farmer; $2,000/577 (parents); b. Barbour 1847, brother of James C.

COONTZ, Samuel Morgan Dallas
Sympathizer; refugee in eastern Va. during war; half-brother *Adam Godwin served Co. H, 62nd Va. Mtd. Inf. (CSA). Farmer; $1,850/672 (parents); b. Barbour 1844; Methodist-Protestant Church; joined Southern Methodists after war; Democrat; m. Isabella F. Poe 1871; living Barbour 1899. Son of Samuel Adam and Sarah (Stalnaker) Coontz; grandson of John and Delila (England) Coontz.

COOPER, John S.
Listed Barbour Light Horse; NFR; brother *Jonas Unionist; brother-in-law *Simon Radabaugh served 133rd W. Va. Mil.; brother-in-law William Clem Confederate sympathizer. $N/G; b. Randolph Co., W. Va. 1839; m. Catherine Radabaugh 1858. Son of Samuel and Jane (Simon) Cooper. Cf. Unionists.

CORDER, Alpheus
Listed Barbour Light Horse; drafted 2-65, never inducted; brother-in-law *Ervin Chrislip listed Barbour Light Horse. Farmer; $0/208; b. Fauquier Co., Va. 1835; Baptist; m. Julie Anne Chrislip 1858; moved to Ill. 1870's. Son of Joseph and Jane (Board) Corder, b. Fauquier Co., settled Barbour 1838; grandson of Joseph and Martha Corder, immigrants from England.

CORDER, William
Sympathizer; arrested 8-61; released 9-61; re-arrested 3-62 for "secessionist activity;" released 8-62. Farmer; $15,000/2,198; b. Barbour 1817; Baptist; m. Trena Devers 1839; d. Barbour 1881. Son of William and Sarah (Cole) Corder; father slave owner, b. Fauquier Co., Va., settled Barbour 1814; grandson of Joseph and Martha Corder.

CORDER, Joshua Simmons
Sympathizer; home burned by Federal troops. Farmer and slave owner; $2,000/286; b. Barbour 1820, brother of William; Baptist; m. Virginia Ann Grant 1850; living Barbour 1899.

CORDER, James W.
Sympathizer; drafted 2-65, never inducted. Farmer; $10,000/1,454; b. Barbour 1824, brother of William; Baptist; m. Mary E. Bond 1854; d. Barbour 1905.

CORDER, Edward M.
Listed sgt., Barbour Light Horse; transf. to Co. I, 14th Va. Cav.; re-enlisted Co. B, 1st Partisan Rangers 5-21-62; AWOL 7-29-62; detailed to recruit in W. Va. 2-14-63; com. Capt., Co. D, 20th Va. Cav. 5-3-63; KIA Winchester 9-19-64. Farmer; $12,000/9,694 (parents); b. Barbour 1833, brother of William; Baptist.

CORDER, Wilson Patton
Enl. Co. D, 20th Va. Cav. 5-12-63. Farmer; $15,000/3,009 (parents); b. Barbour 1843; Baptist; Democrat; m. Mary E. Hudkins 1870; d. Barbour 1931. Son of Joseph and Catherine (Patton) Corder, slave owners; grandson of William and Sarah (Cole) Corder.

CORDER, William Ervin
Enl. Co. D, 20th Va. Cav. 5-1-63. Farmer; $15,000/3,009 (parents); b. Barbour 1845, brother of Wilson; Baptist; m. Marietta Hudkins; d. Barbour 1936.

CORDER, Elam Talbott
Listed sgt., Barbour Light Horse; transf. to Co. H, 31st Va. Inf; prom. to sgt.; wd. Port Republic 6-9-62; POW Spotsylvania 5-12-64; released 5-12-65; brother-in-law *George Dickenson served Co. E, 62nd Va. Mtd. Inf. (CSA). Farmer; $2,000/390 (parents); b. Barbour 1840; Baptist; m. Martha Hodges; moved to Upshur Co., W. Va. after war where living 1880. Son of Albert and Margaret (Talbott) Corder; father b. Fauquier Co., Va.; grandson of Joseph and Jane (Board) Corder.

CORDER, Robert
Enl. Co. E, 62nd Va. Mtd. Inf. 8-26-62; on roll to 4-30-63; NFR. Farmer; $2,000/390 (parents); b. Barbour 1844, brother of Elam T.

CORLEY, Thomas Jefferson
Com. Lt., Co. C, 25th Va. Inf.; wd. Port Republic 6-9-62; d. of diarrhea 1-63. Farmer; $1,000/281; b. Bath Co., Va. 1804; m. Susan Rhea; came to Barbour 1845. Son of John and Catherine (Snead) Corley, b. Bath Co.; grandson of Manoah and Jane (Fogg) Corley, immigrants from Ireland.

CORLEY, Jesse Lee
Enl. Co. G, 11th Va. Cav. 9-8-62; POW 4-8-65; released on oath Clarksburg, W. Va. 4-10-65. Farmer; $1,000/289 (parents); b. Bath Co., Va. 1842, son of Thomas and Susan (Rhea) Corley; m. Jemima Jane Vanscoy 1866; d. Barbour 1860's.

COTTRILL, Elijah
Listed Barbour Light Horse. Farm laborer; $0/0; b. Barbour or Harrison Co., W. Va. 1839; Methodist-Protestant Church; m. Margaret Lindsay 1863; returned to Harrison Co. 1870's where living 1880. Son of Eura Cottrill, b. Harrison Co.; grandson of Joshua and Elisabeth Cottrill; grandfather b. Hampshire Co., Va., settled Barbour.

CRIM, Michael
Sympathizer; killed by men of Co. B, 2nd W. Va. Inf. 10-21-61 for aiding guerrillas; brother-in-law *Isaac Strickler served Co. E, 62nd Va. Mtd. Inf. (CSA). Farmer; $0/840; b. Rockingham Co., Va. 1806; Baptist; came to Barbour 1840's; m. Catherine Strickler 1848. Son of Peter and Elisabeth (Shaver) Crim; father b. Rockingham Co.; grandson of Peter Crim, immigrant from Holland.

CRIM, Joseph Napolean Bonaparte
Sympathizer; elec. Justice of the Peace 1860, refused to serve after 1861; arrested and released; drafted 2-65, never inducted; brothers-in-law *James and *Jaspar Hall served Co. H, 31st Va. Inf. (CSA). Merchant; $1,250/2,759; b. Rockingham Co., Va. 1835, son of Michael and Catherine (Strickler) Crim; Baptist; Democrat; m. Almira Hall 1855; d. Barbour 1915.

CROSS, Daniel
Enl. Co. H, 31st Va. Inf. 5-29-61; wd. Alleghany 12-13-61, d. 12-16-61; brother *Levi served Co. F, 15th W. Va. Inf. (USA); brother-in-law *John Barnhouse served Co. K, 31st Va. Inf. (CSA). Farmer; $2,000/649 (father); b. Barbour 1831. Son of Barton and Deborah (Moore) Cross. Cf. Unionists.

CROSS, George W.
Enl. Co. E, 62nd Va. Mtd. Inf.; wd. Cold Harbor 6-1-64. Tenant; $0/233; b. Barbour 1833, brother of Daniel; Democrat; m. Elisabeth Digman Moore 1856; living Barbour 1880.

CROSS, William M.
Sympathizer; arrested 5-30-63 for sheltering wounded Confederate soldier (the soldier was killed); released Fort Delaware 1865; drafted 3-65, never inducted; brothers-in-law *Hamilton and *Jacob Fink served CSA. Tenant and minister United Brethren Church; $0/155; b. Barbour 1838, brother of Daniel; m. 1) Sarah Catherine Fink 1859; 2) Christina Delauder Fitzwater 1896; d. Barbour 1920.

CROSS, Simpson
Enl. Co. K, 31st Va. Inf. 5-18-61; des. 4-19-62; re-enlisted Co. E, 62nd Va. Mtd. Inf. 8-26-62; sur. Clarksburg, W. Va. 5-9-65. Farmer; $1,000/649 (father); b. Barbour 1842, brother of Daniel; Democrat; m. Elvira Poling 1869; living Barbour 1880.

CROSS, Jacob B.
Enl. Co. H, 62nd Va. Mtd. Inf. 8-1-62; des. 10-18-62; returned voluntarily 4-1-

63; paroled Staunton, Va. 5-12-65. Farmer; $2,000/649 (father); b. Barbour 1844, brother of Daniel; m. Emily Philips 1870; living Barbour 1880.

CROSS, Charles G.
Enl. Co. E, 62nd Va. Mtd. Inf. 3-14-64; transf. to Co. A, 18th Va. Cav. 4-1-64; POW Beverly, W. Va. 10-31-64; released on oath Camp Chase, Ohio 6-12-65. Farmer; $2,000/649 (father); b. Barbour 1846, brother of Daniel; m. Nancy Moore 1868; moved to Highland Co., Va. after 1880; d. 1927.

CROSS, John E.
Enl. Co. E, 62nd Va. Mtd. Inf. 8-26-62; transf. to Co. H 4-16-63; paroled Staunton, Va. 5-17-65; NFR; brother-in-law William Grogg served Co. F, 25th Va. Inf. (CSA). Tenant; $0/115 (parents); b. Barbour 1845; m. Eliza Grogg 1864. Son of Barton and Julie Ann Cross; grandson of Barton and Deborah (Moore) Cross.

CROSS, Stephen
Sympathizer; arrested for disturbing religious worship 1868. $0/115 (parents); b. Barbour 1849, brother of John E.; m. Elisabeth Keller 1870; living Barbour 1880.

CROSS, Nathaniel
Enl. Co. K, 31st Va. Inf. 5-29-61; des. 5-20-62; brother-in-law *John Philips served Co. H, 62nd Va. Mtd. Inf. (CSA) and Co. A, 1st W. Va. Cav. (USA). Tenant; $0/220; b. Barbour 1829; m. Emily Ann _____; living Barbour 1870. Son of John and Nancy Ann (Pittman) Cross; grandson of John and Barbara (Boarer) Cross. Cf. Unionists.

CROSS, Henson
Listed Lt., Barbour Light Horse; NFR. Farmer; $0/220 (father); b. Barbour 1834, brother of Nathaniel.

CROSS, William Willis
Enl. Co. H, 62nd Va. Mtd. Inf. 8-1-62; des. 10-18-62; returned voluntarily 4-1-63; paroled Staunton, Va. 5-15-65. Farmer; $0/220 (father); b. Barbour 1841, brother of Nathaniel; m. Sarah E. _____; living Barbour 1870.

CROUSE, Squire
Listed Barbour Light Horse; enl. Co. H, 10th W. Va. Inf. (USA). Cf. Unionists.

DANIELS, William Wesley
Elec. Sheriff 1860, refused to serve after 1861; listed Barbour Light Horse; enl. Co. D, 20th Va. Cav. 5-1-63; elec. Lt. 6-1-63; prom. to Capt. 1864; wd. 10-64; brother-in-law *Charles Callahan served Co. E, 62nd Va. Mtd. Inf. (CSA). Farmer; $5,000/1,231 (parents); b. Rockingham Co., Va. 1834; came to Barbour 1840's; m. Louvernia Arnold 1868; living Barbour 1880. Son of John and Nancy (Brown) Daniels, b. Va.; grandson of Joseph Daniels.

DANIELS, John Henry
Enl. Co. D, 20th Va. Cav. 5-1-63; prom. to cpl.; reduced to ranks; POW Highland Co., Va. 8-20-63; exch. 2-65; listed Chimborazo Hospital, Richmond, 3-7-65; paroled 5-10-65. Farmer; $5,000/1,231 (parents); b. Barbour 1845, half-brother of William; m. Jennie W. Holt 1872; moved to Ore. after 1880. Son of John and Elisabeth (Hawkins) Daniels.

DANIELS, Andrew Jackson
Enl. Co. D, 20th Va. Cav. 5-1-63; POW Philippi 7-18-63 by men of Co. H, 10th W. Va. Inf.; released Fort Delaware 5-9-65; brother-in-law *Ervin Chrislip listed Barbour Light Horse. $3,050/720 (parents); b. Alleghany Co., Va. 1838; came to Barbour from Augusta Co., Va. 1840's; m. Mary E. ____; moved to Upshur Co., W Va. after war where d. 1895. Son of Joseph and Prudence Daniels, b. Va.; grandson of Joseph Daniels.

DAUGHERTY, William Harrison
Listed Barbour Light Horse; arrested 1-13-63 as hostage for *James Trayhern; transf. to Camp Chase, Ohio 4-29-63; held an additional six months on orders of Governor Pierpont after other hostages released; drafted 3-65, never inducted; brother *Jacob served Co. N, 6th W. Va. Inf. (USA). Farmer; $1,500/802; b. Rockingham Co., Va. 1825; came to Barbour 1840's; m. Ann Margaret Pfau 1847; d. Barbour 1870's. Son of Joshua and Hannah (Turkeyheim) Daugherty. Cf. Unionists.

DICKENSON, Samuel H.
Enl. Co. E, 62nd Va. Mtd. Inf. 8-26-62; left sick in Barbour 8-26-63 during raid; brother-in-law *Salathiel Talbott served same company; brother-in-law *Richard Hudkins listed Barbour Light Horse. Farmer; $4,000/1,593 (father); b. Barbour 1831; Methodist-Episcopal Church; m. Mary Jane Euritt; living Barbour 1880. Son of Robert and Elisabeth (Swadley) Dickenson; father b. Pendleton Co., W. Va., settled Barbour 1830's; grandson of Samuel and Rachel (Davis) Dickenson; grandfather b. Pendleton Co.; great-grandfather immigrated from Holland.

DICKENSON, George J. Washington
Listed Barbour Light Horse; wd. Philippi 6-3-61; re-enlisted Co. E, 62nd Va. Mtd. Inf. 8-26-62; listed AWOL 5-4-64; brothers-in-law *Elam and *Robert Corder served Confederate Army. Farmer; $4,000/1,593 (father); b. Barbour 1834, brother of Samuel; Methodist-Episcopal Church, joined Southern Methodists after war; m. 1) Mary Corder; 2) Deniza J. Corder 1864; d. Barbour 1904.

DICKENSON, Demetrius W.
Listed Barbour Light Horse; re-enlisted Co. E, 62nd Va. Mtd. Inf. 8-26-62; prom. to cpl.; d. of typhoid fever Richmond 9-5-63. Farmer; $4,000/1,593 (father); b. Barbour 1842, brother of Samuel; Methodist-Episcopal Church.

DIGMAN, Philip
Sympathizer; elec. Assessor 1860, refused to serve after 1861; brother-in-law *Edward Hill served 62nd Va. Mtd. Inf. (CSA); brother-in-law *Samuel Holsberry and sister-in-law *Sarah (Holsberry) Digman Confederate sympathizers. Tenant; $800/330; b. Barbour 1816; Methodist-Protestant Church; m. Emily Teter 1859; moved to Braxton Co., W. Va. where d. 1899. Son of Charles and Elisabeth (Stalnaker) Digman; father b. Frederick Co., Md.; grandson of William and Nancy Digman.

DIGMAN, Alpheus S.
Enl. Co. K, 31st Va. Inf. 5-18-61; disch. for disability 6-14-62; brother-in-law *Jesse Poling served Co, E, 62nd Va. Mtd. Inf. (CSA). Tenant; $0/84; b. Barbour 1822, brother of Philip; Methodist-Protestant Church; m. Rachel Poling; living Barbour 1880.

DIGMAN, Thoman Benton
Enl. Co. K, 31st Va. Inf. 12-22-61; des. 4-19-62; returned voluntarily; wd. Cold Harbor 6-1-64; one of five men of company to surrender at Appomattox 4-9-65; brother-in-law *Andrew Valentine served Co. E, 62nd Va. Mtd. Inf. (CSA); brother-in-law *Adam Montgomery served Co. H, 7th W. Va. Inf. (USA). Farmer; $2,000/155 (parents); b. Barbour 1841; m. Ota____; post war minister Methodist-Protestant Church; left county 1870's, returned and d. Barbour 1927. Son of Samuel and Sarah (Sturm) Digman; father b. Barbour; grandson of Charles and Elisabeth (Stalnaker) Digman.

DIGMAN, Sarah (Holsberry)
Sympathizer; home described as "a place of great notoriety for harboring... rebels;" brother *Samuel Holsberry and brother-in-law *Philip Digman

Confederate sympathizers; son-in-law *Andrew Valentine served Co. E, 62nd Va. Mtd. Inf., taken prisoner at her home. $2,000/700 (husband); b. Barbour 1818; m. George Digman 1836; d. Barbour 1870's. Daughter of John and Margaret (Poling) Holsberry; father b. Pa., settled Barbour; granddaughter of John Holsberry, immigrant from Germany.

DILWORTH, James David
Capt., 169th Va. Mil., called out 5-61; brother John served Co. A, 1st West Virginia Cavalry (USA); son Anthony Lt., Co. D, 10th Va. Cav. (CSA); stepsons *Nathaniel and *Elam Poling served Co. K, 31st Va. Inf. (CSA). Farmer; $12,000/1,522; b. Barbour 1799; Methodist-Episcopal Church, joined Southern Methodists after war; Democrat; m. 1) Emily Davis; 2) Margaret Wamsley 1817; 3) Elisabeth Vannoy Poling 1860; d. Barbour 1875. Son of William and Margaret (Anderson) Dilworth; father immigrant from Germany, settled N.J., then Barbour.

DILWORTH, Wesley
Listed sgt., Barbour Light Horse; NFR. Farmer; 6,000/1,009 (parents); b. Barbour 1836; Methodist-Episcopal Church. Son of David and Nancy (Davis) Dilworth; grandson of William and Margaret (Anderson) Dilworth.

DILWORTH, David
Enl. Co. H, 31st Va. Inf. 6-7-61; wd. Second Bull Run 8-29-62; commanded company in August, 1864, then numbering nine men; des. 1-15-65, took oath and released next day. Farmer; $6,000/1,009 (parents); b. Barbour 1840, brother of Wesley; Methodist-Episcopal Church; Democrat; m. Sarah Sutton 1873; d. Barbour 1880.

DOUGLAS, Erwin
Enl. Co. D, 20th Va. Cav. 5-1-63; prom. to cpl.; POW 1863; exch.; on roll to 12-31-64. Farmer; $3,000/400 (parents); b. Barbour 1846; m. Martha A. Fridley 1879; d. Barbour 1915. Son of Earl and Rosannah (Hickman) Douglas; father b. Harrison Co., W. Va.; grandson of Levi and Nancy Ann (Merrick) Douglas; grandfather b. Md., settled Barbour.

DOUGLAS, Worthington
Sympathizer; arrested for disturbing religious services 1868. Farmer; $3,000/400 (parents); b. Barbour 1849, brother of Erwin; m. Caroline Marks 1870; living Barbour 1880 (listed as in jail).

DURRETT, Braxton Byrd
Sympathizer; arrested 1861 and sent to Camp Carlisle, W. Va.; released; refugee in eastern Va. during war. Farmer and slave owner; $2,000/2,799; Democrat; b. Spotsylvania Co., Va. 1820; m. Ann E. Williams 1844; came to Barbour 1840's; d. Barbour 1895. Son of Jonathon and Sarah (Lively) Durrett; father b. Spotsylvania Co.; grandfather immigrant from France.

ELLIOTT, Samuel P.
Guerrilla; arrested 1-13-63 as hostage for *James Trayhern; transf. to Camp Chase, Ohio 4-29-63; d. in prison 6-5-63. Merchant and slave owner; $17,000/12,227; b. Loudoun Co., Va. 1804; Methodist-Episcopal Church; m. Elisabeth Scranage; came to Barbour from Taylor Co., W. Va. 1829. Son of David and Mary (Cole) Elliott; father b. Loudoun Co., settled Taylor Co. 1814; grandson of John and Ester (Beatty) Elliott; grandfather immigrant from Scotland.

ELLIOTT, James Baxter
Sympathizer. Merchant; $17,300/12,227 (parents); b. Barbour 1837, son of Samuel and Elisabeth (Scranage) Elliott; Methodist-Episcopal Church; post-war minister Southern Methodists; Democrat; m. 1) Anna Rebecca Johnson 1871; 2) Myra Reed Wilson 1888; d. Barbour 1915.

ELLIOTT, Alexander Hess
Sympathizer; appointed Deputy Sheriff 1867, removed from office by order of Judge William Harrison on charges of war-time secessionist sympathies. $17,300/12,227 (parents); b. Barbour 1843, brother of James; Methodist-Episcopal Church; Democrat; d. Barbour 1873.

ELLIOTT, William
Guerrilla; brother-in-law Edgar Parsons served Co. E, 25th Va. Inf. (CSA); son-in-law *James Knotts Confederate sympathizer; father-in-law Solomon Parsons and brothers-in-law *Edwin and James Parsons Unionists. Farmer and slave owner; $17,850/9,750; b. Loudoun Co., Va. 1802, brother of Samuel; Baptist; Democrat; m. Rebecca B. Parsons 1833; d. Barbour 1883.

ELLIOTT, Edgar C.
Enl. Co. D, 3rd Va. State Line 8-17-62; re-enlisted Co. C, 19th Va. Cav. 3-15-63; disch.; re-enlisted Co. D, 20th Va. Cav. 4-1-64; AWOL 8- to 10-64; paroled Staunton, Va. 5-10-65; brother-in-law *Bernard Fisher served Co. H, 7th W. Va. Inf. (USA). Farmer; $17,850/9,750 (parents); b. Barbour 1836, son of William and Rebecca (Parsons) Elliott; Baptist; m. Mary J. Fisher 1856; d. Barbour 1902.

ELLIOTT, Solomon Parsons
Enl. Co. D, 3rd Va. State Line 11-16-62; re-enlisted Co. C, 19th Va. Cav. 3-15-63; transf. to Co. D, 20th Va. Cav. 4-1-64; prom. to Lt. 5-21-64; listed sick Harrisonburg Hospital 11-64; recommended for retirement; d. 1866. Farmer; $17,850/9,750 (parents); b. Barbour 1838, brother of Edgar; Baptist.

ELLIOTT, Truman Theodore
Enl. Co. D, 20th Va. Cav. 4-1-64; POW Fisher's Hill 9-23-64. Farmer; $17,850/9,750 (parents); b. Barbour 1844, brother of Edgar; Baptist; Democrat; m. Mary Columbia Lynch 1868; living Barbour 1880.

ELLYSON, Louisa
Sympathizer; arrested near Buckhannon, W. Va. 12-64 as spy; newspaper reporter described her as "quite a young girl, with a lurking look in her eyes, and is supposed to have been quite active in her demonstrations on Government telegraph poles;" in addition to brothers listed below, brothers Samuel and John served 19th Va. Cav. (CSA). $5,000/755 (parents); b. Barbour 1829, daughter of Gideon and Elisabeth (Stevens) Ellyson; m. Jackson Woodyard; d. 1895. Father b. Barbour; granddaughter of Zachariah and Mary (Votaw) Ellyson, b. New Kent Co., Va., settled Pa., then Barbour in 1790's.

ELLYSON, Robert F.
Enl. Co. E, 62nd Va. Mtd. Inf. 8-26-62; transf. to Co. H 4-1-63; prom. to sgt.; wd. New Market 5-15-64; sur. Clarksburg, W. Va. 5-4-65. Farmer; $5,000/755 (parents); b. Barbour 1840, brother of Louisa; m. 1) Sarah Cool 1861; 2) Almira Jane Woodford; moved to Gilmer Co., W. Va. after war where listed Civil War veterans 1890.

ELLYSON, Edward G.
Enl. Co. E, 62nd Va. Mtd. Inf. 8-26-62; transf. to Co. H 4-1-63; POW Grafton, W. Va. 8-31-63; d. Camp Chase, Ohio 10-18-63. Farmer; $5,000/755 (parents); b. Barbour 1842, brother of Louisa.

ENGLAND, Albert
Enl. Co. E, 62nd Va. Mtd. Inf. 3-29-62; transf. to Co. H 4-1-63; des. 4-12-63. Farmer; $2,800/488 (parents); b. Barbour 1846; m. Osie England 1866; living Barbour 1880. Son of Henry and Mary (Alexander) England; father b. Barbour; grandson of James and Elisabeth England, b. Pa., settled Barbour 1787.

ENGLAND, Archibald
Enl. Co. E, 62nd Va. Mtd. Inf. 3-29-62; transf. to Co. H; POW 12-14-62; exch.; des. 4-12-63; arrested 4-29-63 and sent to Camp Chase, Ohio, released after a

few weeks; NFR; brother-in-law *Daniel Felton Unionist; brother-in-law *Middleton Mitchel served Co. F, 15th W. Va. Inf. (USA). Tenant; $0/169; b. Barbour 1836; m. Minerva ____. Son of *John and Elisabeth (Coontz) England; parents b. Barbour; grandson of James and Elisabeth England.

ENGLAND, John
Enl. Co. D, 20th Va. Cav. 4-1-64; POW Alleghany Co., Va. 5-64; took oath and released 8-24-64; NFR. Farmer; $1,500/171 (parents); b. Barbour 1841, brother of Archibald.

ENGLAND, Solomon
Sympathizer; arrested for disrupting religious serviced 1868. $1,000/175 (parents); b. Barbour 1847; m. Virginia B. Johnson 1869; NFR. Son of Henry and Jane England; father b. Barbour; grandson of Henry and Mary (Paxon) England.

EVERSON, Thomas Hart Benton
Enl. Co. C, 3rd Va. State Line; re-enlisted Co. D, 19th Va. Cav. 3-8-63; transf. to Co. B, 20th Va. Cav. 3-17-63; on rolls to 10-31-64. Farmer; $1,000/200 (parents); b. Fayette Co., Pa. 1840; came to Barbour 1850's from Harrison Co., W. Va.; m. Ruth Ice 1865; moved to Calhoun Co., W. Va. after 1880 where d.1909. Son of Eli and Elisabeth (Dunn) Everson; father b. Westmoreland Co., Pa., settled Harrison Co. 1848, then Barbour 1850's; grandson of Nathaniel and Elisabeth (Nash) Everson of Chester Co., Pa.

EVIC, Granville
Enl. Co. H, 31st Va. Inf. 9-21-61; wd. 1862 and disch.; POW Highland Co., Va. while on way home and sent to Camp Chase, Ohio as a civilian prisoner; stepfather *John R. Thompson and brother-in-law *Daniel Reed served Co. H, 62nd Va. Mtd. Inf. (CSA). Farm laborer; $0/0; b. Barbour 1840; m. Olive Anderson 1865; d. Barbour 1870's. Son of Christian and Lydia (Ours) Evic; father b. Pendleton Co., W. Va., settled Harrison Co., W. Va. 1830's, then Barbour; grandson of Francis Evic, b. Pendleton Co., settled Harrison Co.; great-grandson of Christian and Margaret Evic; Christian immigrant from Holland.

FINK, Hamilton
Enl. Co. E, 62nd Va. Mtd. Inf. 3-1-62; wd. Fisher's Hill 9-23-64; wd. Waynesboro 12-28-64; paroled Staunton, Va. 5-24-65; brother-in-law *William Cross Confederate sympathizer. Farm laborer; $0/0; b. Barbour 1842; m. Emaline Ramsey 1867; moved to Tucker Co., W. Va. 1880's. Son of Elias and Mary (Delawder) Fink; father b. Rockingham Co., Va., settled Hardy Co., W. Va., then Barbour.

FINK, Jacob P.
Enl. Co. E, 62nd Va. Mtd. Inf. 3-1-64; wd. Beverly, W. Va. 10-31-64; paroled Staunton, Va. 5-24-65. Farm laborer; $0/0; b. Barbour 1845, brother of Hamilton; m. 1) Arabella Wood 1869; 2) Orppa J. Dayton 1878; moved to Upshur Co., W. Va. where living 1880.

FITZWATER, Joseph
Enl. Co. E, 62nd Va. Mtd. Inf.; AWOL 5-1-64; POW Highland Co., Va. 5-29-64. Farmer; $0/705 (parents); b. Hardy Co.W. Va.1837; came to Barbour 1840's; m. 1) Martha Goodwin 1865; 2) Christina Cross 1874; living Barbour 1880. Son of William and Sarah (Shireman) Fitzwater, b. Hardy Co.; grandson of George and Mary Ann Fitzwater, b. Va.

FITZWATER, William W.
Enl. Co. E, 62nd Va. Mtd. Inf. 8-26-62; POW Barbour 2-63 while recruiting; exch.; paroled Staunton, Va. 5-17-65; brother-in-law George Nestor served same company; brother-in-law John Nestor Confederate sympathizer; brother-in-law Samuel Nestor served Co. B, 11th W. Va. Inf. (USA); brothers-in-law *Thomas Wilson and *Simon Philips Unionists. Tenant; $0/60; b. Hardy Co. 1828; came to Barbour 1840's; m. Harriet Nestor; moved to Tucker Co., W. Va. after war, then to Highland Co., Va. after 1880 where d. 1903. Son of John and Barbara (Harris) Fitzwater, b. Hardy Co.; grandson of George and Mary Ann Fitzwater.

FRIDLEY, Richard
Enl. Co. I, 14th Va. Cav. 1-25-62; POW Greenbrier Co., W. Va. 11-26-62; d. Camp Chase, Ohio 3-2-63. Farmer; $800/229 (parents); b. Rockingham Co., Va. 1833; came to Barbour 1850's. Son of David and Mary Fridley; grandson of Isaac and Elisabeth (Sellers) Fridley, b. Va.

GAINER, Marion
Enl. Co. E, 62nd Va. Mtd. Inf. 8-26-62; prom. to sgt.; POW Barbour 3-21-64 by Home Guard; brother-in-law *Nicolas Holsberry served same company; father-in-law *Samuel Holsberry Confederate sympathizer. Farmer; $1,000/307 (parents); b. Barbour 1835; m. Nancy Holsberry 1856; living Barbour 1880. Son of Jackson and Rachel (Vannoy) Gainer; parents b. Barbour; grandson of Bryan and Nancy (Black) Gainer; grandfather immigrant from Ireland, settled Md., then Va.

GAINER, Solomon W.
Enl. Co. K, 31st Va. Inf. 5-18-61; POW Greenbrier Co., W. Va. 10-3-61; exch.; prom. to sgt. 7-1-64; one of five men of company to surrender at Appomattox 4-9-65; brothers-in-law *Emory Poling and *Richard Johnson Confederate

sympathizers. Farmer; $1,500/335 (father); b. Barbour 1841; Methodist-Episcopal Church, joined Southern Methodists after war; m. Mary J. _____; moved to Ok. in 1880's where d. 1934. Son of Samuel and Elisabeth (Carpenter) Gainer; parents b. Barbour; grandson of Bryan and Nancy (Black) Gainer.

GAINER, Haymond C.
Enl. Co. E, 62nd Va. Mtd. Inf. 5-63; des. 1863 and sur.; released on oath 11-22-63; father-in-law *Asa Philips served Co. I, 17th W. Va. Inf. (USA). Farmer; $2,500/449 (parents); b. Barbour 1843; m. Syrena Philips 1864; living Barbour 1880. Son of Bryan and Sarah (Vannoy) Gainer; grandson of Bryan and Nancy (Black) Gainer.

GALL, Andrew Jackson.
Gave speeches favoring secession at mass meeting, Stewart's Run, Barbour 2-61; arrested 8-61 and released; arrested 3-62 for "secessionist activities;" released 8-62; enl. Co. H, 62nd Va. Mtd. Inf. 9-1-62; des. 9-18-62; re-enlisted Co. D, 20th Va. Cav. 7-20-63; on roll to 12-31-64; brother *George Unionist sympathizer; brother-in-law *Jacob Shank Confederate sympathizer. Farm laborer; $0/0; b. Pendleton Co., W. Va. 1829; Methodist-Episcopal Church, joined Southern Methodists after war; Democrat; m. Mary V. Corder 1867; living Barbour 1899. Son of John and Margaret (Arbogast) Gall. Cf. Unionists.

GALL, Lafayette E.
Major, 169th Va. Mil., called out 5-61; enl. Co. D, 20th Va. Cav. 5-1-63; POW Barbour 7-7-63; released 7-16-63; brother-in-law *Charles Rankin served Co. H, 7th W. Va. Inf. (USA). Farmer; $1,200/123; b. Barbour 1834, brother of Andrew; Methodist-Episcopal Church; m. 1) Elisabeth Rankin 1858; 2) Henrietta Robinson; moved to Lewis Co., W. Va. after war where listed Civil War veterans 1890.

GALL, Burton M.
Arrested 8-61 and sent to Camp Carlisle, W. Va.; released 8-27-61; arrested 3-62; released 8-62; enl. Co. D, 20th Va. Cav. 12-11-63; on roll to 12-31-64. Farm laborer; $0/0; b. Barbour 1838, brother of Andrew; Methodist-Episcopal Church; m. Eliza Ann Hall 1867; living Barbour 1880.

GODWIN, Robert S.
Enl. Co. K, 31st Va. Inf. 5-18-61; prom. to cpl.; wd. in head Alleghany 12-13-61; wd. in hip Port Republic 6-9-62; POW Spotsylvania 5-12-64; released 6-27-65. Tenant; $0/90 (parents); b. Tucker Co., W. Va. 1840; Baptist; m. Sarah Ann Philips 1867; d. Barbour 1918. Son of Isaac and Mary (Coffman) Godwin;

father b. Preston Co., W. Va., settled Tucker Co., then Barbour 1854; grandson of Robert and Mary (Barb) Godwin; grandfather b. Md., settled Preston Co. 1805, then Barbour 1836.

GODWIN, Jacob
Enl. Co. H, 31st Va. Inf. 5-18-61; wd. Gaines Mills 6-27-62; on roll 8-64. Tenant; $0/90 (parents); b. Tucker Co., W. Va. 1842, brother of Robert; m. Melissa Corley 1866; NFR.

GODWIN, Jacob B.
Enl. Co. K, 31st Va. Inf. 6-22-61; des. 7-61; returned voluntarily; brother Joseph Capt., Co. C, 6th W. Va. Inf. (USA). Tenant; $0/13; b. Preston Co., W. Va. 1822; m. Emily Stemple 1841; d. Barbour 1921. Son of Robert and Mary (Barb) Godwin.

GODWIN, Reuben
Enlisted Co. K, 31st Va. Inf. 5-18-61; des. 7-61; returned voluntarily 5-63; wounded Cold Harbor 6-1-64; d. 6-8-64. Tenant; $0/13 (parents); born Tucker Co., W. Va. 1842, son of Jacob and Emily (Stemple) Godwin.

GODWIN, Adam
Enl. Co. H, 62nd Va. Mtd. Inf. 6-1-62; POW Barbour 12-15-63; exch. 9-18-64; hospitalized Richmond to 11-64; half-brother *Samuel Coontz Confederate sympathizer. Farm laborer; $0/0; b. Barbour 1844; m. Emily Cross 1868; moved to Tucker Co., W. Va. 1869 where living 1880. Son of Sarah Coontz; father b. Md.

GODWIN, Andrew Jackson
Enl. Co. H, 62nd Va. Mtd. Inf. 8-1-62; des. 9-62; returned voluntarily; POW Barbour 12-15-63 and released on oath; drafted 3-65, never inducted; brother-in-law *Nathaniel Cross served Co. K, 31st Va. Inf. Farmer; $0/110; b. Tucker Co., W. Va. 1838; m. Sarah Cross 1860; living Barbour 1880. Son of John and Mary Godwin.

GOLDEN, Eldridge G.
Enl. Co. H, 31st Va. Inf. 5-14-61; des. 7-61; brother-in-law *Jaspar Poling served Co. E, 62nd Va. Mtd. Inf. (CSA); brother-in-law *Franklin Poling served Co. H, 31st Va. Inf. (CSA). Farmer; $1,000/230; b. Page Co., Va. 1826; came to Barbour 1830's; m. 1) Ruhama ____; 2) Dorothy Bartlett; d. Barbour 1908. Son of George and Elisabeth Golden; parents and grandparents b. Va.

GOLDEN, John J.
Enl. Co. H, 31st Va. Inf. 5-14-61; hospitalized 8-64; listed AWOL 9-64; arrested and returned to company; des. 3-21-65. Farmer; $50/119 (parents); b. Page Co., Va. 1832, brother of Eldridge; moved to Harrison Co., W. Va. after war.

GOLDEN, James Madison
Enl. Co. H, 31st Va. Inf. 5-14-61; POW Alleghany 12-13-61; exch.; POW Barbour 2-63 by men of Co. A, 6th W. Va. Inf. while on furlough; exch.; hospitalized Mt. Jackson, Va. 8-64. Farmer; $50/119 (parents); b. Page Co., Va. 1839, brother of Eldridge; m. Louisa Jane Cool 1867; moved to Jackson Co., W. Va. after war, then to Roane Co., W. Va. 1870's; d. Jackson Co. 1923.

GOLDEN, Francis Marion
Enl. Co. C, 31st Va. Inf. 5-27-61; prom. to sgt.; wd. Second Bull Run 8-29-62; wd. Wilderness 5-6-64; POW Winchester 9-24-64; paroled 4-16-65. Apprentice shoemaker; $0/0; b. Barbour 1842, brother of Eldridge; m. Conna Reed 1870; moved to Harrison Co., W. Va. after war where d. 1917.

GREATHOUSE, Alexander W.
Enl. Co. D, 20th Va. Cav. 5-1-63; paroled Staunton, Va. 5-19-65; brother-in-law *James Swick Unionist. $0/0; b. Barbour 1840; m. Margaret C. Gum 1865; moved to Highland Co., Va. after war. Son of Enos and Maria Greathouse; father b. Barbour or Harrison Co., W, Va.; grandson of John and Milly (Gillespie) Greathouse; great-grandson of William and Barbara Greathouse; William immigrant from Prussia, settled Harrison Co.

HALL, James Dickenson
Sympathizer; gave pro-secessionist speeches mass meeting Stewart's Run, Barbour 2-61; refugee at Staunton, Va. during war; brother Leonidas secessionist delegate to Richmond Convention for Wetzel Co., W. Va. Farmer; $9,000/4,020; b. Upshur Co., W. Va. 1807; m. Mary J. Callahan 1832; d. 1861. Son of Samuel and Elisabeth (Owens) Hall; father b. Pendleton Co., W. Va. settled Upshur Co., then Barbour; grandson of Thomas and Elisabeth (Dickenson) Hall; grandfather b. Md., settled Pendleton Co. 1790's, then Barbour.

HALL, James Edward
Enl. Co. H, 31st Va. Inf.; prom. to Lt. 6-21-62; POW near Gettysburg 7-5-63; exch. 2-65; appointed regimental adjutant; sur. Appomattox 4-9-65; brother-in-law *Joseph Crim Confederate sympathizer. Farmer; $6,250/3,452 (parents); b. Barbour 1841; Methodist-Episcopal Church, joined Southern Methodists after

war; m. *Elisabeth Wilson 1869; d. Barbour 1915. Son of John and Harriet (Rightmire) Hall; grandson of Samuel and Elisabeth (Owens) Hall.

HALL, Jaspar L.
Enl. Co. H, 31st Va. Inf. 5-14-61; des. 1861; refugee in eastern Virginia. Farmer; $6,250/3,452 (parents); b. Barbour 1845, brother of James E.; Methodist-Episcopal Church; moved to New Mexico 1880's.

HALL, Fletcher
Enl. Co. H, 62nd Va. Mtd. Inf. 4-7-63; KIA Beverly, W. Va. 10-31-64; brother-in-law *Martin Ward served same company. Miller; $5,000/678 (parents); b. Barbour 1840; Methodist-Episcopal Church. Son of David and Nancy (Reger) Hall; father b. Upshur Co., W. Va.; grandson of David and Elisabeth (Skidmore) Hall; great-grandson of Thomas and Elisabeth (Dickenson) Hall.

HALL, Abraham R.
Enl. Co. H, 62nd Va. Mtd. Inf. 8-1-62; color guard cpl. 4-11-62; POW Randolph Co., W. Va. 12-6-63; released Fort Delaware 6-20-65. $5,000/678 (parents); b. Barbour 1842, brother of Fletcher; m. Jennie ____; moved to Ill. after war where living 1880.

HALL, William B.
Listed Lt., Barbour Light Horse; enl. Co. D, 20th Va. Cav. 5-1-63; listed AWOL 9-24-64; POW Philippi 10-18-64 by men of 6th W. Va. Inf.; brother *Stephen and brother-in-law *Isaac Post Unionists. Farmer; $8,500/4,444; b. Barbour 1826; m. Martha K. Moffet; living Barbour 1880. Son of Lewis and Rachel (Johnson) Hall; father b. Pendleton Co., W. Va.; grandson of John and Elisabeth (Gregg) Hall; great-grandson of Thomas and Elisabeth (Dickenson) Hall.

HALL, Wilbur F.
Enl. Co. E, 62nd Mtd. Inf. 8-26-62; color guard cpl. 4-11-63; d. Augusta Co., Va. 3-15-64; brother Nathan served in same company; brother William Unionist. Farmer; $0/220; b. Taylor Co., W. Va. 1839; m. Priscilla Marquess 1860; came to Barbour during war. Son of Nathan and Mary (Means) Hall; grandson of Nathan and Elisabeth (Robinson) Hall, b. Va.

HARDIN, Bonaparte
Enl. Co. K, 31st Va. Inf. 6-22-61; des. New Market 5-25-62; NFR. Farm laborer; $0/0; b. Fayette Co., Pa. 1846; came to Barbour 1850's from Preston Co., W. Va. Son of John Hardin and Elisabeth Bailey, b. Fayette Co., settled Preston Co. 1840's.

HARRIS, Jacob
Sympathizer; brother-in-law *David Anglin Confederate sympathizer. Tenant; $1,100/282; b. Hardy Co., W. Va. 1834; came to Barbour from Upshur Co., W. Va. 1850's; m. Mary Jane Anglin 1855; moved to Gilmer Co., W. Va. 1873 where living 1880. Son of George and Elisabeth (Yankey) Harris; father b. Hardy Co., settled Upshur Co. 1830's, then Barbour 1850's, then Wood Co. 1870's; grandparents b. Va.

HARRIS, Silas
Enl. Co. E, 62nd Va. Mtd. Inf. 8-26-62; AWOL 2-20 to 4-30-63; wd. left arm Barbour 4-24-64; sur. Clarksburg, W. Va. 5-20-65. Tenant; $0/47 (parents); b. Upshur Co., W. Va. 1845, brother of Jacob; moved to Harrison Co., W. Va. after war.

HARRIS, Jaspar W.
Enl. Co. E, 62nd Va. Mtd. Inf. 8-26-62; wd. New Market 5-15-64; paroled Staunton, Va. 5-23-65. Farmer; $800/182; b. Barbour 1840; Baptist; m. Nancy J. Clark 1858; living Barbour 1908. Son of Isaac and Drusilla Harris; father b. Barbour; grandson of John and Catherine (Hymes) Harris, b. Hardy Co., W. Va. great-grandson of Simeon and Hannah (Smith) Harris; Simeon first Baptist preacher in Barbour, b. Hardy Co., settled Barbour 1780's.

HARRIS, Gideon Draper Camden
Enl. Co. K, 31st Va. Inf. 5-18-61; des. 4-19-62; com. Lt., 139th W. Va. Mil. 8-16-62. Cf. Unionists.

HARRIS, David W.
Enl. Co. H, 31st Va. Inf. 5-14-61; des. 4-19-62; brother-in-law Henry Lewis Capt., Co. B, 10th W. Va. Inf. (USA); brothers-in-law *James, John, Henry and Lewis Wentz served Union army. Farmer; $1,500/160; b. Hanover Co., Va. 1825; Methodist-Protestant Church; came to Barbour 1840's; m. Mary Francis Rose; d. Upshur, W. Va. 1883. Son of David and Elisabeth (Grubb) Harris; father b. Hanover Co., settled Barbour, then Upshur Co.; grandparents b. Va.

HARSH, Adam G.
Enl. Co. K, 31st Va. Inf. 5-29-61; des. 4-19-62; brother *Samuel served Barbour Home Guard; father-in-law *Jacob Bolyard Confederate sympathizer. Farmer; $500/301; b. Barbour 1835; m. Nancy E. Bolyard 1856; moved to Tucker Co., W. Va. after war where living 1880. Son of Jacob and Sarah (Stemple) Harsh; father b. Preston Co., W. Va.; grandson of Frederick and Sarah (Core) Harsh; grandfather immigrant from Germany, settled Preston Co.

HARTMAN, James T.
Sympathizer; elec. Circuit Court Clerk 1860; refused to serve after 1861; brother Joel Unionist; brother-in-law *Abraham Burner served Co. H, 62nd Va. Mtd. Inf. (CSA); brother-in-law George Burner served Bat. E, 1st W. Va. Art. (USA). $1,500/741; b. Pendleton Co., W. Va. 1818; Presbyterian; came to Barbour 1840's; m. Mary Hull Burner 1844; moved to Ritchie Co., W. Va. 1883 where d. 1894. Son of William and Mary (Sharps) Hartman; father b. Pa, settled Pendleton Co., then Barbour.

HARTMAN, Austin J.
Enl. Co. D, 20th Va. Cav. 2-1-64; POW Beverly, W. Va. 10-31-64; released Camp Chase, Ohio 6-12-65. $1,500/741 (parents); b. Barbour 1846, son of James and Mary (Burner) Hartman; Presbyterian; m. Margaret Virginia Reger 1872; moved to Harrison Co., W. Va. after 1880 where d. 1931.

HARVEY, Jeremiah
Listed cpl., Barbour Light Horse. Tenant; $0/1,744; b. Hampshire Co., W. Va. 1820; Methodist-Episcopal Church; m. Nancy Irons in Hardy Co., W. Va. 1840; came to Barbour shortly after; d. Barbour 1899. Son of Rezin and Elisabeth (Queen) Harvey; father b. Md., settled Barbour.

HARVEY, John M.
Enl. Co. D, 20th Va. Cav. 5-1-63; prom. to cpl.; AWOL 10-64; POW Philippi 10-24-64; released on oath 10-28-64; brother Benjamin served Co. A, 133rd W. Va. Mil.; brother-in-law *John Furr served Co. D, 6th W. Va. Inf. (USA). Farmer; $0/190 (parents); b. Upshur Co., W. Va. 1843; Baptist; m. Elisabeth Burr Haskins 1874; living Barbour 1880. Son of James and Ester (Bean) Harvey, b. Hampshire Co., W. Va.; grandson of Rezin and Elisabeth (Queen) Harvey.

HARVEY, Marshall T.
Enl. Co. D, 20th Va. Cav. 5-1-63; POW Barbour 7-18-63 by men of Co. H, 10th W. Va. Inf.; released Fort Delaware 5-10-65. Farmer; $0/190 (parents); b. Barbour 1843, brother of John M.; Baptist; Democrat; m. Ruhama Cool Ward 1872; moved to Upshur Co., W. Va. after 1880 where d. 1915.

HEATHERLY, John N.
Listed Barbour Light Horse; drafted 2-65, never inducted; brother-in-law *James Swick Unionist. Tenant; $0/90 (parents); b. Barbour 1834; m. Ruth D. Swick 1859; living Barbour 1880. Son of John and Virginia (Zinn) Heatherly; parents b. Barbour; grandson of James and Nancy (Anglin) Heatherly, b. Va.

HEDRICK, Isaac R.
Enl. Co. E, 62nd Va. Mtd. Inf. 8-26-62; des.; returned voluntarily; paroled Staunton, Va. 5-15-65; brother Adam served Co. K, 25th Va. Inf. (CSA). Farm laborer; $0/0; b. Pendleton Co., W. Va. 1838; came to Barbour 1850's; returned to Pendleton Co. after war where m. Rachel Davis; living Pendleton Co. 1880. Son of Adam and Jezabel (Hinkle) Hedrick; grandson of Frederick and Mary Hedrick; great-grandson of Charles and Rebecca (Conrad) Hedrick; great-great-grandson of Charles Hedrick.

HERSHMAN, Abraham
Sympathizer; arrested 1-13-63 as hostage for *James Trayhern; released shortly after on parole; son-in-law *Marshall Boyles served Barbour Home Guard (USA). Doctor and Methodist minister; $5,000/767; b. Hardy Co., W. Va. 1814; m. Mary Sagar; came to Barbour 1840's; organized first Southern Methodist church in Barbour; d. Barbour 1876. Son of John and Hannah (Sagar) Hershman; grandson of John and Magdalena (Ziegler) Hershman; great-grandson of Mathias Hershman, b. on passage to America, settled Hardy Co. from Pa.

HICKMAN, Wellington
Listed Barbour Light Horse; brother James served Co. B, 20th Va. Cav. (CSA); son-in-law *John Furr served Co. D, 6th W. Va. Inf. (USA). Tenant; $0/265; b. Barbour or Harrison Co., W. Va. 1816; m. 1) Nancy Reed 1837; 2) Eleanor Reed 1844; d. Barbour 1860's. Son of Arthur and Jane (Parker) Hickman; father b. Harrison Co.; grandson of Sotha and Eliza (Davis) Hickman, b. Del., settled Harrison Co. from Md. 1770's.

HICKMAN, Thomas
Enl. Co. D, 20th Va. Cav. 5-1-63; drowned while crossing Potts Creek, Va. 5-14-64. Tenant; $0/265 (parents); b. Barbour 1847, son of Wellington and Eleanor (Reed) Hickman.

HICKMAN, James P.
Enl. Co. H, 31st Va. Inf.; wd. Gaines Mill 6-27-62; d. 7-15-62. Farm Laborer; $0/0; b. Harrison Co., W. Va. 1838; came to Barbour 1850's. Son of Elias and Jemima (Davisson) Hickman; grandson of Sotha and Margaret (Cain) Hickman; great-grandson of Sotha and Eliza (Davis) Hickman.

HICKMAN, Lewis
Listed Barbour Light Horse; enl. Co. D, 20th Va. Cav. 5-1-63; elec. Lt. 5-3-63; on roll to 10-31-64. Tenant; $0/1,046; b. Harrison Co., W. Va. 1839, brother of James P.; m. Martha _____; moved to Rockbridge Co., Va. 1866 where d. 1916.

HICKMAN, John S.
Enl. Co. D, 20th Va. Cav. 5-1-63; prom. to Lt. 6-1-63; resigned commission 1-24-64 and re-enlisted as a pvt.; paroled Staunton, Va. 5-25-65. Farmer; $3,791/900 (parents); b. Harrison Co., W. Va. 1838; came to Barbour during war; d. Harrison Co. 1871. Son of James and Nancy (Bird) Hickman; grandson of Sotha and Margaret (Cain) Hickman.

HICKMAN, James M.
Enl. Co. D, 20th Va. Cav. 5-1-63; prom. to sgt. 7-1-63; on rolls to 12-31-64. Farmer; $3,791/900 (parents); b. Harrison Co., W. Va. 1842, brother of John S; m. Henrietta Houghton 1866; returned to Harrison Co. after war where d. 1911.

HILL, Jamison
Sympathizer; arrested 1861 and sent to Camp Carlisle, W. Va.; released; drafted 3-65, never inducted; brothers-in-law *Henry and *Hannibal Hill served Confederate Army. Farmer; $2,500/376; b. Barbour 1836; m. Emily Hill; living Barbour 1880. Son of William and Sarah (Johnson) Hill; parents b. Pendleton Co., W. Va.; grandson of John and Barbara (Buller) Hill, settled Pendleton Co., then Barbour..

HILL, Jacob
Enl. Co. K, 31st Va. Inf.; appointed Lt. 5-61; lost election for Lt. 5-1-62 and dropped from roll; returned to Barbour and killed 9-19-63. Farmer; $2,500/884; b. Barbour 1837, brother of Jamison.

HILL, Francis Marion
Enl. Co. K, 31st Va. Inf. 5-18-61, prom. to sgt. 7-64; POW Fort Stedman, Va. 3-25-65; released 6-17-65. Farmer; $2,500/884 (parents); b. Barbour 1839, brother of Jamison; m. Sarah M. Ramsey 1870; living Barbour 1880.

HILL, Edward J.
Enl. Co. E, 62nd Va. Mtd. Inf. 8-26-62; transf. to Co. H 9-1-62; left sick in Barbour 8-26-63; brother-in-law *Philip Digman Confederate sympathizer; brother-in-law *Alpheus Digman served Co. K, 31st Va. Inf. (CSA). Farmer; $1,000/429; b. Barbour 1826; m. Catherine Digman 1847; living Barbour 1880. Son of Frederick and Matilda (Coontz) Hill; grandson of John and Barbara (Buller) Hill.

HILL, Henry
Enl. Co. K, 31st Va. Inf.; des. 7-61; returned voluntarily; on rolls to 12-62; NFR. $N/G; b. Barbour 1835, brother of Edward.

HILL, Hannibal
Enl. Co. H, 31st Va. Inf. 5-14-61; prom. to sgt.; com. Capt., Co. E, 62nd Va. Mtd. Inf. 8-26-62; wd. New Market 5-15-64; wd. left side and arm and POW Beverly, W. Va. 10-31-64; escaped and recaptured 2-15-65; "A young West Virginia mountaineer of reckless daring." Laborer; $0/0; b. Barbour 1842, brother of Edward; m. Apoline V. Smith 1869; moved to Texas 1875 where d. 1895.

HITE, John Henry
Enl. Co. I, 14th Va. Cav. 5-20-61; transf. to Barbour Light Horse 5-26-61, then back to 14th Cav. after Light Horse disbanded; prom. to sgt. 4-9-63; prom. to Lt. 4-1-64; accidentally wd. 8-28-64; d. Winchester Hospital 9-3-64. Farmer; $20,000/1,077 (parents); b. Augusta Co., Va. 1840. Son of Thomas and Eveline (Sterrett) Hite; father slave owner, b. Rockingham Co., Va., settled Barbour 1840's; grandson of John and Cornelia (Reagan) Hite, b. Rockingham Co.; great-grandson of John and Sarah (Etling) Hite, settled Va. from N.Y.

HITE, William Franklin
Enl. Co. I, 14th Va. Cav. 10-16-62; POW Greenbrier Co., W. Va. 10-16-64; exch. 4-8-64; paroled Harrisonburg, Va. 5-27-65. Farmer; $20,000/1,077 (parents); b. Augusta Co., Va. 1844, brother of John Henry; returned to Augusta Co. after war, then to Calif. where d. 1916.

HOFFMAN, Jaspar N.
Enl. Co. E, 62nd Va. Mtd. Inf. 8-26-62; prom. to sgt.; POW 12-7-62; exch.; paroled Staunton, Va. 5-16-65; NFR. Farmer; $3,100/922 (parents); b. Barbour 1838. Son of Anthony and Martha (Wells) Hoffman; father b. Loudoun Co., Va.; grandson of John and Margaret (Hoff) Hoffman; grandfather b. N.J., settled Loudoun Co., then Barbour 1797.

HOFFMAN, Jacob F.
Enl. Co. E, 62nd Va. Mtd. Inf. 8-26-62; paroled Staunton, Va. 5-17-65. Farmer; $3,100/922 (parents); b. Barbour 1842, brother of Jaspar; m. Christina Ellen Smith 1877; moved to Marshall Co., W. Va. 1880's where listed Civil War veterans 1890.

HOLDEN, John Benton
Enl. Co. H, 31st Va. Inf.; des. 8-62; re-enlisted Co. D, 20th Va. Cav. 6-1-63; POW Fisher's Hill 9-23-64; exch. 3-19-65; des. and sur. Clarksburg, W. Va. 5-1-65; brother Franklin served Co. G, 62nd Va. Mtd. Inf. (CSA); sister *Elisabeth Atherton Unionist. Farmer; $3,000/613 (father); b. Barbour 1841; Baptist; m.

Columbia Chenoweth 1869; d. Barbour 1902. Son of John and Prudence (Kittle) Holden; father b. Harrison Co, W. Va.; grandson of Alexander and Nancy (Townsend) Holden; grandfather b. N.J.., settled Harrison Co. 1790's.

HOLLAND, Wellington
Enl. Co. B, 31st Va. Inf. 5-21-61; appointed Lt. 7-1-61; dropped in election 5-1-62; brother Nathan served 62nd Va. Mtd. Inf. and 18th Va. Cav. (CSA); brother-in-law *Benjamin McCoy Unionist. Wheelwright; $2,000/47; b. Pendleton Co., W. Va. 1816; Methodist-Episcopal Church; came to Barbour 1858; m. 1) Rachel Hinkle; 2) Elisabeth McCoy Zinn 1860; moved to Upshur Co., W. Va. after war where d. 1880. Son of Joseph and Margaret (Usher) Holland, b. Va.

HOLLAND, William F.
Sympathizer. $2,000/47 (parents); b. Pendleton Co., W. Va. 1838, son of Wellington and Rachel (Hinkle) Holland; Methodist-Episcopal Church, joined Methodist-Protestant Church after war; m. Hannah Criss 1861; moved to Upshur Co., W. Va. 1877 where d. 1914.

HOLLAND, Levi T.
Enl. Co. D, 20th Va. Cav. 7-15-63; POW Beverly, W. Va. 10-29-64; released Camp Chase, Ohio 6-12-65; brother-in-law *Joseph Jones served Co. H, 31st Va. Inf. (CSA). Carpenter; $N/G; b. Va. 1827; Democrat; came to Barbour 1850's where m. Margaret Jones 1853; living Barbour 1880. Parents b. Va.

HOLSBERRY, Samuel
Sympathizer; elec. Justice of the Peace 1860, refused to serve after 1861; arrested 1-13-63 as hostage for *James Trayhern; transf. to Camp Chase, Ohio 4-29-63; released 1-24-64; sister *Sarah Digman Confederate sympathizer; son-in-law *Marion Gainer served Co. E, 62nd Va. Mtd. Inf. (CSA); brothers-in-law *Philip Digman and *Alpheus Corder Confederate sympathizers; brother-in-law *Edward Hill served 62nd Va. Mtd. Inf. (CSA). Farmer; $1,400/753; b. Barbour 1812; Methodist-Episcopal Church, joined Southern Methodists after war; m. Magdelena Digman 1833; d. Barbour 1878. Son of John and Margaret (Poling) Holsberry; father b. Pa., settled Barbour; grandson of John Holsberry, immigrant from Germany,

HOLSBERRY, Nicolas
Enl. Co. E, 62nd Mtd. Inf. 8-26-62; left sick at home during raid into Barbour 8-63; returned; wd. in thigh Fisher's Hill 9-23-64; paroled Staunton, Va. 5-25-64. Farmer; $675/282; b. Barbour 1834, son of Samuel and Magdelena (Digman) Holsberry; Methodist-Episcopal Church; m. Matilda Gainer 1856; living Barbour 1880.

HOLT, Sarah Jane (Woods).
Sympathizer; brother *Samuel Woods and brothers-in-law *Charles and *William Holt served Confederate army. $4,650/178 (husband); b. Quebec Province, Canada 1825; Methodist-Episcopal Church; moved to Pa. 1830's; came to Barbour 1840's where m. 1) Stephen Holt 1850; 2) Jacob H. Burner 1871; post-war postmistress; d. Barbour 1920. Daughter of Adam and Jane (Long) Woods, immigrants from Ireland.

HOLT, Charles Asbury
Com. Lt. and Adj., 25th Va. Inf.; resigned 4-63; com. Capt., Co. K, 62nd Va. Mtd. Inf.; wd. in right leg New Market 5-15-64; hospitalized to end of war; sister-in-law *Sarah Jane (Woods) Holt Confederate sympathizer; brother-in-law Frederick Berlin served 133rd W.Va. Militia. Student, VMI; $2,260/4,193 (parents); b. Rockbridge Co., Va. 1836; m. Elizabeth Heeler 1866; moved to Augusta Co., Va. after war where d. 1907. Son of Thomas and Mary Minerva (Graham) Holt, slave owners, b. Augusta Co., settled Barbour 1850's; grandson of Richard and Margaret (Couthorne) Holt, b. Augusta Co.

HOLT, William F.
Enl. Co. H, 31st Va. Inf. 5-14-61; wd. in hand Port Republic 6-19-62; disch. 7-12-62; NFR. Tinner; $2,260/4,193 (parents); b. Augusta Co. 1842, brother of Charles.

HOOKER, James
Enl. Co. K, 19th Va. Cav. 2-64; POW Beverly, W. Va. 10-29-64; d. Camp Chase, Ohio 3-26-65; brother *William served Co. H, 10th W. Va. Inf. (USA). Domestic servant; $0/0 (mother); b. Bath Co., Va. 1847; came to Barbour 1850's. Son of Richard and Nancy Hooker, b. Bath Co.

HOWDERSHELT, John W.
Enl. Co. K, 31st Va. Inf. 5-19-61; des. 7-61; re-enlisted Co. H, 62nd Va. Mtd. Inf. 8-1-62; POW Tucker Co., W. Va. 10-28-62; exch. 11-20-62; des. Barbour 11-63; brothers-in-law John and Nathan Loughry served Union army. Laborer; $0/0; b. Barbour 1841; m. Mary A. Loughry 1863; moved to Preston Co., W. Va. after war where living 1880. Son of John and Elisabeth (Ferguson) Howdershelt; father b. Fauquier Co., Va.; grandson of John and Rebecca (Turner) Howdershelt.

HUDKINS, William Wesley
Listed bugler, Barbour Light Horse; drafted 2-65, never inducted. Farmer; $3,500/697 (parents); b. Barbour 1836; Baptist, joined Methodist-Episcopal Church after war; m. Margaret Brossius 1861; living Barbour 1870. Son of Eli

and Mary (Ranier) Hudkins; father b. Barbour; grandson and Henry and Mary (Isner) Hudkins; great-grandson of Bennett and Susan (Boatwright) Hudkins, b. Md., settled Barbour 1780's.

HUDKINS, John M.
Enl. Co. D, 20th Va. Cav. 5-1-63; POW Barbour 9-27-63 by men of Home Guard; noted as having taken oath previously; d. of bronchitus Rock Island Prison, Ill. 3-18-64. Farmer; $3,500/697 (parents); b. Barbour 1843, brother of William Wesley; Baptist.

HUDKINS, Richard D.
Listed Barbour Light Horse; pension claim for war-time service in 169th Mil. rejected 1902; brothers-in-law *Samuel, *George and *Demetrius Dickenson served Confederate army. Farmer; $2,000/488; b. Barbour 1837; Methodist-Episcopal Church; m. 1) Harriet Dickenson; 2) Nancy E. Green 1874; living Barbour 1880. Son of Bennett and Nancy (Eurit) Hudkins; grandson of Richard and Elisabeth (Ingram) Hudkins; great-grandson of Bennett and Susan (Boatwright) Hudkins.

HUMPHREYS, Robert G.
Listed Barbour Light Horse; drafted 2-65, never inducted. Farmer; $1,400/303; born Albemarle Co., Va. 1827; came to Barbour 1850's where m. Elisabeth Reed 1853; living Barbour 1880. Son of Meriweather and Susan (Thurston) Humphreys; father b. Albemarle Co., settled Upshur Co., W. Va.; great-grandson of David Humphreys, immigrant from Scotland.

HUMPHREYS, Thomas S.
Sympathizer; son-in-law *Emmanuel Stone served Co. H, 31st Va. Inf. (CSA). Tenant; $0/258; b. Alleghany Co., Va. 1812; m. Matilda Hudson 1834; came to Barbour 1840's from Pocahontas Co., W. Va.; moved to Randolph Co., W. Va. after war where living 1880. Parents b. Va.

HUMPHREYS, Matilda (Hudson)
Sympathizer; Tenant; $0/258; b. Augusta Co., Va. 1816, wife of Thomas S.; living Randolph Co., W. Va. 1880. Daughter of Richard and Elisabeth (Reddon) Hudson, b. Augusta Co., settled Pocahontas Co., W. Va.; granddaughter of George Hudson, b. Augusta Co.

HUMPHREYS, William Madison
Enl. Co. H, 31st Va. Inf. 5-19-61; des. Tenant; $0/258 (parents); b. Alleghany Co., Va. 1839, son of Thomas and Matilda (Hudson) Humphreys; m. Laura _____; d. Barbour 1905.

HUMPHREYS, Lorenzo Dow
Enl. Co. H, 31st Va. Inf. 5-14-61; wd. in leg Cedar Creek 8-1-64; leg later amputated. Tenant; $0/258 (parents); b. Barbour 1842, brother of William; m. Hulda Hartman 1870; moved to Lewis Co., W. Va. after war where living 1880.

HUMPHREYS, Richard F.
Enl. Co. F, 31st Va. Inf. 5-31-63; transf. to Co. H; KIA Spotsylvania 5-14-64. Tenant; $0/258 (parents); b. Barbour 1844, brother of William.

HUMPHREYS, Oliver C.
Sympathizer; attempted to warn Confederates at Philippi 6-3-61. Tenant; $0/258 (parents); b. Barbour, 1849, brother of William; m. 1) Marcilla Sturms 1869; 2) Florida ____; moved to Randolph Co., W. Va. after the war where living 1880.

HYMES, Gilbert Simon
Enl. Co. E, 62nd Va. Mtd. Inf. 8-26-62; prom. to sgt.; wd. left leg Williamsport 7-7-63; wd. New Market 5-15-64; paroled Staunton, Va. 5-1-65. Tenant $0/54; b. Barbour 1842; Democrat; m. Susan Malinda Fitzwater 1866; living Barbour 1899. Son of John and Malinda (Philips) Hymes; grandson of George Hymes, b. Hardy Co., W. Va., settled Barbour.

ICE, Thomas
Sympathizer. Farmer; $2,000/539; b. Marion Co., W. Va. 1808; came to Barbour 1850's with wife Sarah Virginia; d. 1860's. Son of Abraham and Mary (Leuman) Ice; b. Marion Co.; grandson of William and Margaret (Higginbotham) Ice; great-grandson of Frederick and Ellen Ice, settled Monongalia Co., W. Va. 1760's.

ICE, William T.
Sympathizer; drafted 3-65, never inducted. Attorney; $1,500/500 (parents); b. Marion Co., W. Va. 1840; Baptist; Democrat; came to Barbour 1864; m. Columbia Jarvis 1866; living Barbour 1899. Son of Andrew and Elisabeth (Alexander) Ice; father b. of Marion Co.; grandson of Thomas and Drusilla (White) Ice; great-grandson of Frederick and Ellen Ice.

ISNER, Thomas H.
Enl. Co. E, 62nd Va. Mtd. Inf. 8-26-62; d. during or shortly after war; brothers *Hamilton and *Washington served U. S. Army. Tenant; $0/50; b. Barbour 1824; Methodist-Episcopal Church; m. Caroline Ferguson 1844. Son of John and Mary (Hudkins) Isner, b. of Barbour; grandson of William Isner, settled Barbour 1770's.

ISNER, Henry
Enl. Co. E, 62nd Va. Mtd. Inf. 8-26-62; des. 10-24-62; sur. Beverly, W. Va. 8-16-63; d. of typhoid fever Rock Island Prison, Ill. 3-21-64. Tenant; $0/50; b. Barbour 1830, brother of Thomas; Methodist-Episcopal Church; m. Julie Ann Shireman.

ISNER, William
Enl. Co. H, 31st Va. Inf. 5-14-61; prom. to sgt.; prom. to Lt. 7-62; wd. Spotsylvania 5-30-64; d. 6-21-64. Tenant; $250/45 (mother); b. Barbour 1836, brother of Thomas; Methodist-Episcopal Church.

JARVIS, Elisabeth (Rightmire)
Sympathizer; home ransacked 6-61, then seized by Federal army 4-63; refugee in eastern Va. 6-63; sister *Julia Butcher and brother-in-law Edward Armstrong Confederate sympathizers; son-in-law *Nathan Taft Unionist. Widow; $3,000/340; b. Barbour 1803; Baptist; m. Solomon Jarvis 1822; living Barbour 1880. Daughter of John and Ann (Ashby) Rightmire, b. Va.

JARVIS, William D. F.
Enl. Co. H, 31st Va. Inf. 5-14-61; prom. to sgt.; cited for bravery at Alleghany 12-13-61; disch. for disability 3-12-64; sur. and gave oath Philippi 5-22-65. Merchant; $3,000/340 (mother); b. Taylor Co., W. Va. 1835; d. 1911. Son of Solomon and Elisabeth (Rightmire) Jarvis; father b. Harrison Co., W. Va.; grandson of Solomon and Margaret (Haythorn) Jarvis, b. Md.; great-grandson of John and Sarah (Hood) Jarvis, settled Harrison Co. 1788.

JENKINS, William Kester
Listed Capt. Barbour Light Horse; arrested Barbour 6-61 after company disbanded; released on oath; brother-in-law *William Daniels Capt., Co. D, 20th Va. Cav. Farmer; $0/35; b. Pendleton Co., W. Va. 1824; Methodist-Episcopal Church, joined Southern Methodists after war; Democrat; came to Barbour 1840's; m. 1) Rhoda Daniels 1848; 2) Mary J. Callahan Reed 1872; living Barbour 1899. Son of William and Jane (Kester) Jenkins; father immigrant from England.

JENKINS, Henry Middleton
Listed Barbour Light Horse; com. Lt., 169th W. Va. Mil. 5-15-62, never called into service. Cf. Unionists.

JETT, Wesley
Enl. Co. D, 20th Va. Cav. 5-1-63; POW Piedmont 6-4-64; exch. 3-12-65 and immediately hospitalized Richmond; d. of diarrhea 3-20-65. Farm laborer;

$930/584 (parents); b. Barbour 1837; came to Barbour 1860's from Ritchie Co., W. Va. Son of Wesley and Nancy (Lipscomb) Jett; father b. Barbour, settled Ritchie Co. 1840's; grandson of John and Sarah (Smith) Jett; grandfather b. Fauquier Co., Va., settled Barbour.

JOHNSON, William
Sympathizer; elec. to House of Delegates 1860 and retained seat at Richmond through the war; fought at Laurel Hill, retreating to Monterey, Va. where remained as refugee. Tradesman; $1,200/310; b. Barbour 1810; Methodist-Episcopal Church, joined Southern Methodists after war; m. 1) Lydia Ann Wells 1833; 2) Catherine Strickler Crim (widow of *Michael Crim) 1869; d. Barbour 1893. Son of Levi and Rebecca (Cross) Johnson; father b. Loudoun Co., Va., settled Barbour 1797; grandson of Robert and Mary (Vannoy) Johnson; grandfather b. N.J.

JOHNSON, Mortimor C.
Enl. Co. H, 31st Va. Inf. 5-14-61; prom. to cpl.; des. 4-19-62; re-enlisted Co. A, 18th Va. Cav. 6-1-62; com. Lt., Co. H, 62nd Va. Mtd. Inf.; prom. to Capt. 4-4-63; KIA Randolph Co., W. Va. 12-6-63; brothers-in-law *Nathaniel, *Elam and *Emory Poling served Co. K, 31st Va. Inf. (CSA). Tradesman; $0/0; b. Barbour 1836, son of William and Lydia Ann (Wells) Johnson; Methodist-Episcopal Church; m. Rebecca Poling.

JOHNSON, Isaac Vandeventer
Enl. Co. H, 31st Va. Inf. 5-14-61; prom. to Lt.; wd. in leg Alleghany 12-13-61; resigned commission; served quartermaster, Imboden's brigade. Clerk; $480/25; b. Barbour 1837, brother of Mortimor; Baptist; joined Southern Methodists after war; Democrat; m. 1) Fanny Link 1874; 2) Fanny Kemper 1893; moved to Roanoke Co., Va. 1890's.

JOHNSON, Thomas Benton
Enl. Co. H, 31st Va. Inf. 5-14-61; des. 11-15-61; POW Barbour 11-25-61; exch. 11-10-62; disch. 11-18-62, suffering from typhoid fever; arrested Randolph Co., W. Va. 1-3-63 by men of Co. A, 1st W. Va. Cav. with *James Lynch; said to have d. in prison. Plasterer; $1,200/310 (father); b. Barbour 1840, brother of Mortimor.

JOHNSON, Joseph Linden
Enl. Co. E, 62nd Va. Mtd. Inf., serving as drummer; sur. Beverly, W. Va. 5-11-65. $1,200/310 (father); b. Barbour 1847, brother of Mortimor; Methodist-Episcopal Church, joined Southern Methodists after the war; Democrat; m. 1) Ellen Rebecca Crim 1869; 2) Susan M. McCartney 1879; d. Barbour 1923.

JOHNSON, John Gordon
Sympathizer; father-in-law Job Parsons Confederate sympathizer; son-in-law *Hiram Smith served Co. H, 31st Va. Inf. (CSA). Farmer; $4,000/1,375; b. Barbour 1816, brother of William; Methodist-Episcopal Church, joined Southern Methodists after war; Democrat; m. Catherine Parsons 1839; d. Barbour 1902.

JOHNSON, Richard M.
Sympathizer; hid Confederate soldiers home on furlough; brother-in-law *Solomon Gainer served Co. K, 31st Va. Inf. (CSA). Farmer; $0/120; b. Barbour 1840, son of John and Catherine (Parsons) Johnson; Methodist-Episcopal Church; joined Methodist-Episcopal Church, South after war; Democrat; m. Nancy Gainer 1859; living Barbour 1880.

JOHNSON, William Worthington
Enl. Co. D, 20th Va. Cav. 5-1-63; on roll to 12-31-64. Farmer; $4,000/1,375 (parents); b. Barbour 1848, brother of Richard; Methodist-Episcopal Church; Democrat; m. Alice Parsons; moved to Idaho after 1880.

JOHNSON, Peter
Sympathizer; pre-war County Surveyor, refused to serve after 1861; arrested 1-13-63 as hostage for *James Trayhern; transf. to Camp Chase, Ohio 4-29-63; released 1-24-64; sister *Osa Philips Confederate sympathizer; son-in-law*Hamilton Poling served Co. E, 62nd Va. Mtd. Inf. (CSA); brother-in-law *Adamirin Stemple served Co. K, 31st Va. Inf. (CSA). Farmer; $1,720/575; b. Barbour 1810; Democrat; m. 1) Mary Holsberry 1830; 2) Sarah Stemple 1854; d. Barbour 1887. Son of John and Elisabeth (Poling) Johnson; father b. Loudoun Co., Va.; grandson of Robert and Mary (Vannoy) Johnson.

JOHNSON, Martin C.
Listed Barbour Light Horse; transf. to Co. K, 31st Va. Inf. 5-18-61; prom. to cpl.; des. 4-19-62; re-enlisted Co. E, 62nd Va. Mtd. Inf.; des. Braxton Co., W. Va. 9-17-63; enl. U. S. Vols. Rock Island Prison, Ill.; NFR. $1,720/575 (parents); b. Barbour 1843; German Baptist. Son of Peter and Mary (Holsberry) Johnson.

JOHNSON, Reason
Sympathizer; hid Confederate soldiers. Farmer; $1,000/298; b. Barbour 1835, brother of Martin; m. Mariah Coberly; living Barbour 1880.

JOHNSON, Garrett
Guerrilla; indicted for guerrilla activities in Tucker Co., W. Va. 9-7-63. Farmer;

$13,750/2,445; b. Barbour 1813, brother of William; m. 1) Elisabeth Thompson; 2) Alice ___; d. Barbour 1864.

JOHNSON, Enoch B.
Enl. Co. E, 62nd Va. Mtd. Inf.; scout and mail courier; paroled Staunton, Va. 5-17-65; NFR. Farmer; $1,660/859; b. Barbour 1820, brother of William; German Baptist; m. Rebecca Coontz 1838.

JOHNSON, Frederick M.
Enl. Co. K, 31st Va. Inf. 5-18-61; prom. to cpl. 7-1-64; wd. in arm McDowell 5-8-62; wd. in face Freemans Ford 8-22-62; one of five men of company to surrender at Appomattox 4-9-65; NFR. Farmer; $1,660/859 (parents); b. Barbour 1841, son of Enoch and Rebecca (Coontz) Johnson; German Baptist.

JOHNSTON, Abraham
Enl. Co. A, 25th Va. Inf.; transf. to Co. E, 62nd Va. Mtd. Inf. 8-26-62; wd. Fisher's Hill 9-23-64. Farmer; $0/770; b. Taylor Co., W. Va. 1825; Baptist; came to Barbour 1850's; m. 1) Elisabeth ___; 2) Martha ___; 3) Martha E. Russell 1866; d. Barbour 1871. Son of Abraham and Hannah Johnston; grandson of Peter and Eleanor (Peters) Johnston, settled Taylor Co. 1780's.

JONES, Joseph R.
Enl. Co. H, 31st Va. Inf. 5-14-61; POW Kernstown 7-24-64; exch. 3-2-65 and returned to Barbour; brother-in-law *Levi Holland served Co. D, 20th Va. Cav. (CSA). Tenant; $0/155; b. Barbour 1837; m. Zilda Cade 1861; living Barbour 1880. Son of Solomon and Elisabeth (Kirby) Jones; father b. Fluvanna Co., Va.; grandson of John and Martha (Humphreys) Jones.

JONES, William W.
Sympathizer; elec. Justice of the Peace 1860, refused to serve after 1861. Farmer; $1,600/394; b. Fluvanna Co., Va. 1817; Democrat; m. Rebecca Johnson; living Barbour 1880. Son of Solomon and Elisabeth Jones, b. Va.

JONES, Flavius Josephus
Enl. Co. E, 62nd Va. Mtd. Inf. 5-9-63; wd. Williamsport 7-9-63; hospitalized for a year, then disch.; father-in-law *John Coontz Confederate sympathizer. Shoemaker; $1,600/394 (parents); b. Barbour 1840, son of William and Rebecca (Johnson) Jones; Baptist; m. Amanda Coontz 1859; d. Barbour 1926.

JONES, Lewis Coleman
Enl. Co. E, 62nd Va. Mtd. Inf. 5-9-63; on roll to 12-31-64; brother-in-law *Minor Sharps served Co. D, 20th Va. Cav. (CSA); brother-in-law *James

Sharps served Co. F, 17th W. Va. Inf. (USA). Tenant; $1,600/394 (parents); b. Barbour 1843, brother of Flavius; Baptist; m. Emaline Sharps 1862; living Barbour 1880.

JONES, William H.
Enl. Co. H, 31st Va. Inf. 5-14-61; prom. to sgt.; wd. right leg Bethesda Church 5-30-64; leg amputated; d. Farmville General Hospital 6-21-64; brother *Solomon Lt., 169th W. Va. Mil.. Tenant; $350/130 (parents); b. Bath Co., Va. 1842. Son of John and Delphia Jones, b. Va., settled Barbour 1840's.

JONES, Isaac
Listed Barbour Light Horse; enl. Co. H, 31st Va. Inf. 5-29-61; KIA Mechanicsville 5-30-64; brother-in-law *Adam Starcher served Co. A, 18th Va. Cav. (CSA). Tenant; $0/127 (parents); b. Rockingham Co., Va. 1832. Son of Paschal and Anna (Black) Jones, b. Va., settled Barbour 1840's.

JONES, Elliott
Listed Barbour Light Horse; enl. Co. H, 31st Va, Inf.; wd. Antietam 9-17-62; on roll to 12-64. Tenant; $0/127 (parents); b. Rockingham Co., b. 1835, brother of Isaac; living Barbour 1870.

KELLAR, Adam
Enl. Co. E, 62nd Va. Mtd. Inf. 3-29-63; des. 11-63; sur. and took oath 11-22-63; father-in-law *Jacob Bennett Unionist; brother-in-law *Thomas Moran Confederate sympathizer. Farmer; $1,400/195; b. Barbour 1836; m. Lydia Bennett 1857; moved to Gilmer Co., W. Va. after war where living 1880. Son of Samuel and Nancy Keller, b. Va.

KELLEY, William D.
Enl. Co. H, 31st Va. Inf. 5-14-61; d. of pneumonia Staunton, Va. 11-8-62; father Unionist sympathizer; brothers *Dyer and *Loman served U. S. Army. Farmer; $8,500/1,037 (parents); b. Barbour 1834, son of *Samuel and Delia (Poling) Kelley. Cf. Unionists.

KENT, John T.
Enl. Co. H, 31st Va. Inf. 5-14-61; des. 7-61; re-enlisted Co. C, 13th Va. Inf. 4-22-62; in hospital 5-62; des. and re-enlisted Co. D, 20th Va. Cav. 5-1-63; transf. to Co. E, 62nd Va. Mtd. Inf. 3-64; POW Fisher's Hill 9-23-64; released on oath Clarksburg, W. Va. 11-13-64; Farm laborer; $0/0; b. Loudoun Co., Va. 1843; Presbyterian; came to Barbour with family of *Thomas Jefferson Anderson; m. Sarah C. _____; living Barbour 1880. Son of Benjamin Harrison and Malinda (Henry) Kent; grandson of Benjamin and Sarah Kent, b. Loudoun Co.

KERR, George W.
Listed Barbour Light Horse. Farmer; $150/105; b. Pocahontas Co., W. Va. 1818; Presbyterian; m. 1) Louisa Reed 1849; 2) Elisabeth Wotring 1865; 3) Mary Ann Pew 1873; living Barbour 1880. Son of Robert and Ann Eliza (Arbogast) Kerr; father b. Pocahontas Co.; grandson of Daniel and Mary (Kirkpatrick) Kerr, b. Rockbridge Co., Va.; great-grandson of Robert and Elisabeth (Bailey) Kerr, immigrants from England.

KITTLE, Benjamin Wilson Jr.
Sympathizer; arrested 12-63 on charges of "bushwacking" and sent to Camp Chase, Ohio where d. 8-5-64; brothers Squire, Marshall and George served Co. D, 62nd Va. Mtd. Inf., Marshall and George KIA; brother Edward served Co. F, 31st Va. Inf., KIA Wilderness. Blacksmith; $0/258; b. Randolph Co., W. Va. 1819; m. Emily Clarke 1840; came to Barbour 1850's. Son of Benjamin and Nancy (Stalnaker) Kittle; grandson of Jacob and Mary Kittle; great-grandson of Abraham and Christina (Westfall) Kittle, b. N.Y., settled Randolph Co. from N.J. 1770's.

KNIGHT, Benjamin J.
Listed Barbour Light Horse; claim for war time service in 169th Mil. rejected 1902; brother *William served Co. N, 6th W. Va. Inf. (USA). Farmer; $1,000/238 (parents); b. Taylor Co., W. Va. 1836; Baptist; m. Martha Jenkins 1863; living Barbour 1880. Son of Thomas and Catherine (Rosier) Knight. Cf. Unionists.

KNISELY, Lafayette M.
Enl. Co. D, 20th Va. Cav. 5-1-63; prom. to sgt. 7-1-63; on roll to 12-31-64; brother Holdridge served in same company; brother George served Co. I, 14th Va. Cav. (CSA). Farm laborer; $0/0; b. Harrison Co., W. Va. 1832; moved to Ill. 1840's; returned to Harrison Co. 1850's where m. Sarah Jane Arnold 1856; moved to Barbour 1859; living Barbour 1880. Son of Jacob and Prudence (Chidester) Knisely; father b. Pa.; grandson of George and Annie (Eib) Knisely, settled Harrison Co., then Ritchie Co., W. Va.

KNOTTS, James
Sympathizer; father-in-law *William Elliott Confederate sympathizer; brothers-in-law *Edgar, *Solomon and *Truman Elliott served 20th Va. Cav. (CSA). Tenant; $0/75; born Taylor Co., W. Va. 1833; Methodist-Episcopal Church, joined Southern Methodists after war; came to Barbour 1850's where m. Melvina Elliott 1857; d. Barbour 1895. Son of James and Susanna (Miller) Knotts; grandson of James Absalom and Anne (Myers) Knotts, b. Va.

LANG, David Berkeley
Scout for Confederate army 1861-1862; com. Major, 62nd Va. Mtd. Inf.; prom. to Lt. Col.; KIA Stephenson's Depot 9-5-64; described by comrades as "A cool and brave officer, respected and beloved by his men;" "Lang was as kind, gentle and modest as he was brave and dashing;" "His honor and worth as a friend, his courage and daring as a soldier, his efficiency, skill and daring as an officer, cannot easily be overdrawn;" Cousin Theodore Lang Major, 3rd W. Va. Inf. (USA) and author of Loyal West Virginians. Farmer; $2,000/565; b. Harrison Co., W. Va. 1831; Methodist-Episcopal Church; m. Elisabeth Powell 1851; came to Barbour 1859. Son of Lemuel and Sereptia (Berkeley) Lang, b. Harrison Co.; grandson John and Nancy Lang, b. Va., settled Harrison Co.

LANG, Arthur Wellington
Enl. Co. I, 14th Va. Cav. 7-1-61; wd. in shoulder Cheat Mountain 7-19-61;POW near Lexington 6-10-64; exch. 3-10-65; paroled Staunton, Va. 5-12-65; brother Alstorpheus served Co. C, 31st Va. Inf. (CSA). Mechanic; $0/320 (parents); b. Harrison Co., W. Va. 1840; came to Barbour 1850's; m. 1) Margaret Teter 1878; 2) C. M. Parr 1883; moved to Roane Co., W. Va. after war. Son of Henderson and Mary (Ferris) Lang; grandson of John and Nancy Lang.

LANHAM, Jaspar
Enl. Co. H, 62nd Va. Mtd. Inf. 4-24-63; des. Barbour Co. 11-63; enl. Co. M, 3rd W. Va. Cav. (USA). Cf. Unionists.

LANTZ, William Jacob
Enl. Co. D, 20th Va. Cav. 6-27-63; des. 9-63; wife's parents *Thomas and *Elisabeth Wood Unionists; brother-in-law *William Wood served Co. F, 3rd W. Va. Inf. (USA). Tenant; $0/40; b. Barbour 1833; m. Martha Wood; living Barbour 1880. Son of Henry and Elisabeth (Rodabaugh) Lantz; father b. Rockingham Co., Va.; grandson of George and Mary (Woodford) Lantz; grandfather b. Shenandoah Co., Va., settled Barbour 1811.

LANTZ, George W.
Enl. Co. H, 62nd Va. Mtd. Inf. 4-26-63; des.; re-enlisted Co. D, 20th Va. Cav. 8-9-63; POW 1863; brother John served same company. Tenant; $50/150 (mother); b. Barbour 1843; m. Margaret E. Yeager 1871; moved to Randolph Co., W. Va. 1870's where d. 1904. Son of William and Nancy (Lanham) Lantz; grandson of George and Mary (Woodford) Lantz.

LANTZ, Henry
Enl. Co. H, 62nd Va. Mtd. Inf. 4-7-63; KIA Williamsport 7-7-63. Tenant; $50/150 (mother); b. Barbour 1846, brother of George.

LEMMON, William H.
Listed Barbour Light Horse; enl. Bat. E, 1st W. Va. Art. (USA). Cf. Unionists.

LIPSCOMB, Flavius C.
Enl. Co. D, 20th Va. Cav. 5-1-63; AWOL 9-63; detailed as teamster 2-16-64; paroled Staunton, Va. 5-25-65; brother-in-law *John Adams served Co. C, 17th W. Va. Inf. (USA). Tenant; $0/0; b. Ritchie Co., W. Va. 1835; came to Barbour 1850's where m. Sarah Adams 1853; moved to Harrison Co., W. Va. 1870's where living 1880. Son of John and Martessa (Costolo) Lipscomb; father b. King George Co., Va.; grandson of Ambrose and Winifred (Mardis) Lipscomb; grandfather b. King William Co., Va., settled Preston Co., W. Va. 1808.

LOHR, Henry
Enl. Co. K, 31st Va. Inf. 5-18-61; des. 4-19-62; enl. Co. H, 10th W. Va. Inf. (USA); des. 9-9-62; rejoined 31st Va. Inf. 5-63; wd. Gettysburg 7-3-63; des. 10-10-63 and returned to Barbour. Cf. Unionists.

LYNCH, James Edward
Enl. Co. H, 31st Va. Inf. 5-14-61; POW Rich Mountain by men of 1st W. Va. Cav. 1-12-63; released Camp Chase, Ohio 5-27-63. Merchant; $600/150; b. Harrison Co., W. Va. 1824; m. Margaret Johnson 1845; moved to Taylor Co., W. Va. after war where d. 1870's.

MARKS, Owen
Sympathizer; arrested 1868 for disturbing religious services. Blacksmith; $0/27; b. Barbour 1831; Baptist; m. 1) Sarah Knight; 2) Matilda Burns 1881; living Barbour 1880. Son of Benjamin and Mary (Jenkins) Marks; father b. Ky.

MARKS, Lemuel
Listed Barbour Light Horse; brothers-in-law *Noah, *Edward and *Emery McCauley Unionists. Blacksmith; $60/150; b. Barbour 1838, brother of Owen; Baptist; Democrat; m. 1) Elisabeth Cleavenger 1855; 2) Drusilla McCauley 1860; 3) Indiana Talbot Lough (widow of *William Lough) 1871; living Barbour 1880.

MARSH, Benjamin
Enl. Co. K, 31st Va. Inf. 5-18-61; d. of disease 3-3-62. Pauper ("Ben had no home, just lived anywhere"); $0/0; b. Tucker Co., W. Va. 1838. Grandson of Benjamin and Sarah (Minear) Marsh; grandfather b. Loudoun Co.,, Va. settled Tucker Co. 1790's.

MARTIN, Enoch Charles
Enl. Co. K, 31st Va. Inf. 5-18-61; des. 5-25-62 ("My year was up."); arrested Ritchie Co., W. Va. 6-26-62 by men of 6th W. Va. Inf.; exch. 10-15-62; des. again; POW Pocahontas Co., W. Va. by men of 87th Pa. Inf.; d. of variola Alton Prison, Ill. 2-3-63; brother *Zephania served Co. G, 14th W. Va. Inf. (USA). Farmer; $500/95; b. Barbour Co. 1838. Son of Henson and Jane (Currence) Martin. Cf. Unionists.

MARTINEY, Joseph
Sympathizer; elec. Assessor 1860, refused to serve after 1861. Farmer; $800/333; b. Randolph Co., W. Va. 1820; m. Margaret Finline 1845; d. Barbour 1894. Son of William and Mahala (Stalnaker) Martiney; grandson of William and Eunice (Eastburn) Martiney, b. Va.

MARTINEY, Samuel
Listed Barbour Light Horse. Farmer; $2,000/895; b. Randolph Co., W. Va. 1839, brother of Joseph; m. Elisabeth Crim 1865; d. 1870's.

MASON, Edward J.
Enl. Co. E, 62nd Va. Mtd. Inf. 5-9-63; des. 10-4-64 and returned to Barbour; drafted 3-65, never inducted. Farmer; $2,000/723 (parents); b. Taylor Co., W. Va. 1842; Baptist; m. Barbara Rohrbaugh 1868; living Barbour 1870. Son of Sanford and Rosanna (Fleming) Mason, settled Barbour 1847; grandson of Thomas and Lydia (Goodwin) Mason; great-grandson of Thomas Mason, b. N. H., settled Taylor Co. 1790's.

MASON, Elmore J.
Enl. Co. C, 26th Va. Cav. 4-20-63; des. 8-1-63; re-enlisted Co. E, 62nd Va. Mtd. Inf.; d. of dysentery Harrisonburg, Va. 1-23-64. Farmer; $2,000/572 (parents); b. Taylor Co., W. Va. 1844, brother of Edward; Baptist.

MATHEWS, Amos
Enl. Co. K, 31st Va. Inf. 5-29-61; AWOL 4-21-62; returned to company; wd. Richmond 3-22-65; POW when city evacuated. Farmer; $2,000/572 (parents); b. Preston Co., W. Va. 1837; came to Barbour 1840's; m. Bede Poling 1860; d. Barbour 1907. Son of Isaac and Catherine (Bennett) Mathews; father b. Preston Co.; grandson of Joseph and Elisabeth (Criss) Mathews, b. Va., settled Preston Co.

MATHEWS, Eugenius
Enl. Co. K, 31st Va. Inf. 5-18-61; d. 1-17-62 of wounds received Greenbrier 10-3-61. Farmer; $2,000/572 (parents); b. Barbour 1842, brother of Amos.

MAY, Francis Marion
Sympathizer; arrested 9-5-62 for uttering "treasonable language" on affidavit signed by brother; released 7-13-63; drafted 3-65, never inducted. Tenant; $0/10; b. Preston Co., W. Va. 1826; m. Sydney Pierce; came to Barbour 1850's where living 1880. Son of Henry and Ellen (Gibson) May; father b. Preston Co.; grandson of George May, settled Preston Co. "at an early date."

McCLASKEY, William
Sympathizer; appointed Deputy Sheriff 1860, refused to serve after 1861; arrested 6-61; released on oath a few weeks later; drafted 3-65, never inducted; brother James Unionist. Farmer; $9,000/625; b. Monongalia Co., W. Va. 1821; Methodist-Episcopal Church; Democrat; m. Catherine Proudfoot 1843; d. Barbour 1886. Son of William and Rebecca (Howell) McClaskey; parents b. Va., moved to Allegany Co., Md., then Monongalia Co., then Barbour 1835.

McCLASKEY, Catherine (Proudfoot)
Sympathizer. $9,000/625; b. Barbour 1824; wife of William McClaskey; d. Barbour 1876. Daughter of Thomas and Elisabeth (Robinson) Proudfoot; granddaughter of John and Leanor (Hitt) Proudfoot.

McCLASKEY, Elisabeth Ann
Sympathizer; arrested 7-62 for destroying flag of Co. K, 6th W. Va. Inf.; NFR. $9,000/625 (parents); b. Barbour 1846, daughter of William and Catherine (Proudfoot) McClaskey; Methodist-Episcopal Church.

McGILL, Cornelius
Enl. Co. K, 31st Va. Inf. 5-18-61; des. 7-61; NFR. Farmer; $0/72; b. Preston Co., W. Va. 1839; came to Barbour 1850's; m. Catherine Ann _____; Son of Eli and Emily McGill; grandson of Ferdinand McGill, b. Va., settled Preston Co. 1820's; great-grandson of Charles and Hannah McGill; great-grandfather immigrant from Ireland.

McGUFFIN, Samuel
Sympathizer; narrowly escaped arrest. Farmer; $1,200/478; b. Augusta Co., Va. 1808; came to Barbour 1840's with wife Catherine; living Barbour 1880. Son of James and Elisabeth (Erwin) McGuffin, b. Augusta Co.; grandson of Robert and Elisabeth (King) McGuffin; grandfather b. Pa., settled Augusta Co.

McKINNEY, Joseph M.
Enl. Co. F, 20th Va. Cav. 5-10-63; POW Alleghany Co., Va. 12-18-63; released Camp Chase, Ohio 5-8-65; NFR. Tenant; $0/103; b. Harrison Co., W. Va. 1828; m. Judith Mowery 1849; came to Barbour 1850's. Son of Joseph and Mary (Jones) McKinney; grandson of Thomas and Catherine (Houff) McKinney, b. Loudoun Co., Va., settled Harrison Co.

McLEAN, Fleming
Enl. Co. C, 26th Va. Cav. 4-20-63; des. and re-enlisted Co. E, 62nd Va. Mtd. Inf. 5-9-63; POW Pocahontas Co., W. Va. 3-9-65; released on oath Camp Chase, Ohio 6-13-65. Farmer; $3,200/502 (mother); b. Randolph Co., W. Va. 1845; Methodist-Episcopal Church; moved to Idaho after war. Son of William and Hannah (Weese) McClean; father b. Randolph Co.; grandson of Daniel and Anna (Wilmoth) McClean; grandfather settled Randolph Co. from Hardy Co., W. Va.

MILLER, William Fairfax
Sympathizer; arrested 1-13-63 as hostage for *James Trayhern; transf. to Camp Chase, Ohio 4-29-63; released 1-24-64. Farmer; $400/145; b. Va. 1826; German Baptist; came to Barbour 1950's with wife Nancy; living Barbour 1880. Parents b. Va.

MINEAR, Hickman
Enl. Co. H, 31st Va. Inf. 5-14-61; des. 7-61. Apprentice to *Thompson Surghnor; $0/0; b. Va. 1840; came to Barbour 1850's; m. Mary Ann ____; moved to Doddridge Co., W. Va. after war where living 1880. Parents b. Va.

MONTGOMERY, John J.
Sympathizer; arrested 3-31-62 for "aiding rebels; Union man shot near his home; a bad character;" released on oath 11-4-62; sons *Adam and *Michael served U. S. Army. Ferryman; $300/140; b. Barbour 1812; Methodist-Protestant Church; m. Mary Edwards 1831; d. Barbour 1870's. Son of John Montgomery, b. Md., settled Barbour.

MOORE, Anthony H.
Enl. Co. E, 62nd Va. Mtd. Inf. 8-26-62; des. 1865; drafted into Co. D, 7th W. Va. Inf. 3-13-65; des. 6-25-65; brother-in-law *David Waggoner served Co. H, 31st Va. Inf. (CSA). Farmer; $800/562 (parents); b. Barbour 1840; m. Lydia Waggoner 1865; moved to Gilmer Co., W. Va. after war where living 1880. Son of Isaac and Bethiah (Wells) Moore; grandson of William and Rachel (Philips) Moore, b. Va.

MOORE, Martin
Enl. Co. K, 31st Va. Inf. 5-18-61; wd. Alleghany 12-31-61; wd. in hand Port Republic 6-9-62; wd. in arm Bloody Angle 5-12-64; hospitalized Staunton, Va. where paroled 5-15-65; NFR. Tenant; $0/35 (parents); b. Tyler Co., W. Va. 1840; came to Barbour 1850's. Son of Samuel and Nancy (Wilson) Moore, b. Barbour; grandson of Martin and Juda Moore, b. Barbour; great-grandson of Daniel and Deborah (Poling) Moore, b. Md., settled Barbour.

MOORE, Wilson
Enl. Co. K, 31st Va. Inf. 5-27-61; wd. in ankle Port Republic 6-9-62; wd. Fredericksburg 12-13-62, d. three days later. Tenant; $0/35 (parents); b. Tyler Co., W. Va. 1841, brother of Martin.

MOORE, William H.
Enl. Co. E, 62nd Va. Mtd. Inf. 8-26-62; on roll to 4-63. Farmer; $0/157; b. Barbour 1823; Methodist-Episcopal Church; m. Barbara _____; living Barbour 1880. Son of John and Susan (Hill) Moore; grandson of William and Catherine (Button) Moore; grandfather b. Md.; great-grandson of Daniel and Deborah (Poling) Moore.

MOORE, Jaspar E.
Enlisted Co. E, 62nd Va. Mtd. Inf. 8-26-62; prom. to sgt. major; POW Barbour 12-1-63; released Fort Delaware 6-15-65. Farmer; $800/245 (parents); b. Barbour 1839, half-brother of William; Methodist-Episcopal Church; m. Rachel Elisabeth Holsberry 1866; living Barbour 1880. Son of John and Mary Susanna (Willet) Moore.

MOORE, Adam
Enl. Co. E, 62nd Va. Mtd. Inf. 5-9-63; sur. Beverly, W. Va. 5-15-65; paroled Clarksburg, W. Va. 5-20-65. Farmer; $800/245 (parents); b. Barbour 1845, brother of Jaspar; Methodist-Episcopal Church; m. Mary Jane Dobbins 1867; moved to Gilmer Co., W. Va. after war where listed Civil War veterans 1890.

MOORE, Jesse Marshall
Enl. Co. K, 31st Va. Inf. 5-18-61; wd. Freeman's Ford 8-22-62 (officially listed as KIA); assigned as brigade teamster; sick in hospital 1864; disch. 4-20-65; brother *Eli served Co. D, 17th W. Va. Inf. (USA). Farm laborer; $0/0; b. Barbour 1841; m. Margaret _____; living Barbour 1880. Son of William and Sarah (Bennett) Moore; grandson of Eli Moore, b. Hampshire Co., W. Va. settled Barbour.

MOORE, Granville W.
Enl. Co. K, 31st Va. Inf. 5-27-61; des. 7-61; returned voluntarily 4-14-62; wd. Gaines Mill 6-27-61; wd. Freeman's Ford 8-22-62; des. and re-enlisted Co. E, 62nd Va. Mtd. Inf.; returned to 31st Va. Inf. 2-28-64; hospitalized 5- to 8-64; paroled Appomattox 4-9-65. Farm laborer; $0/0; b. Barbour 1841, brother of Jesse; m. Christina Montgomery 1859; moved to Preston Co., W. Va. 1870's where living 1880.

MOORE, Henry
Enl. Co. E, 62nd Va. Mtd. Inf.; des. and sur. 11-22-63. Tenant; $0/95 (parents); b. Barbour 1849, brother of Jesse; living Barbour 1870.

MORAN, Thomas
Sympathizer; arrested 12-17-62 on charges of "disloyalty;" transf. to Camp Chase, Ohio 4-29-63; transf. to Fort Delaware 7-14-63; released; drafted 3-65, never inducted; brother-in-law *Adam Keller served Co. E, 62nd Va. Mtd. Inf. (CSA). Farmer; $1,000/308; b. Ireland 1827; came to Barbour 1850's; m. Leanna Keller 1858; living Barbour 1880. Son of John and Sarah Moran.

MORRALL, Lair Davis
Sympathizer; elec. Circuit Court Clerk 1860, refused to serve after 1861; served on committee drafting pro-secessionist resolutions Philippi 3-61; refugee in Buckingham Co., Va. during war. Farmer; $14,840/9,982; b. Pendleton Co., W. Va. 1814; Presbyterian; came to Barbour 1840's where m. Elisabeth Harper 1843; d. Barbour 1889. Son of Samuel and Elisabeth (Davis) Morrall; father b. Pendleton Co., settled Randolph Co., W. Va. 1830's; grandson of Samuel and Mary (Davis) Morrall, b. Pendleton Co.

MORRALL, Elisabeth (Harper)
Sympathizer; arrested 5-62. $14,840/9,982; b. Pendleton Co. 1818, wife of Lair D. Morrall; Presbyterian; d. Barbour 1893. Daughter of Henry and Elisabeth (Mouse) Harper; father b. Pendleton Co., W. Va. settled Randolph Co., W. Va. 1820's; granddaughter of Jacob Harper, b. Pendleton Co.; great-granddaughter of Philip Harper, immigrant from Germany.

MORRISON, William McKendra
Enl. Co. D, 20th Va. Cav. 5-1-63; paroled Staunton, Va. 5-14-65. Farmer; $5,260/1,372; b. Lewis Co., W. Va. 1817; m. 1) Cassandra Arnold; 2) Susan Fox 1866; d. Barbour 1882. Parents b. Va.

MORRISON, William Columbus
Enl. Co. D, 20th Va. Cav. 5-1-63; POW Beverly, W. Va. 10-31-64; d. of pneumonia Camp Chase, Ohio 2-65. Farmer; $5,260/1,372 (parents); b. Barbour 1844, son of William and Cassandra (Arnold) Morrison.

MURPHY, Herbert
Enl. Co. A, 25th Va. Inf. 5-31-61; wd. Alleghany 12-13-61; wd. in side Fredericksburg 12-13-62; POW Beverly, W. Va. 5-2-63; released on oath 5-17-63 and returned to company; POW Spotsylvania 5-12-64; released on oath 5-17-65; brother Andrew served Co. H, 62nd Va. Mtd. Inf. (CSA); brother-in-law *Albert Price served Co. D, 20th Va. Cav. (CSA); brothers-in-law *William and *Isaac Price served Co. F, 15th W. Va. Inf. (USA). Farmer; $0/95; b. Randolph Co., W. Va. 1841; Baptist; Democrat; came to Barbour 1850's where m. Amanda Jane Price 1859; returned to Randolph Co. after war where d. 1890. Son of David and Hester (Knotts) Murphy; father b. Culpepper Co., Va., settled Monongalia Co., W. Va. then Randolph Co.; grandson of David and Lydia (Roe) Murphy, b. Culpepper Co., settled Barbour.

MURPHY, Amanda Jane (Price)
Sympathizer; hid wounded Confederate soldiers in her home; carried mail across lines; brother *Albert served Co. D, 20th Va. Cav. (CSA); brothers *William and *Isaac and brother-in-law *Levi Cross served Co. F, 15th W. Va. Inf. (USA). $0/95; b. Barbour 1844, wife of Herbert Murphy; living Randolph Co., W. Va. 1880. Daughter of William and Ann (Poling) Price. Cf. Unionists.

MURPHY, William H.
Enl. Co. E, 62nd Va. Mtd. Inf. 8-26-62; des. Barbour 2-63; drafted 2-65, never inducted. Farmer; $6,000/948 (parents); b. Barbour 1840; Democrat; m. Amanda Keller 1865; living Barbour 1880. Son of Harrison and Elisabeth (Martin) Murphy; father b. Culpepper Co. Va.; grandson of David and Lydia (Roe) Murphy.

MURPHY, Martha Anne
Sympathizer; arrested 12-64 charged with cutting telegraph lines and spying; d. of typhoid fever Wheeling Prison, W. Va. 12-22-64. $1,800/235 (parents); b. Barbour 1838. Daughter of John and Martha (Snyder) Murphy; granddaughter of William and Leander (Poe) Murphy, b. Fauquier Co., Va., settled Taylor Co, W. Va., 1800.

MURPHY, Eugenius
Enl. Co. A, 25th Va. Inf. 5-28-61; des. 12-7-61 with five others and gave information on Confederate positions to Federal commander; all five described

by former comrades as "the meanest cusses outside the polluted gates of Hell." Farmer; $1,800/235 (parents); b. Barbour 1840, brother of Martha Anne; m. Mary E. Gainer 1862; moved to Randolph Co., W. Va. after war where living 1880.

MURPHY, William Riley
Sympathizer; arrested 6-61. Farmer; $1,800/230 (parents); b. Taylor Co., W. Va. brother of Martha Anne; refugee in Monterey, Va.; m. Hester A. Myers 1869; post-war German Baptist minister; living Barbour 1880.

MUSTOE, William
Listed Barbour Light Horse; enl. Co. H, 31st Va. Inf. 5-14-61; prom. to sgt. 7-62; in hospital 4- to 12-63; wd. 1864. Farmer; $2,500/658 (parents); b. Highland Co., Va. 1837; Methodist-Episcopal Church; m. Martha E. Byrd 1867; living Barbour 1880. Son of Chambers and Margaret (Gibson) Mustoe; father b. Bath Co., Va., settled Barbour 1838; grandson of Anthony Mustoe, b. Va., settled Augusta Co., then Bath Co.

MUSTOE, David
Enl. Co. F, 11th Va. Cav. 3-31-62 (may have enlisted 5-61 while company was at Philippi); AWOL 2-7-63; in hospital 6-13-63; POW Beverly, W. Va. 1-17-64; took oath and released Wheeling, W. Va. 2-2-64. Farmer; $2,500/658 (parents); b. Barbour 1840, brother of William; m. Ester M. Davis; moved to Mo. after war where d. 1903.

MUSTOE, James H.
Enl. Co. F, 11th Va. Cav. 3-31-62 (may have enlisted 5-61 while company was at Philippi); on roll to 2-63, des. Farmer; $2,500/658 (parents); b. Barbour 1840, brother of William; m. Nancy J. Hudkins 1864; moved to Mo. 1870's where living 1880.

NICOLA, John
Sympathizer; arrested 3-31-62 and sent to Camp Chase, Ohio on charges of "aiding rebels; guerrillas at his house;" released on oath 11-4-62; son-in-law *Johnson Wilson served Co. H, 31st Va. Inf. (CSA). Miller; $0/26; b. Preston Co., W. Va. 1800; m. Mary Boger; came to Barbour 1854; d. 1874. Son of Jacob and Catherine (Willet) Nicola; father b. Somerset Co., Pa., settled Preston Co.

NICOLA, Jacob B.
Sympathizer; arrested 3-31-62 with father and sent to Camp Chase, Ohio; released on oath 11-4-62. $500/500; b. Preston Co., W. Va. 1833, son of John

and Mary (Boger) Nicola; m. 1) Susan ____; 2) Mary Guseman Hays 1882; returned to Preston Co. after war where living 1880.

NUTTER, John
Enl. Co. H, 62nd Va. Mtd. Inf. 8-1-62; wd. New Market 5-15-64. Farmer; $1,500/300 (parents); b. Barbour 1841; Baptist; m. Rachel Angeline Thompson 1867; living Barbour 1880. Son of Charles and Malinda (Cross) Nutter; grandson of George and Delila (Costilow) Nutter; great-grandson of Christopher and Rebecca (Morehead) Nutter, settled Barbour from Harrison Co., W. Va.; great-great-grandson of Thomas and Sarah (Godwin) Nutter; Thomas b. Sussex Co., N.J., moved to Augusta Co., Va., then Fayette Co., Pa., then Harrison Co.

NUTTER, David C.
Sympathizer; arrested and sent to Camp Chase, Ohio 6-61; released; arrested 1862; Farmer; $1,200/540; b. Barbour 1827; Methodist-Episcopal Church; m. 1) Louisa ____; 2) Seruptia Hinkle 1862; moved to Harrison Co., W. Va. after 1880 where d. 1894. Son of George and Delila (Costilow) Nutter.

NUTTER, Burrell
Enl. Co. E, 62nd Va. Mtd. Inf. 8-26-62; served as color guard; wd. New Market 5-15-64; POW Barbour 12-11-64; released Camp Chase, Ohio 5-10-65. Farmer; $2,500/866 (parents); b. Barbour 1842; Methodist-Episcopal Church; living Barbour 1880. Son of Daniel and Harriet Nutter.

NUTTER, Theodore
Enl. Co. E, 62nd Va. Mtd. Inf. 8-26-62; wd. New Market 5-15-64; wd. Cold Harbor 6-1-64; paroled Staunton, Va. 5-1-65. Farmer; $2,500/866 (parents); b. Barbour 1845, brother of Burrell; Methodist-Episcopal Church; m. Melissa Wolf 1870; living Barbour 1880.

OVERFIELD, John H.
Enl. Co. D, 20th Va. Cav. 6-1-63; not listed subsequent rolls. Tenant; $0/242; b. Harrison Co., W. Va. 1846; Methodist-Protestant Church; m. Nancy Holt 1872; living Barbour 1880. Son of John and Susan (Trimble) Overfield; grandson of Peter and Deborah Overfield, settled Harrison Co. from Bath Co., Va.

PARKS, Granville
Com. Lt., 169th W. Va. Mil.; later arrested on charges of secessionist sympathies. Cf. Unionists.

PAUGH, Wilson M.
Listed cpl., Barbour Light Horse; enl. Co. D, 20th Va. Cav. 5-1-63; detailed as orderly to regimental commander; on roll to 12-31-64; NFR; brother-in-law *William Benson served same company. Tenant; $0/53 (mother); b. Barbour 1838; Methodist-Episcopal Church. Son of Isaac and Elisabeth (Methaney) Paugh; grandson of Joseph and Jane Paugh, b. N.J., settled Barbour.

PAUGH, Harrison D.
Enl. Co. H, 31st Va. Inf.; wd. Second Bull Run 8-29-62; wd. Antietam 9-17-62; in hospital 1863; NFR. Farmer; $2,500/337 (parents); b. Barbour 1841; Methodist-Protestant Church. Son of John and Ann (McPherson) Paugh; grandson of Joseph and Jane Paugh.

PAUGH, Richard
Enl. Co. K, 31st Va. Inf. 5-29-61; des. 7-61; NFR. Farmer; $0/42; b. Va. 1827; m. Harriet ____.

PAYNE, John W.
Sympathizer; led crowds at Philippi searching for anti-secessionist delegates returning from Richmond Convention 4-61; refugee in Wythe Co., Va. during war; sons *Nathan and *William Unionists; son *James served Co. N, 6th W. Va. Inf. (USA); son-in-law *William Price Unionist. Bank clerk; $0/150; b. Barbour 1803; Baptist; m. Margaret Bennett 1823; living Barbour 1880. Son of Henry and Elisabeth (Smith) Payne, b, Va.

PHILIPS, Franklin Coontz
Enl. Co. K, 31st Va. Inf. 5-29-61; prom. to sgt.; POW New Creek 9-28-64; released on oath 10-31-64, but returned to regiment; sur. Appomattox 4-9-65, one of five men in company. Farmer; $1,500/754 (parents); b. Barbour 1840; m. Ingabe N. Harris 1865; moved to Randolph Co., W. Va. after war where d. 1914. Son of William and Delila (Coontz) Philips; grandson of John and Bethiel (Wells) Philips; great-grandson of Thomas and Susanna (Kittle) Philips. Cf. Unionists.

PHILIPS, Obediah
Enl. Co. H, 31st Va. Inf. 5-14-61; prom. to sgt.; des. 4-19-62; brother *Simeon Unionist; brother-in-law *Jacob Philips Confederate sympathizer. Farmer; $300/3,391; b. Barbour 1831; m. Elisabeth ____; d. Barbour 1863. Son of Joseph and Mary (Harris) Philips; grandson of John and Bethiel (Wells) Philips.

PHILIPS, Courtland
Enl. Co. K, 31st Va. Inf. 5-18-61; wd. in foot Freeman's Ford 8-22-62; wd. in hip and POW Gettysburg 7-3-63; exch.; hospitalized 4- to 8-64; POW Strasburg, Va. 10-19-64; released 6-16-65. Tenant $0/54; b. Barbour 1842; m. Amanda Harris 1869; moved to Tucker Co., W. Va. 1870's; moved to Md. after 1880's where d. 1925. Son of _____ and Zipporah Philips; grandson of Joseph and Mary (Harris) Philips.

PHILIPS, Granville
Enl. Co. E, 62nd Va. Mtd. Inf. 8-26-62; des. 11-4-62; enl. Co. N, 6th W. Va. Inf. (USA). Cf. Unionists.

PHILIPS, Bennett
Enl. Co. K, 31st Va. Inf. 5-29-61; des. 7-61; brother *Asa Philips served Co. I, 17th W. Va. Inf. (USA). Farmer; $500/235; b. Barbour 1820; m. 1) Ann Fitzwater 1841; 2) Almira (Philips) Philips (widow of *Isaac N. Philips) 1884; moved to Preston Co., W. Va. after war, then to Tucker Co., W. Va. where d. 1912. Son of Jacob and Sarah (Bennett) Philips; grandson of Isaac and Elisabeth (Kittle) Philips; great-grandson of Thomas and Susannah (Kittle) Philips.

PHILIPS, Osa (Johnson)
Sympathizer; distributed illegal mail; brother *Peter Johnson Confederate sympathizer. $1,000/217 (husband); b. Barbour 1816; Methodist-Episcopal Church; m. 1) James Philips 1838; 2) Isaac Poling 1878; d. Barbour 1887. Daughter of John and Elisabeth (Poling) Johnson; father b. Loudoun Co., Va.; granddaughter of Robert and Mary (Vannoy) Johnson; grandparents b. N.J., settled Loudoun Co., then Barbour.

PHILIPS, John Riley
Enl. Co. K, 31st Va. Inf. 5-18-61; appointed Lt.; 7-1-61; indicted for treason Wheeling, W. Va. 9-20-61; wd. Greenbrier 10-2-61; wd. and cited for bravery Alleghany 12-13-61; elec. Capt. 5-1-62; wd. in hip Gaines Mill 6-27-62; wd. in shoulder Antietam 9-17-62; wd. in leg Fredericksburg 12-13-62; wd. right hip Wilderness 5-6-64; disch. for disability 2-24-65; paroled 7-3-65. Farmer; $1,000/217 (parents); b. Barbour 1839; Methodist-Episcopal Church; Democrat; m. Elisabeth E. Parks 1867; author of A History of Valley Furnace; d. Barbour 1894. Son of James and Osa (Johnson) Philips; grandson of Jacob and Sarah (Bennett) Philips.

PHILIPS, Jesse Jr.
Enl. Co. H, 62nd Va. Mtd. Inf. 6-1-62; des. 10-23-62; son *Issac served Co. A, 1st W. Va. Cav. (USA). Farm laborer; $0/4; b. Barbour 1819; m. Mary Wilt

1838; living Barbour 1880. Son of Jesse and Margaret (Kittle) Philips; grandson of Henry and Lydia (Harris) Philips; great-grandson of Thomas and Susannah (Kittle) Philips.

PHILIPS, John E.
Enl. Co. H, 62nd Va. Mtd. Inf. 6-1-62; des. 10-23-62; enl. Co. A, 1st W. Va. Cav. (USA). Son of Jesse and Mary (Wilt) Philips. Cf. Unionists.

PHILIPS, Jacob B.
Sympathizer; arrested 6-63 and killed by guards; brother-in-law *Obediah Philips served Co. H, 31st Va. Inf. (CSA); brother-in-law *Simon Philips Unionist. Farmer; $2,000/470; b. Barbour 1828, brother of Jesse Jr.; m. Mary Ann Philips.

PHILIPS, Albert G.
Enl. Co. K, 31st Va. Inf. 5-19-61; des. 7-61; rejoined regiment; des. 4-19-62; rejoined regiment; on roll to 10-63. Farmer; $1,000/619 (parents); b. Barbour 1841; m. Almarine Philips 1865; moved to Tucker Co., W. Va. 1870's where listed Civil War verterans 1890; d. 1912. Son of Black and Nancy (Philips) Philips; grandson of Jesse and Margaret (Kittle) Philips.

PHILIPS, George H.
Enl. Co. D, 62nd Va. Mtd. Inf.; transf. to Co. A 4-15-63; POW Beverly, W. Va. 2-8-65; released on oath 6-13-65; brother-in-law Perry Hillyard served Co. A, 25th Va. Inf. (CSA); brother-in-law *Jesse Teter Unionist. Farmer; $1,500/615; b. Barbour 1818; Baptist; m. Martha Hillyard 1847; living Barbour 1880. Son of Thomas and Margaret (Westfall) Philips; grandson of Thomas and Susannah (Kittle) Philips.

PHILIPS, William A.
Enl. Co. C, 20th Va. Cav. 6-9-63; des. 3-1-64. Farmer; $1,500/165; b. Barbour 1822, brother of George; m. Elisabeth Coffman 1842; living Barbour 1880.

PHILIPS, George Coffman
Enl. Co. C, 20th Va. Cav. 6-9-63; listed sick Chimborazo Hospital, Va. 11-63; des. and sur. Philippi 2-9-65; released on oath 3-7-65. Farmer; $1,500/165 (parents); b. Barbour 1846, son of William and Elisabeth (Coffman) Philips; m. Alice _____; living Barbour 1870.

PHILIPS, Andrew Jackson
Enl. Co. K, 31st Va. Inf. 5-29-61; des. 7-61; brother-in-law John E. Canfield served Co. E, 62nd Va. Mtd. Inf. (CSA). Farmer; $500/104 (parents); b.

Barbour 1835; m. Rebecca Cross Philips 1865; living Barbour 1880. Son of John and Eleanor (Smith) Philips.

PICKENS, John
Listed Barbour Light Horse. Farmer; $23,782/3,300; b. Highland Co., Va. 1828; m. Hannah A. Corder 1847; living Barbour 1880. Son of Alexander and Margaret (Wiley) Pickens, b. Highland Co.; grandson of Alexander and Sarah Pickens, b. Va.

PITZER, John M.
Enl. Co. K, 31st Va. Inf. 6-22-61; des. 4-19-62; re-enlisted Co. E, 62nd Va. Mtd. Inf. 12-20-62; returned to 31st Va. Inf. 2-8-64; POW; bother-in-law *Henry Shaffer served Co. K, 31st Va. Inf. (CSA). Farmer; $500/65; b. Marion Co., W. Va. 1822; m. 1) Elisabeth Shaffer 1841; 2) Elisabeth Hartman 1865; d. Barbour 1868. Son of John and Hetta (Martin) Pitzer; grandson of John and Elisabeth (Price) Pitzer, settled Marion Co., then Barbour 1830's.

PITZER, Richard George
Enl. Co. K, 31st Va. Inf. 6-22-61; des. 4-19-62; re-enlisted Co. E, 62nd Va. Mtd. Inf. 12-20-62; returned to 31st Va. Inf. 2-8-64. Farmer; $500/65 (parents); b. Barbour 1844, son of John and Elisabeth (Shaffer) Pitzer; m. Matilda Summerfield 1866; living Barbour 1880.

POLING, William Black
Enl. Co. H, 31st Va. Inf. 10-3-61; disch. for old age 6-16-62. Farmer; $995/56; b. Allegany Co., Md. 1805; m. Jane Philips 1830; d. Barbour 1860's; son of Samuel and Margaret (Black) Poling; grandson of Martin and Rachel Poling, b. Md.; great-grandson of Samuel and Margaret (Greitje) Poling; Samuel b. Del., settled Allegany Co., Md., then Barbour.

POLING, Valentine Black
Enl. Co. E, 62nd Va. Mtd. Inf. 8-26-62; on roll to 12-31-64; father-in-law *Jacob Bennett and brother-in-law *Jonathon Bennett served Co. K, 31st Va. Inf. (CSA). Farmer; $100/71; b. Barbour 1832, son of William B. and Jane (Philips) Poling; m. Rachel Bennett 1854; d. Barbour 1898.

POLING, Samuel
Enl. Co. H, 31st Va. Inf. 5-14-61; prom. to cpl.; prom. to sgt.; KIA Spotsylvania 5-12-64. Farmer; $995/56 (parents); b. Barbour 1833, brother of Valentine.

POLING, Hamilton
Enl. Co. E, 62nd Va. Mtd. Inf. 8-26-62; des.; drafted 3-65, never inducted; father-in-law *Peter Johnson Confederate sympathizer; brother-in-law *Martin Johnson served same company. Farmer; $0/0; b. Barbour 1834; m. Almira Johnson 1860; post-war Methodist-Protestant minister; Democrat; d. Barbour 1912. Son of Roger and Mary (Sturm) Poling; parents b. Barbour; grandson of Martin and Rachel Poling.

POLING, Nicolas
Enl. Co. K, 31st Va. Inf. 5-18-6 prom. to sgt.; appointed Lt. 1-1-62; wd. in shoulder Gettysburg 7-3-63; wd. Mechanicsville 5-20-64; wd. in groin and POW Winchester 9-19-64; exch. 10-31-64; listed unfit for duty; paroled 5-11-65. Farmer; $400/256 (parents); b. Barbour 1838, brother of Hamilton; Methodist-Protestant Church; m. Catherine Smith 1868; NFR.

POLING, Alexander
Enl. Co. E, 62nd Va. Mtd. Inf. 8-26-62; on roll to 12-31-64; NFR. Farmer; $2,500/624 (parents); b. Barbour 1840; Methodist-Protestant Church. Son of David and Margaret (Sturm) Poling; father b. Barbour; grandson of Martin and Lettice Ann (Marsh-Wright) Poling; grandfather b. Md.; great-grandson of Martin and Rachel Poling.

POLING, Jesse B.
Enl. Co. E, 62nd Va. Mtd. Inf. 8-26-62; paroled Staunton, Va. 5-10-65; brothers Nicolas and Jacob served Co. C, 11th W. Va. Inf. (USA); brothers-in-law *Henry Lohr and *Alpheus Digman served 31st Va. Inf. (CSA). Farmer; $1,400/225 (parents); b. Barbour 1838; m. 1) Barbara Ann Lohr 1857; 2) Martha Schoonover Hill; d. Barbour 1883. Son of Amos and Sarah (Sturm) Poling; parents b. Barbour; grandson Martin and Lettice Ann (Marsh-Wright) Poling.

POLING, Israel
Enl. Co. E, 62nd Va. Mtd. Inf. 8-26-62; POW Barbour 8-23-63; released on oath Rock Island Prison, Ill. 6-16-65. Farmer; $500/266; b. Barbour 1830; Methodist-Episcopal Church; joined Methodist-Protestant Church after war; Democrat; m. Rachel Limbers 1847; living Barbour 1880. Son of Barnett and Jane (Sturm) Poling; father b. Md.; grandson of William and Rachel (Poling) Poling; b. Md.; great-grandson of Peter and Hannah Poling, b. Del., settled Barbour.

POLING, Isaac S.
Enl. Co. E, 62nd Va. Mtd. Inf. 8-26-62; POW 12-7-63; exch. 6-64; on roll to 12-31-64. Farmer; $1,500/506 (parents); b. Barbour 1832, brother of Israel;

Methodist-Episcopal Church; Democrat; m. Louisa May Rogers 1867; d. Barbour 1897.

POLING, Franklin A.
Enl. Co. H, 31st Va. Inf. 5-14-61; des. 4-62; four of wife's brothers served Confederate army. Farmer; $500/170; b. Barbour 1838, brother of Israel; Methodist-Episcopal Church; m. Francis Golden 1858; moved to Wood Co., W. Va. after war where living 1880.

POLING, Nathaniel
Enl. Co. K, 31st Va. Inf. 5-18-61; prom. to sgt.; appointed Lt. 5-61; failed to win election as Lt. 5-1-62 and re-enlisted as a pvt.; wd. in ribs Gettysburg 7-3-63; wd. and POW Winchester 9-19-64; exch.; sur. Harrisonburg, Va. 5-2-65; stepfather *James Dilworth Capt., 169th Va. Mil.; brothers-in-law *Wesley Bean and *Mortimer Johnson served Confederate army. Farmer; $1,300/1,063; b. Barbour 1833; m. 1) Alzina Ervine 1865; 2) Barbara Goff 1870; 3) Mary Ann Hershman Boyles (widow of *Marshall Boyles); d. Barbour 1897. Son of James and Elisabeth (Vannoy) Poling; parents b. Barbour; grandson of Martin and Mary (Poling) Poling, b. Md.; great-grandson of Peter and Hannah Poling.

POLING, Emory
Sympathizer; brother-in-law *Solomon Gainer served Co. K, 31st Va. Inf. (CSA). Farmer; $1,200/565; b. Barbour 1834, brother of Nathaniel; Methodist-Episcopal Church, joined Southern Methodists after war; m. Catherine Gainer; d. Barbour 1866.

POLING, Elam T.
Enl. Co. K, 31st Va. Inf. 5-18-61; AWOL 9-26-61; wd. Spotsylvania 5-12-64; hospitalized to 8-64; POW Harpers Ferry 9-30-64; released on oath 1-16-65. Farmer; $2,000/220; b. Barbour 1841, brother of Nathaniel; Methodist-Episcopal Church; m. Minerva Stalnaker 1865; NFR.

POLING, Anthony
Enl. Co. K, 31st Va. Inf. 5-18-61; des. 7-61; brother-in-law *Elliott Stalnaker served Co. E, 62nd Va. Mtd. Inf. (CSA). Farmer; $0/200; b. Barbour 1839; m. Sarah Stalnaker 1857; living Barbour 1880. Son of Jonathon and Jane (Gainer) Poling, b. Barbour; grandson of Martin and Mary (Poling) Poling.

POLING, Euram
Enl. Co. K, 31st Va. Inf. 5-18-61; des. 7-61; re-enlisted Co. E, 62nd Va. Mtd. Inf. 8-26-62; POW 12-6-62; exch. 4-63; d. Harrisonburg, Va. 8-20-64. Farmer;

$500; b. Barbour 1831; m. Alanish Poling. Son of Martin and Margaret (Payne) Poling; father b. Md.; grandson of Samuel Poling, b. Md., settled Barbour.

POLING, Jaspar
Enl. Co. E, 62nd Va. Mtd. Inf. 8-26-62; POW Barbour 12-6-62; exch. 4-63; des. 11-23-63, took oath and returned to Barbour; four of wife's brothers served Confederate army. Tenant; $0/127; b. Barbour 1840, brother of Euram; m. Elisabeth Golden 1859; moved to Wood Co., W. Va. after war where living 1880.

POST, George W.
Enl. Co. D, 20th Va. Cav. 7-1-63; prom. to sgt. 7-1-63; POW Highland Co., Va. 12-12-63; released on oath Camp Chase, Ohio 1-16-65; brother Stephen and brother-in-law Albinius Marple served in same company; brother-in-law Stewart Queen Unionist. Farmer; $9,500/2,750 (parents); b. Upshur Co., W. Va. 1840; came to Barbour during war; m. Mary A. Woodford 1860; living Barbour 1880. Son of Daniel and Mary (Hevener) Post; grandson of Abraham and Christina Post; parents and grandparents b. Va.

PRICE, Albert
Enl. Co. D, 20th Va. Cav. 4-1-64; POW Fisher's Hill 9-23-64; exch. or escaped; POW Beverly, W. Va. 10-31-64; released on oath Camp Chase, Ohio 6-12-65; sister *Amanda Murphy secessionist; brothers *William and *Isaac and brother-in-law *Levi Cross served Co. F, 15th W. Va. Inf. (USA). Farmer; $2,000/500 (parents); b. Barbour 1847; Methodist-Episcopal Church; m. Sophia Boner 1866; living Barbour 1880. Son of William and Ann (Poling) Price. Cf. Unionists.

RADABAUGH, Benjamin J.
Listed Barbour Light Horse; brother-in-law *Simon Radabaugh served 133rd W. Va. Mil. (USA). Farmer; $1,850/362; b. Barbour 1838; m. 1) Elisabeth Radabaugh 1859; 2) Mary E. Martin 1866; moved to Ohio 1870's. Son of Benjamin and Fanny (Post) Radabaugh; parents b. Hardy Co., W. Va.; grandson of George and Sarah (Heavener) Radabaugh; great-grandson of Adam and Catherine (Simmons) Radabaugh.

RADCLIFF, John Cather
Enl. Co. D, 20th Va. Cav. 5-1-63; sur. Staunton, Va. 5-10-65. Farmer; $3,000/1,040; b. Barbour 1810; m. Letitia Leach 1835; d. Barbour 1860's. Son of Jonathon and Sarah (Cather) Radcliff, b. Harrison Co., W. Va.; grandson of John and Catherine (Coburn) Radcliff.

RADCLIFF, John Milton
Listed cpl., Barbour Light Horse; arrested Vinton Co., Ohio 9-62 on charges of "uttering treasonable language;" released; enl. Co. D, 20th Va. Cav. 5-1-63; prom. to sgt. 7-1-63; des. 10-5-64; sur. Weston, W. Va. 12-3-64; released on oath 12-5-64. Farmer, $3,000/1,040 (parents); b. Barbour 1841, son of John and Letitia (Leach) Radcliff; m. Margaret Callahan 1867; moved to Roane Co., W. Va. after war where living 1880.

REED, Nathan I.
Listed Barbour Light Horse; drafted 2-65, never inducted; pension claim for wartime service 169th Mil. rejected 1902; brother John and brothers-in-law *Jacob Pringle and Joseph Engle served Co. F, 11th W. Va. Inf. (USA). Farmer; $0/140; b. Barbour 1836; m. Mary Ann Catherine Engle 1857; moved to Roane Co., W. Va. 1876 where d. 1907. Son of Alexander and Mary Ann (Reeder) Reed, b. Barbour; grandson of David Reed; Reeds of Barbour largely descended from early settlers of Virginia; earliest known ancestor is Andrew Reed of 17th Century Westmoreland Co., Va.

REED, Daniel
Listed Barbour Light Horse; enl. Co. H, 62nd Va. Mtd. Inf. 8-1-62; prom. to cpl.; POW Randolph Co., W. Va. 12-6-63; exch. 10-31-64; on roll to 12-64; brother-in-law *Granville Evic served Co. H, 31st Va. Inf. (CSA). Farmer; $0/40 (parents); b. Barbour 1840, brother of Nathan; m. Jemima Evic 1861; moved to Roane Co., W.Va. after war where living 1880.

REED, William
Listed Barbour Light Horse. Farmer; $1,500/224 (parents); b. Barbour 1836; m. Lucinda ____; moved to Taylor Co., W. Va. after war where living 1880. Son of Ashabell and Louvina (Pepper) Reed; father b. Loudoun Co., Va.; grandson of Jonathon and Sarah Reed.

REED, Peter T.
Enl. Co. H, 62nd Va. Mtd. Inf. 8-1-62; prom. to sgt. 3-24-63; POW Randolph Co., W. Va. 12-6-63; released on oath Fort Delaware 6-20-65. Tenant; $0/85 (parents); b. Barbour 1842; m. Sarah Shaw 1865; moved to Upshur Co., W. Va. after war where living 1880. Son of Alpheus and Jane Reed; parents and grandparents b. Va.

REED, Milton D.
Secretary, pro-secessionist meeting Stewart's Run, Barbour 2-61; listed Barbour Light Horse; brother-in-law *Felix Stewart listed Barbour Light Horse. Carpenter; $408/140 (mother); b. Barbour 1836; Baptist; Republican; m.

Margaret J. Stewart 1866; living Barbour 1880. Son of Peter and Ruth (Lewellyn) Reed; parents and grandparents b. Va.

REED, Philander
Listed Barbour Light Horse; drafted 2-65, never inducted; NFR. Farmer; $0/183; b. Barbour 1839, brother of Milton; Methodist-Episcopal Church; m. Lucinda Euritt 1859.

REED, James W. D.
Enl. Co. D, 20th Va. Cav. 6-1-63; on roll to 12-31-64. Farmer; $0/144 (parents); b. Barbour 1839; m. Sarah C. Reed 1866; living Barbour 1880. Son of Madison and Samantha Reed; grandson of Peter and Sarah Reed.

REED, John W.
Enl. Co. D, 20th Va. Cav. 6-1-63; on rolls to 12-31-64; NFR. Farmer; $0/144 (parents); b. Barbour 1843, brother of James.

REED, Margaret
Sympathizer; carried information to Confederate army on Union troops at Buckhannon, W. Va. before Jones-Imboden Raid; arrested soon after for waving rebel flag; sent to Wheeling Prison; NFR; brother-in-law *William Bartlett listed Barbour Light Horse; brother-in-law *Simon Radabaugh served 133rd W. Va. Mil. Laborer; $0/0 (parents); b. Rockingham Co., Va. 1840. Daughter of William and Lucinda Reed, b. Va., settled Barbour 1850's.

REED, John C.
Enl. Co. B, 17th Va. Cav. 8-25-62; transf. to Co. K; prom. to sgt. 1-63; reduced to ranks 10-1-63; wd. Moorefield, W. Va. 8-7-64. Farmer; $775/130 (parents); b. Randolph Co., W. Va. 1845; Methodist-Episcopal Church; m. Sarah Cleavenger 1867; moved to Upshur Co., W. Va. after war where d. 1900. Son of Anthony and Rachel Reed; parents and grandparents b. Va.

REED, Alexander D.
Enl. Co. A, 46th Btln. Va. Cav. 7-11-63; des. same day; drafted into Co. F, 7th W. Va. Inf. (USA). Cf. Unionists.

REEDER, Gideon J.
Enl. Co. E, 62nd Va. Mtd. Inf. 8-26-62; paroled Staunton, Va. 5-10-65; NFR; brother-in-law Amos Wilfong served 133rd W. Va. Mil.. Farmer; $791/400 (father); b. Barbour 1844. Son of William and Rachel (Martin) Reeder; father b. Barbour; grandson of Thomas and Margaret Reeder; grandfather b. Loudoun Co., Va.; great-grandson of Joseph and Barbara Reeder of Loudoun Co.

REGER, Albert Gallatin
Listed Capt., Barbour Greys (Co. H, 31st Va. Inf.); com. Major, 25th Va. Inf. 5-61; listed sick 10-61; resigned commission 3-25-62; refugee Fluvanna Co., Va. serving as tax collector; brother John chaplain, 7th W. Va. Inf. (USA). Attorney; $1,200/270; b. Upshur Co., W. Va. 1818; Methodist-Episcopal Church; Democrat; m. Mary Seay 1844; State Senator 1852-1856; returned to Upshur Co. 1880's where d. 1892. Son of Abram and Sarah (Brake) Reger; grandson of John and Elisabeth (West) Reger; great-grandson of Jacob and Barbara (Crites) Reger, immigrants from Germany to Hardy Co., W. Va. 1765, settled Upshur Co. 1780's.

REGER, Anthony
Sympathizer; vice-president of pro-secessionist meeting Stewart's Run, Barbour 2-61. Farmer; $3,000/1,174; b. Upshur Co., W. Va. 1822; Methodist-Episcopal Church; m. 1) Mary Ann Ours Lynch 1836; 2) Rachel Pickens 1836; 3) Catherine Bradley Long 1894; returned to Upshur Co. where d. 1904. Son of Abram and Mary (Reeder) Reger; grandson of Jacob and Barbara (Crites) Reger.

REGER, Gideon
Sympathizer; gave pro-secessionist speeches mass meeting Stewart's Run, Barbour 2-61; listed Barbour Light Horse; drafted 2-65, never inducted; NFR. Farmer; $3,000/1,174 (parents); b. Upshur Co., W. Va. 1840, son of Anthony and Rachel (Pickens) Reger; Methodist-Episcopal Church.

REGER, Jacob
Enl. Co. H, 62nd Va. Mtd. Inf. 8-1-62; brother-in-law *Johnson Ward Unionist. Farmer; $7,300/1,378; b. Upshur Co., W. Va. 1806, brother of Anthony; m. Nancy Martin 1826; d. Barbour 1870's.

REGER, Martin
Listed Barbour Light Horse; brother-in-law *Abraham Burner served Co. H, 62nd Va. Mtd. Inf. (CSA); brother-in-law George Burner served Bat. E, 1st W. Va. Art. (USA). Tenant; $7,300/1,378; b. Upshur Co., W. Va. 1835, son of Jacob and Nancy (Martin) Reger; m. Martha Burner 1857; returned to Upshur Co. 1870's where living 1880.

REGER, Ezra
Listed Barbour Light Horse; enlisted Co. H, 62nd Va. Mtd. Inf.; promoted to Lt. 4-4-63; d. of disease Augusta Co. 3-4-64. Farmer; $7,300/1,378; born Upshur Co. 1842, brother of Martin.

REGER, Joel
Listed Barbour Lighthorse; enl. Co. H, 62nd Va. Mtd. Inf.; prom. to cpl. 4-5-63; des. 1864. Farmer; $7,300/1,378; b. Upshur Co., W. Va. 1844, brother of Martin; m. Jennifer Ann Chrislip 1864; moved to Calif. 1870's where d. 1921.

REGER, Granville J.
Enl. Co. C, 14th Va. Cav. 5-16-62 while student at Loch Willows Academy, Churchville, Va.; prom. to sgt. 10-1-62; wd. Droop Mountain 11-10-63; prom. to Lt; commanding company 2-64; sur. Appomattox 4-9-65, only man in company. Student; $0/0; b. Upshur Co., W. Va. 1840; moved to Mo. after war where m. Martha _____. Son of Isaac and Eliza (McCoy) Reger; grandson of Abram and Mary (Reeder) Reger.

RIDER, Michael Morgan
Enl. Co. H, 31st Va. Inf. 5-14-61; prom. to sgt.; elec. Lt. 5-1-62; wd. Gaines Mill 6-27-62; d. 7-2-62; brother Bennett served as U. S. Postmaster in Harrison Co. during war. Farmer; $4,000/987 (parents); b. Bath Co., Va. 1837; Methodist-Episcopal Church. Son of John Wesley and Sarah (Bird) Rider, b. Bath Co.; grandson of John and Sarah (Matheny) Rider, b. Bath Co., settled Barbour 1840's.

RIDGEWAY, Amos
Enl. Co. K, 31st Va. Inf. 4-26-63; hospitalized for fever 10-63; paroled Staunton, Va. 5-15-65. Mechanic; $0/220 (parents); b. Monongalia Co., W. Va. 1846; came to Barbour 1850's; m. Mary Ann Snider; moved to Pendleton Co., W. Va. after war, then to Ind. where d. 1903. Son of Henry and Eliza (Ridgeway) Ridgeway; grandson of Noah and Jane (Horton) Ridgeway, b. Monongalia Co.; great-grandson of Lott and Catherine (Frazer) Ridgeway; immigrants to Pa., settled Monongalia Co.

RILEY, Patrick
Enl. Co. H, 31st Va. Inf. 5-14-61; wd. in thigh McDowell 5-8-62; wd. Sommerville Ford 9-14-63. Boarder; $0/0; b. Ireland 1834; came to Barbour 1850's with wife Bridgett; moved to Randolph Co., W. Va. after war where living 1880.

ROBINSON, Smith D.
Enl. Co. A, 25th Va. Inf. 5-24-61; POW 4-62; exch. 5-62; re-enlisted Co. C, 3rd Va. State Line; re-enlisted Co. D, 19th Va. Cav. 3-8-63; POW Highland Co., Va. 12-17-64; released on oath 6-12-65; father Unionist; brothers *Thomas and *Simon served U.S. Army. $0/62 (parents); b. Barbour 1838; m. Drusilla Duckworth 1867; living Barbour 1880. Son of *James and Lydia Robinson. Cf. Unionists.

ROBINSON, Allison D.
Enl. Co. H, 31st Va. Inf. 5-14-61; KIA Antietam 9-17-62 while color bearer. Tenant; $0/146 (parents); b. Barbour 1838. Son of Henry and Emily (Reed) Robinson; parents b. Barbour; grandson of Job and Nancy (Thompson) Robinson; grandfather b. N.J.; great-grandson of James and Elisabeth (Davis) Robinson, b. N.J., settled Barbour.

RUSSELL, Charles W.
Sympathizer; arrested Beverly, W. Va. 7-63 by men of 10th W. Va. Inf.; sent to Camp Chase, Ohio; of twelve men arrested with him, only Russell and two others survived imprisonment. Toll keeper; $1,400/125; b. Frederick Co., Va. 1819; settled Lewis Co., W. Va. where m. Mary E. Collett 1847; came to Barbour 1850's; settled Randolph Co., W. Va. after war where d. 1885. Son of Isaac and Matilda (Perry) Russell, b. Va.

RYMER, George
Enl. Co. H, 31st Va. Inf.   Farmer; $2,000/267; b. Va. 1819; Methodist-Protestant Church; m. Virginia Jane Matheny 1837; d. Barbour 1870's.

SARGEANT, Hezekiah
Listed Barbour Light Horse; enl. Co. A, 18th Va. Cav. 6-1-62; POW Randolph Co., W. Va. by men of 8th Ohio Cav. 2-19-65; released Cumberland, Md. 9-22-65, the last Confederate from Barbour to be released from captivity. Farmer; $1,000/518; b. Barbour 1825; Methodist-Protestant Church; m. 1) Ruhamy Wells 1849; 2) Anna Day 1858; 3) Permelia ____; moved to Webster Co., W. Va. after war where living 1880. Son of John and Margaret Sargeant, b. Pa., settled Barbour.

SARGEANT, Jacob
Enl. Co. D, 20th Va. Cav. 6-27-63; des. and sur. Buckhannon, W. Va. 8-23-64. Farmer; $1,500/625 (parents); b. Barbour 1844; m. 1) Letha E. Simon 1858; 2) Alina F. Simpson 1873; moved to Lewis Co., W. Va. 1870's where living 1880. Son of Isaiah and Barbara (Shockey) Sargeant; parents b. Va.; grandson of John and Margaret Sargeant.

SEARS, Alexander
Enl. Co. E, 62nd Va. Mtd. Inf. 8-26-62; prom. to cpl.; d. 1864; brothers John, *James, *Israel and *Abel served Union Army. Laborer; $0/0; b. Hardy Co., W. Va. 1838. Son of John and Ruth (Orrihood) Sears. Cf. Unionists.

SEE, David Kennison
Sympathizer; arrested 1863; d. of typhoid fever Camp Chase, Ohio 3-17-64. Tenant; $0/139; b. Hardy Co., W. Va. 1838; United Brethren Church; came to

Barbour 1840's; m. Mary Jane Thorn. Son of Adam and Amelia (Randall) See; grandson of Adam See, b. Hardy Co.

SHAFFER, Jacob
Sympathizer; farm burned by Unionists, livestock seized; drafted 3-65, never inducted; brother Henry Unionist. Farmer; $1,000/195; b. Preston Co., W. Va. 1818; German Baptist; came to Barbour 1841 when m. Margaret Wilson; d. Barbour 1906. Son of Arnold and Susanna Shaffer; father b. Germany; grandson of John Peter and Elisabeth Shaffer, immigrants from Germany, settled Preston Co. 1790's.

SHAFFER, Henry
Enl. Co. K, 31st Va. Inf. 6-22-61; des. next day; POW Barbour 7-61; released on oath 10-61; drafted 3-65, never inducted; brother-in-law *John Pitzer served same company. Farmer; $N/G; b. Barbour 1834; Baptist; m. Nancy Pitzer 1852; moved to Tucker Co., W. Va. after war where listed Civil War veterans 1890; d. 1913. Son of John and Mary (Nestor) Shaffer; father b. Germany; grandson of John Peter and Elisabeth Shaffer.

SHANK, Jacob
Sympathizer; home burned by Federal soldiers; brothers-in-law *Andrew, *Burton and *Lafayette Gall served Confederate army; brother-in-law *George Gall Unionist. Farmer; $1,200/326; b. Berkeley Co. 1815; Methodist-Episcopal Church, joined Southern Methodists after war; came to Barbour 1840's where m. Susan Gall 1849; living Barbour 1899. Son of John and Elisabeth (Johnson) Shanks, b. Va.; grandson of Christian Shank, immigrant from Germany.

SHARPS, Minor S.
Enl. Co. D, 20th Va. Cav. 4-1-64; des. and POW near Harper's Ferry 7-64, claiming to have been conscripted; sent to Elmira Prison; released on oath 5-29-65; brother *James served Co. K, 17th W. Va. Inf. (USA). Farmer; $3,000/719 (parents); b. Taylor Co., W. Va. 1846; m. Rosanna Sluss 1867; NFR. Son of William and Matilda (Bailey) Sharps. Cf. Unionists.

SHAW, Hezekiah
Listed Barbour Light Horse; enl. Co. C, 4th W. Va. Cav. (USA). Cf. Unionists.

SHIREMAN, Harrison
Enl. Co. E, 62nd Va. Mtd. Inf. 8-26-62; des. 2-22-63. Tenant; $0/30 (parents); b. Hardy Co., W. Va. 1837; m. Elisabeth Fitzwater; living Barbour 1880. Son of John and Sarah (Hines) Shireman, b. Hardy Co., settled Barbour 1840's; grandparents b. Va.

SHIREMAN, Ferguson
Enl. Co. E, 62nd Va. Mtd. Inf. 8-26-62; sur. Philippi 5-15-65. Tenant; $0/30 (parents); b. Hardy Co., W. Va. 1842, brother of Harrison; returned to Hardy Co. after war where living 1880.

SHIREMAN, Martin
Enl. Co. E, 62nd Va. Mtd. Inf. 8-26-62; des. 1864 and returned to Barbour. Tenant; $0/30 (parents); b. Hardy Co., W. Va. 1843, brother of Harrison; m. Ingaby Johnson 1867; living Barbour 1880.

SIMON, Allen
Listed Barbour Light Horse; brother *Andrew Lt. 169th W. Va. Mil.; brother-in-law *Francis Payne Unionist; NFR. Farmer; $6,000/2,208 (parents); b. Barbour 1840; m. Susan ____. Son of Abram and Mary (Yeager) Simon. Cf. Unionists.

SIMON, Abraham
President, pro-secessionist meeting Stewart's Run, Barbour 2-21; enl. Co. H, 10th W. Va. Inf. (USA). Cf. Unionists.

SMITH, Hiram
Enl. Co. H, 31st Va. Inf.; prom. to sgt.; des. Staunton, Va. 8-62 and returned to Barbour; drafted 2-65, never inducted; brother George served Co. F, 11th W. Va. Inf. (USA); father-in-law *John Johnson and brother-in-law *Richard Johnson Confederate sympathizers; brother-in-law *William Johnson served Confederate Army. Farmer; $1,000/220; b. Barbour 1822; Baptist; m. 1) Eunice ____; 2) Lucinda Johnson 1863; 3) Rebecca Parsons 1880; living Barbour 1880. Son of Henry and Catherine (Lesher) Smith; grandson of William and Barbara (Sprinstone) Smith, b. Va., settled Barbour 1790's.

SMITH, Israel
Enl. Co. E, 62nd Va. Mtd. Inf. 8-26-62; on roll to 12-31-64; brother Levi served Co. D, 62nd Va. Mtd. Inf. (CSA). Farmer; $1,200/331 (mother); b. Barbour 1833; moved to Gilmer Co., W. Va. 1840's; returned to Barbour 1850's; moved to Roane Co., W. Va. after war where living 1880. Son of John and Elisabeth (Philips) Smith; grandson of William and Barbara (Springston) Smith.

SMITH, James W.
Listed Barbour Light Horse; enl. Co. C, 17th Va. Cav. 8-19-62; paroled Clarksburg, W. Va. 9-30-65; NFR; brothers-in-law *Charles and *Reuben Walden listed Barbour Light Horse. Farmer; $200/63; b. Hardy Co., W. Va. 1829; came to Barbour 1850's where m. Mildridge Walden 1856. Son of John. and Sarah (Harris) Smith, b. Va.

STALNAKER, Samuel
Sympathizer; arrested 1-13-63 as hostage for *James Trayhern; released 1-24-64. Farmer; $4,000/824; b. Randolph Co., W. Va. 1797; Methodist-Episcopal Church; m. Isabella Ryan 1818; d. Barbour 1868. Son of William and Margaret (McHenry) Stalnaker; grandson of Jacob and Elisabeth (Truby) Stalnaker, settled Randolph Co. from Augusta Co., Va. 1770's; great-grandson of Samuel Stalnaker, immigrant from Germany.

STALNAKER, Harrison Hagans
Enl. Co. E, 62nd Va. Mtd. Inf.; prom. to Lt.; wd. Fisher's Hill 9-23-64; paroled Staunton, Va. 5-13-65; father-in-law William Parsons Confederate sympathizer; brothers-in-law Nelson, Joseph and David Parsons served Confederate army; brother-in-law *Henry Auvil Confederate sympathizer. Farmer; $4,000/824 (parents); b. Barbour 1827; Methodist-Episcopal Church, joined Southern Methodists after war; m. Catherine Parsons 1850; d. Barbour 1909. Son of James and Elisabeth (Neptune) Stalnaker; grandson of William and Margaret (McHenry) Stalnaker.

STALNAKER, Elliott
Enl. Co. E, 62nd Va. Mtd. Inf. 8-26-62; prom. to Lt.; AWOL 9-1-64; POW Pocahontas Co., W. Va. 3-9-65; brother-in-law *Anthony Poling served Co. K, 31st Va. Inf. (CSA). Tenant; $0/202; b. Barbour 1836, brother of Harrison; Methodist-Episcopal Church; m. Susan Poling 1856; d. Barbour 1870's.

STALNAKER, Wesley W.
Enl. Co. K, 31st Va. Inf. 5-18-61; d. of disease 10-1-61. Farmer; $3,000/967 (parents); b. Barbour 1845. Son of Henry and Hannah (Vannoy) Stalnaker; grandson of Samuel and Elisabeth (Ryan) Stalnaker.

STARKER, Adam O.
Listed Barbour Light Horse; enl. Co. A, 18th Va. Cav. 6-1-61; POW Oakland, Md. 8-15-63 as horse thief; released on oath Camp Chase, Ohio 1-6-64; brothers-in-law *Isaac and *Elliott Jones served Co. H, 31st Va. Inf. (CSA); brothers-in-law Edward Love and John Fisher served 10th W. Va. Inf. (USA). Farmer; $0/140; b. Kanawha Co., W. Va. 1832; came to Barbour 1850's where m. Susan Jones 1856; d. 1860's. Son of Samuel and Eleanor Starker; descendant of Adam Starker, settled Kanawha 1780's.

STEMPLE, James W.
Enl. Co. K, 31st Va. Inf. 5-24-61; des. 7-61; brother-in-law *John Hoffman served Co. F, 3rd W. Va. Inf. (USA); brothers-in-law *James, *Thomas and *George Fry served Barbour Home Guard. Farmer; $2,000/600 (parents); b.

Barbour 1843; Methodist-Protestant Church; m. Mary Ellen Hoffman 1861; d. Barbour 1895. Son of William and Mary (Pifer) Stemple, b. Preston Co., W. Va.; grandson of Martin and Margaret (Montgomery) Stemple; great-grandson of Godfrey and Margaret (Boyles) Stemple; Godfrey immigrant from Germany, settled Preston Co. from Md. 1780's.

STEMPLE, Adamrin J.
Enl. Co. K, 31st Va. Inf. 5-24-61; des. 7-61; brother-in-law *James Sturm served same company; brothers-in-law Isaac and Jaspar Martiney served Co. B, 10th W. Va. Inf. (USA). Farmer; $1,000/433 (parents); b. Barbour 1840; m. 1) Margaret Martiney 1856; 2) Cinderella Martiney 1864; moved to Calhoun Co., W. Va. during war where d. 1889. Son of Isaac and Catherine (Wilt) Stemple; father b. Preston Co., W. Va.; grandson of John and Sarah (Boyles) Stemple; great-grandson of Godfrey and Margaret (Boyles) Stemple.

STEWART, Felix G.
Listed Barbour Ligh Horse; joined U. S. Army. Cf. Unionists.

STEWART, John J.
Enl. Co. K, 31st Va. Inf. 5-24-61; indicted for treason 9-20-61; prom. to sgt-major 6-1-61; wd. Port Republic 6-9-62; KIA Fort Stedman 4-2-65. Farmer; $1,000/132 (parents); b. Harrison Co. 1835. Son of John and Elisabeth Stewart; parents and grandparents b. Va.

STEWART, James J.
Enl. Co. K, 31st Va. Inf.; NFR. Farmer; $1,000/132 (parents); b. Harrison Co., W. Va. 1844, brother of John.

STOCKWELL, Isaac
Enl. Co. K, 31st Va. Inf. 6-22-61; wd. in neck Second Bull Run 8-29-62; brigade teamster 1863; POW Barbour 1-18-65; released Camp Chase, Ohio 5-16-65; brother *Henry served Co. B, 3rd W. Va. Cav. (USA); brother Abraham served Home Guard, Taylor Co. Tenant; $0/54; b. Taylor Co., W. Va. 1832; came to Barbour 1840's; m. Sarah Nestor 1855; moved to Gilmer Co., W. Va. after war where living 1880. Son of Joseph and Rachel Stockwell; father b. Monongalia Co., W. Va.; grandson of John and Matilda Stockwell, settled Monongalia from Fayette Co., Pa.

STOCKWELL, Sarah (Nestor)
Sympathizer; refugee in eastern Va. Tenant; $0/54; b. Barbour 1839, wife of Isaac; living Gilmer Co., W. Va. 1880. Daughter of John and Sarah (Auvil) Nestor; granddaughter of Jacob and Margaret (Durr) Nestor, immigrants from Germany, settled Frederick Co., Md., then Barbour.

STOCKWELL, William Wesley
Enl. Co. K, 31st Va. Inf. 5-18-61; des.; re-enlisted Co. E, 62nd Va. Mtd. Inf. 8-36-62; POW and exch., returning to 31st Va. Inf. 5-18-64; wd. right foot Hatcher's Run 2-7-65; hospitalized Staunton, Va. where paroled 5-16-65; NFR. Farmer; $0/95 (parents); b. Taylor Co., W. Va. 1845, brother of Isaac.

STONE, Emmanuel
Enl. Co. H, 31st Va. Inf. 5-14-61; wd. Gettysburg 7-3-63; des. and sur. Weston, W. Va. 2-9-65, took oath and sent home; NFR; three brothers of wife served Confederate army. Farm laborer; $0/0; b. Monongalia Co., W. Va. 1840; came to Barbour 1850's; m. Elisabeth Humphries 1861. Son of James and Jane Stone.

STREETS, Nathaniel
Enl. Co. K, 31st Va. Inf. 5-24-61; des. and POW 11-7-61; drafted 3-65, never inducted; pension claim for war-time service 169th Mil. rejected 1902; father-in-law *Nathan McDaniel served Co. B, 17th W. Va. Inf. (USA). Farmer; $800/285 (parents); b. Barbour 1842; Methodist-Protestant Church; m. Caroline McDaniel 1865; moved to Preston Co., W. Va. 1870's where living 1880. Son of George and Catherine Streets; father b. Barbour; grandson of Brooks and Margaret (McDonald) Streets, b. Md., settled Barbour.

STRICKLER, Isaac Harrison
Enl. Co. E, 62nd Va. Mtd. Inf.; prom. to sgt.; prom. to Lt.; resigned commission 1864; refugee in Buckingham Co., Va. running store with *Lair D. Morrall; brother Jacob served Confederate militia; mother-in-law *Elizabeth Jarvis Confederate sympathizer; brother-in-law *William Jarvis served Co. H, 31st Va. Inf. (CSA); brother-in-law *Michael Crim Confederate sympathizer; brother-in-law *Nathan Taft Unionist. Merchant and slave owner; $5,750/10,516; b. Page Co., Va. 1816; Baptist; Democrat; came to Barbour where m. Margaret J. Jarvis 1850; d. Barbour 1885. Son of Joseph and Mary (Miley) Stricker; father b. Shenandoah Co. Va.; grandson of Joseph and Barbara (Harnick) Strickler, b. Va.; great-grandson of Abraham Strickler, immigrant from Germany.

STURM, Henry
Com. Capt., Co. K, 31st Va. Inf. 5-61; indicted for treason 9-20-61; lost election for company commander 5-1-62 and dropped from roll; refugee in eastern Va. for rest of war. Farmer; $1,800/415; b. Barbour 1794; m. 1) Elisabeth Stalnaker 1815; 2) Susan Johnson Alexander 1824; d. Barbour 1882. Son of Nicolas and Elisabeth (Gainer) Sturm; grandson of John and Magdelena (Dellinger) Sturm, immigrated from Germany to Md., settled Berkeley Co., Va.

STURM, John M.
Enl. Co. H, 31st Va. Inf. 5-18-61; des.; said to have joined Imboden's brigade, but no record found. Farmer; $100/161; b. Barbour 1833, son of Henry and Susan (Alexander) Sturm; m. Margaret Halsey; moved to Harrison Co., W. Va. after war, then to Calhoun Co., W. Va. where d. 1915.

STURM, Lair Dayton
Sympathizer; arrested Calhoun Co., W. Va. 3-17-64 with *James Sturm on charges of murdering Union soldier; sent to Camp Chase, Ohio; released; drafted 3-65, never inducted. Farmer; $1,880/415 (parents); b. Barbour 1845, brother of John M.; m. Amanda Coontz 1868; living Barbour 1880.

STURM, Henry Jr.
Elec. Justice of the Peace 1863; arrested 2-29-64 by Home Guard on charges of shooting at Union soldiers and sent to Camp Chase, Ohio; son of Nicolas and Ann (McClaskey) Sturm. Cf. Unionists.

STURM, Michael
Sympathizer; arrested 2-29-64 with *Henry Sturm Jr. and sent to Camp Chase, Ohio. Farmer; $2,000/230 (parents); b. Barbour 1842, brother of Henry Jr.; m. Susan Miller 1865; living Barbour 1880.

STURM, Jacob
Guerrilla; indicted for treason Wheeling 9-20-61; POW 1862 and sent to Camp Chase, Ohio. Farmer; $1,800/319; b. Barbour 1816, brother of Capt. Henry Sturm; m. Lettice Ann Poling 1835; d. 1860's.

STURM, Martin Van Buren
Sympathizer; said to have been imprisoned. Farmer; $250/220; b. Barbour 1836, son of Jacob and Lettice (Poling) Sturm; m. Magdalena Stalnaker 1857; moved to Calhoun Co., W. Va. during war where d. 1879.

STURM, James W.
Enl. Co. K, 31st Va. Inf. 10-7-61; des. 4-19-62; arrested Calhoun Co., W. Va. 4-17-64 with *Lair D. Sturm, charged with murder of Federal soldier; sent to Camp Chase, Ohio, then City Point for exchange, but held until released 6-6-65; brother-in-law *Adamrin Stemple served same company. Tenant; $0/23; b. Barbour 1839, brother of Martin; m. Christina Stemple 1857; moved to Calhoun Co. 1870's where d. 1874.

STURM, Amos K.
Enl. Co. K, 31st Va. Inf. 5-18-61; prom. to cpl.; wd. Port Republic 6-9-62; transf. to Co. E, 62nd Va. Mtd. Inf. 8-26-62; on roll to 12-31-64. Farmer; $1,800/319 (parents); b. Barbour 1841, brother of Martin; m. Susan Woodford 1867; moved to Calhoun Co., W. Va. after war.

SURGHNOR, Thompson
Listed Lt., Barbour Light Horse; transf. to Upshur Greys (Co. B, 25th Va. Inf.); POW Laurel Hill 7-13-61; exch.; prom. to sgt.-major 11-1-61; transf. to Co. A, 18th Va. Cav. 6-1-62; wd. in head and POW Beverly, W. Va. 10-31-64; d. next day; father-in-law *Daniel Capito Unionist; brothers-in-law John and Christian Capito served 17th W. Va. Inf. (USA). Editor, Barbour Jeffersonian ("In violence of utterances, it was probably surpassed by no newspaper in Richmond."); $1,600/200; b. Loudoun Co., Va 1821; Catholic; came to Barbour 1850's where m. Martha Capito 1854. Son of James and Harriet (Peyton) Surghnor; parents b. Va.

TALBOTT, Robert Dowden
Sympathizer; vice-president of pro-secessionist mass meeting Hackers Creek, Barbour 1-61; brother *Elam Unionist; in addition to sons listed below, son David served Co. D, 20th Va. Cav. (CSA); father-in-law *John Howe Woodford and brother-in-law *Jacob Woodford Confederate sympathizers; brothers-in-law *George Gall and *John Harvey Woodford Unionists. Farmer; $5,000/1,478; b. Barbour 1801; Baptist; m. 1) Mary Woodford 1818; 2) Clara W. Brandon 1881; d. Barbour 1885. Son of Richard and Margaret (Dowden) Talbott; father b. Fairfax Co., Va. said to have been first permanent settler in Barbour; grandson of William and Elisabeth (Cottrill) Talbott; grandfather immigrant from England.

TALBOTT, John
Sympathizer; arrested 12-27-62 and sent to Camp Case, Ohio; released 7-13-63. Tenant; $0/216; b. Barbour 1819, son of Robert and Mary (Woodford) Talbott; m. 1) Leah Ann Robinson 1837; 2) Susan _____; living Barbour 1870.

TALBOTT, Jacob
Enl. Co. D, 20th Va. Cav. 6-27-63; detailed as teamster; NFR. Tenant; $0/216 (parents); b. Barbour 1842, son of John and Leah Ann (Robinson) Talbott.

TALBOTT, Richard T.
Sympathizer; elec. Justice of the Peace 1860, refused to serve after 1861; member of committee drawing up pro-secessionist resolutions Philippi 3-61; drafted 2-65, never inducted. Farmer; $13,000/2,335; b. Barbour 1821, brother

of John; Baptist; moved to Ill. 1840's where m. Margaret Weber 1849, returning to Barbour same year; moved to Kan. after 1880 where d. 1901.

TALBOTT, Salathiel
Enl. Co. E, 62nd Va. Mtd. Inf. 8-26-62; transf. to Co. D, 20th Va. Cav. 3-1-64; on roll to 12-31-64; brothers-in-law *Samuel, *George amd *Demetrius Dickenson served Co. E, 62nd Va. Mtd. Inf. (CSA). Farmer; $5,000/1,478 (parents); b. Barbour 1832, brother of John; m. Rachel Dickenson 1854; believed to have been forced to flee county after war for role in Trayhern kidnapping; moved to Mo. where d. 1911.

TALBOTT, Francis Marion
Enl. Co. E, 62nd Va. Mtd. Inf. 8-26-62; KIA Leading Creek, Gilmer Co, W. Va.. during Jones-Imboden Raid. Mechanic; $5,000/1,478 (parents); b. Barbour 1835, brother of John; Baptist; m. Elisabeth Linger.

TALBOTT, Perry M.
Enl. Co. H, 31st Va. Inf. 5-14-61; POW Alleghany 12-13-61; exch. Vicksburg 8-62; POW Gettysburg 7-3-63; exch. 1864; paroled Appomattox 4-9-65, one of two men in company. Farmer; $3,500/400; b. Barbour 1845, brother of John; Baptist; m. Mary C. Teter; moved to Upshur Co., W. Va. after war d. 1935.

TALBOTT, Robert R.
Sympathizer; pro-secessionist speaker mass meeting Stewarts Run, Barbour 2-6; step-brother *George Thompson, Capt., Co. H, 31st Va. Inf. (CSA); brother-in-law *John Stickle served Co. B, 6th W. Va. Inf. (USA). Farmer; $600/286; b. Barbour 1823; Methodist-Episcopal Church; Democrat; m. June Virginia Stickle 1844; moved to Upshur Co., W. Va. after 1880 where d. 1900. Son of Elisha and Mildred (Stephens) Talbott; father slave owner, b. Barbour; grandson of Richard and Margaret (Dowden) Talbott.

TALBOTT, Isaac D.
Enl. Co. E, 62nd Va. Mtd. Inf. 8-26-62; prom. to sgt.; father-in-law *Robert Mitchell Unionist; brothers-in-law *Josiah and *Middleton Mitchell served Co. F, 15th W. Va. Inf. (USA). Farmer; $1,800/260; b. Barbour 1825, brother of Robert R.; Methodist-Episcopal Church, joined Baptist Church after war; m. Martha Mitchell 1841; living Barbour 1899.

TALBOTT, Elam
Sympathizer; hid Confederate soldiers on furlough; drafted 2-65, never inducted. Farmer; $300/100; b. Barbour 1829, brother of Robert R.; Methodist-Episcopal Church; m. Keziah Proudfoot 1852; living Barbour 1880.

TALBOTT, Irwin F.
Enl. Co. E, 62nd Va. Mtd. Inf. 8-26-62; des. 11-2-62; drafted 2-65, never inducted. Farmer; $4,000/872; b. Barbour 1843, half-brother of Robert R.; Methodist-Episcopal Church; m. 1) Sabina___; 2) Angelina Lance 1880; living Barbour 1880. Son of Elisha and Elisabeth (Losh) Talbott.

TALBOTT, Enoch H.
Listed Barbour Light Horse. Tenant; $400/80; b. Barbour 1834; m. Susan O'Neal 1855; living Barbour 1880. Son of David and Ruth (Wamsley)Talbott; grandson of Richard and Margaret (Dowden) Talbott.

TALBOTT, Irwin Benton
Enl. Co. E, 62nd Va. Mtd. Inf. 8-26-62; prom. to sgt.; wd. Mt. Crawford 3-1-65; paroled Staunton, Va. 6-3-65. Farmer; $800/150; b. Barbour 1836; Baptist; m. Virginia Caroline Zinn 1870; moved to Randolph Co., W. Va. 1886 where d. 1932. Son of Zachariah and Mary (Ellison) Talbott; grandson of Richard and Margaret (Dowden) Talbott.

TEETS, Noah
Enl. Co. K, 31st Va. Inf. 5-28-61; des. 7-61; drafted 2-65, never inducted. $N/G; b. Hardy Co., W. Va. 1840; came to Barbour 1861; m. Julian Oster 1862; living Barbour 1880. Son of Joseph and Ann Teets; parents and grandparents b. Va.

TETER, Jacob
Sympathizer; arrested and sent to Camp Chase, Ohio 4-28-63; released 5-63; brother *Joseph Unionist; four sons in Union army; son-in-law *David Foy Unionist. Farmer; $2,500/409; b. Barbour 1803; Methodist-Episcopal Church; m. Mary Coberly 1824; d. Barbour 1879. Son of Jacob and Elisabeth (Holden) Teter. Cf. Unionists.

TETER, James
Listed Barbour Light Horse; arrested and sent to Camp Chase, Ohio 4-29-63; transferred to Fort Delaware 7-14-63; released and enl. Co. F, 15th W. Va. Inf. (USA). Cf. Unionists.

TETER, Worthington William
Listed Barbour Light Horse; father Unionist. $1,800/695 (parents); b. Barbour 1849; m. Martha V. Teter 1879; d. Barbour 1906. Son of *Jesse and Elisabeth (Philips) Teter. Cf. Unionists.

THOMPSON, John R.
Enl. Co. H, 62nd Va. Mtd. Inf.; prom. to cpl. 3-1-62; prom. to Lt. 4-3-63; on roll to 12-31-64; step-son *Granville Evic served Co. H, 31st Va. Inf. Tenant;

$0/208; b. Barbour 1823; m. Lydia Ours Evic 1858; moved to Gilmer Co., W. Va. 1870's where living 1880. Parents b. Va.

THOMPSON, George T.
Enl. Co. H, 31st Va. Inf. 5-1-61; appointed Lt. 5-61; wd. and cited for bravery Alleghany 12-13-61; elec. Capt. 5-1-62; wd. Cedar Mountain 8-9-62; POW Stephenson's Depot 7-20-64; released on oath 1-20-65; returned to Barbour and killed by Home Guards; brother *Commodore Capt. 169th W. Va. Mil.; stepbrothers *Isaac and *Irwin Talbott served Co. E, 62nd Va. Mtd. Inf. (CSA); brother-in-law *James Woodford Unionist. Farmer; $3,000/411; b. Barbour 1835, son of Hezekiah and Sarah (Logan) Thompson. Cf. Unionists.

THOMPSON, Albert J.
Enl. Co. H, 31st Va. Inf. 5-14-61; prom. to cpl.; POW Pocahontas Co., W. Va. 4-24-62; d. of consumption Camp Chase, Ohio 6-62. Coal digger; $200/70 (parents); b. Pendleton Co., W. Va. 1843. Son of George and Catherine Thompson, b. Pendleton Co., settled Barbour 1850's; grandson of Joseph and Rachel Thompson, b. Va.

THOMPSON, John P.
Sympathizer; elec. Justice of the Peace 1860, refused to serve after 1861; drafted 3-65, never inducted; wife Confederate sympathizer; father-in-law *Daniel Capito Unionist; brothers-in-law John and Christian Capito served 17th w. Va. Inf. (USA); brother-in-law *Alpheus Wilson Unionist. $0/2,498 (parents); b. Barbour 1826; Baptist; Democrat; m. *Helen Captito 1864; moved to Ohio after 1880. Son of Henry and Mary (Perrell) Thompson; father Baptist minister, b. Barbour; grandson of Henry and Rebecca Thompson, settled Barbour from Monongalia Co., W. Va. 1780's.

THOMPSON, Andrew J.
Enl. Co. H, 31st Va. Inf. 5-14-61; prom. to cpl.; wd. Port Republic 6-9-62; POW Monocasy River 7-15-64; released on oath 5-15-65. Farm servant; $0/60; b. Barbour 1840; m. Osa England 1858; living Barbour 1880. Son of Joseph and Sarah Thompson; parents and grandparents b. Va.

THOMPSON, Josiah
Enl. Co. H, 31st Va. Inf. 5-14-61; POW Greenbrier 10-3-61; exch.; d. of disease 2-6-63. Tenant; $0/90 (parents); b. Barbour 1835. Son of William and Catherine (Moorehead) Thompson; grandson of William and Elisabeth Thompson, b. Fauquier Co., Va., settled Barbour.

THOMPSON, George W.
Enl. Co. H, 31st Va. Inf. 5-14-61; POW Alleghany 12-13-61; exch.; KIA Port Republic 6-9-62. Tenant; $0/90 (parents); b. Barbour 1836, brother of Josiah.

THORNHILL, J. D. C. "Champ"
Enl. Barbour Light Horse; re-enlisted Co. H, 31st Va. Inf. 12-10-61; des. 4-19-62; re-enlisted Co. H, 62nd Va. Mtd. Inf. 6-1-62; transf. to Co. A, 18th Va. Cav.; KIA Winchester 9-19-64; "Comrade Champ Thornhill, as brave a man as ever lived, was shot in the forehead and killed so quickly that he sat perfectly rigid in death until removed;" three brothers of wife served Confederate army. Miller and slave owner; $700/100; b. Rappahannock Co., Va. 1833; came to Barbour 1850's where m. Mariah Boner 1855. Son of Thomas and Margaret Thornhill; father b. Rappahannock Co.; grandson of Thomas Thornhill, b. Orange Co., Va.

THORNHILL, Francis
Sympathizer; arrested and sent to Camp Chase, Ohio; released; drafted 3-65, never inducted. Farmer; $1,050/535; b. Rappahannock Co., Va. 1821; m. Elisabeth Willis; came to Barbour 1850's; Presbyterian; Democrat; d. Barbour 1873. Son of Bryant and Frances (Jones) Thornhill, b. Rappahannock Co.; grandson of Bryant and Thomson Thornhill, b. Va.

THRASHER, Jacob
Listed Barbour Light Horse; POW Philippi 6-3-61; released on oath; re-enlisted Co. C, 26th Va. Cav. 6-23-63; POW 7-23-63; brother Isaac served Co. B, 19th Va. Cav (CSA); brother Richard served Co. F, 33rd Va. Inf. (CSA), KIA Second Bull Run; brother George served Bat. E, 1st W. Va. Art. (USA); brother David served Co. L, 6th W. Va. Cav. (USA). Farm laborer; $0/0; b. Hardy Co., W. Va. 1837; came to Barbour 1850's; listed as patient Weston Insane Asylum, W. Va. 1880. Son of Jacob and Mary Isabel (Roberts) Thrasher, b. Va.

TRIMBLE, Andrew
Sympathizer; home burned 2-8-62; drafted 3-65, never inducted; brother *William Unionist. Farmer; $0/0; b. Pendleton Co., W. Va. 1823; Methodist-Episcopal Church; came to Barbour 1830's; m. Barbara Marple 1842; d. Barbour 1882. Son of John and Sarah (Waybright) Trimble. Cf. Unionists.

TRIMBLE, Alvin Draper
Enl. Co. D, 20th Va. Cav. 5-1-63; POW 7-7-63 and sent to Camp Chase, Ohio; transf. to Fort Delaware 7-14-63. $0/0 (parents); b. Barbour 1846, son of Andrew and Barbara (Marple) Trimble; Methodist-Episcopal Church; m. Amanda J. Stewart 1868; d. Barbour 19-.

UTTERBACK, John
Enl. Co. A, 25th Va. Inf. 1862; re-enlisted or transf. to Co. D, 20th Va. Cav. 5-1-63; wd. three times; POW and released on oath Clarksburg, W. Va. 4-14-65; brother George served Co. F, 3rd W. Va. Inf. and Co. K, 17th W. Va. Inf. (USA). Farm laborer; $0/0; b. Fauquier Co., Va. 1847; Methodist-Episcopal Church; came to Barbour 1850's; moved to Fairfax Co., Va. after war were d. 1929. Son of John Wesley and Juliet (Bailey) Utterback; grandson of Nathanial and Mary (Tomblin) Utterback, b. Fauquier Co.

VALENTINE, Andrew
Enl. Co. E, 62nd Va. Mtd. Inf.; prom. to Lt.; POW Barbour Co. 3-21-64 by Home Guard; exch. 2-26-65; paroled Mt. Jackson, Va. 4-21-65; mother-in-law *Sarah Digman Confederate sympathizer. Farmer; $800/105; b. Randolph Co., W. Va. 1835; Democrat; came to Barbour 1850's where m. Rachel Digman 1858; returned to Randolph Co. 1870's where d. 1887. Son of James and Elisabeth Valentine; grandson of John and Amelia Valentine, b. Va.

VAN METER, Benjamin Franklin
Enl. Co. K, 31st Va. Inf. 6-22-61; d. of disease 1-17-62. Farmer; $700/302; b. Rockingham Co., Va. 1823; m. Catherine _____. Van Meters settled Shenandoah Valley 1730's.

VARNER, John F.
Enl. Co. H, 31st Va. Inf. 3-8-62; des. 12-17-64; released on oath Beverly, W. Va. 12-22-64; wife had three brothers in Confederate army, two in Union army. Farmer; $0/15; b. Pendleton Co., W. Va. 1825; came to Barbour 1850's from Harrison Co., W. Va.; m. Mary Isner 1856; living Barbour 1880. Son of Christian and Rachel (Simmons) Varner; father b. Highland Co., Va.; grandson of George and Elisabeth (Eckhardt) Varner, b. Highland Co.; great-grandson of Adam Varner, settled Highland Co.

WAGGONER, David
Enl. Co. H, 31st Va. Inf. 5-14-61; POW Tucker Co., W. Va. 7-15-61; by one account KIA, other account moved to Doddridge Co., W. Va. after war; brothers-in-law *Anthony Moore and *Page D. Carter served Confederate army; brother-in-law *Adam Vanscoy served Co. F, 3rd W. Va. Cav. (USA). Tenant; $0/175 (parents); b. Rockingham Co., Va. 1844; came to Barbour 1850's from Augusta Co., Va. Son of Jacob and Margaret (Dietrick?) Waggoner; parents and grandparents b. Va.

WALDEN, Charles Wesley
Listed Barbour Light Horse; enl. Co. H, 62nd Va. Mtd. Inf. 4-7-63; prom. to cpl.; POW Beverly, W. Va. 10-31-64; released Camp Chase, Ohio 5-10-65. Farm

laborer; $800/163 (parents); b. Prince William Co., Va. 1840; came to Barbour 1840's; moved to Kan. after war. Son of John and Sophia (Saunders) Walden, b. Henrico Co., Va., settled Barbour 1830's; grandson of George and Elisabeth Walden, b. Caroline Co. Va.; great-grandson of Charles and Mary (Lee) Walden, b. Stafford Co., Va.

WALDEN, Reuben Ellis
Listed Barbour Light Horse. Store clerk; $0/0; b. Prince William Co., Va. 1842, brother of Charles; m. Mary Ann Zinn 1866; living Barbour 1880.

WALLACE, John C.
Enl. Co. H, 31st Va. Inf. 5-14-61; des. 10-63; enl. Bat. H, 1st W. Va. Art. (USA). Cf. Unionists.

WARD, McKinsey
Sympathizer; arrested 1863 for "secessionist activities;" released on oath; brothers Aquilla, *James and *Johnson Unionists; son-in-law Foster Hinkle served Co. I, 3rd W. Va. Cav. (USA); brother-in-law Frederick Sandridge served Co. H, 31st Va. Inf. (CSA); brother-in-law Luther Sandridge served Co. F, 15th W. Va. Inf. (USA). Farmer; $3,000/310; b. Upshur Co., W. Va. 1808; Methodist-Episiscopal Church; m. 1) Phoebe Heavener 1828; 2) Sophia Sandridge Neely Whitely (widow of *Alexander Whitely) 1864; returned to Upshur Co. after war where d. 1888. Son of Job and Tabitha (Cummins) Ward. Cf. Unionists.

WARD, John B.
Enl. Co. H, 62nd Va. Mtd. Inf. 8-1-62. Farmer; $0/217; b. Upshur Co., W. Va. 1833, son of McKinsey and Phoebe (Heavener) Ward; Methodist-Episcopal Church; m. 1) Jane Waugh 1856; 2) Adele ____; moved to Mineral Co., W. Va. where living 1880.

WARD, Martin Van Buren
Listed Barbour Light Horse; enl. Co. H, 62nd Va. Mtd. Inf. 4-7-63; des. 10-13-64; brothers-in-law *Abraham and *Fletcher Hall served Confederate army. Farmer; $800/166; b. Upshur Co., W. Va. 1836, brother of John B.; Methodist-Episcopal Church; m. Olive Hall 1857; returned to Upshur Co. after war where living 1880.

WELCH, John
Listed Barbour Light Horse; brother *Samuel served Co. H, 10th W. Va. Inf. (USA); brother-in-law *William Callahan Confederate sympathizer; brother-in-law *Lewis Rohr Unionist; brother-in-law John Houston served Co. A, 14th W.

Va. Inf. (USA). Tenant; $500/310; b. Barbour 1830; Methodist-Episcopal Church; m. Amanda Watson Devers 1858; d. Barbour 1881. Son of Samuel and Margaret (Ratcliff) Welch. Cf. Unionists.

WELCH, Benjamin Franklin
Sympathizer; arrested and sent to Camp Chase, Ohio 4-29-63; transf. to Fort Delaware 7-14-63 where d. 9-14-63. Farmer; $9,000/1,505 (parents); b. Barbour 1846, brother of John; Methodist-Episcopal Church.

WELLS, Anthony H.
Enl. Co. H, 31st Va. Inf. 5-14-61; disch. for disability 7-18-62; re-enlisted Co. E, 62nd Va. Mtd. Inf. 8-26-62; transf. to Co. H 4-1-63. Farmer; $1,000/441; b. Barbour 1827; Methodist-Episcopal Church; m. Sarah ____; moved to Gilmer Co., W. Va. 1870's where living 1880. Son of Daniel and Elisabeth Wells; father b. Barbour; grandson of Phineas and ____ (Kittle) Wells, Baptist minister settled Barbour.

WELLS, John H.
Listed Barbour Light Horse. Farmer; $N/G; b. Barbour 1829, brother of Anthony; Methodist-Episcopal Church; m. Caroline Wells 1859; d. Barbour 1888.

WELLS, John Monroe
Enl. Co. E, 62nd Va. Mtd. Inf. 8-26-62; des. 11-23-63; released on oath; brother-in-law Elam Heatherly served Co. E, 11th W. Va. Inf. (USA). Farmer; $1,000/142; b. Brown Co., Ill. 1844; Methodist-Episcopal Church, joined German Baptists after war; came to Barbour 1840's; m. Elisabeth Holsberry 1865; living Barbour 1880. Son of Abraham and Sarah Eleanor (Black) Wells, b. Barbour, settled Gilmer Co., W. Va. after war; grandparents b. Va.

WHITELY, Alexander
Enl. Co. H, 31st Va. Inf. 5-14-61; elec. Lt.; KIA Port Republic 6-9-62; brother-in-law Frederick Sandridge served same company; brother-in-law Luther Sandridge served Co. F, 15th W. Va. Inf. (USA). Shoemaker; $0/100; b. Ireland 1830; m. Sophia Sandridge Neely 1858.

WILEY, Alexander
Listed Barbour Light Horse; enl. Co. H, 31st Va. Inf. 5-14-61. Farmer; $2,500/587 (parents); b. Barbour 1840; m. Mariah Henderson 1865; living Barbour 1880. Son of James and Elisabeth (Rider) Wiley; parents settled Barbour from Rockbridge Co., Va. 1820's; descendant of Scotch-Irish settlers to Rockbridge Co. 1760's.

WILLET, James G.
Enl. Co. K, 31st Va. Inf. 5-18-61; prom. to sgt.; listed sick 7-62; des. Fairfax Co., Va. 10-2-62; POW Randolph Co., W. Va. 10-62; exch.; wd. Spotsylvania 5-20-64; d. of wounds 8-31-64; brother-in-law Thomas Gorrell served Co. H, 3rd W. Va. Cav. (USA). Farmer; $0/95 (parents); b. Barbour 1832. Son of David and Mary Willet; father b. Barbour; grandson of David and Mary (Chrislip) Willet; grandfather b. Va.

WILLIAMSON, John R.
Sympathizer; member of committee drafting pro-secessionist resolutions Philippi 3-7-61; brother-in-law Harman Sinsel Delegate W. Va. Constitutional Convention; brother-in-law John Sinsel served Co. F, 3rd W. Va. Inf. (USA). Farmer; $25,000/11,075; b. Barbour 1817; Democrat; m. 1) Lucinda Sinsel; 2) Susan Sinsel; d. Taylor Co. 1876. Son of Archibald and Jane Williamson; father b. Taylor Co., W. Va.; grandfather immigrant from Scotland.

WILLIAMSON, Edwin Draper
Enl. Co. H, 31st Va. Inf. 5-14-61; prom. to cpl.; POW Fort Stedman 3-25-65; released 6-21-65. Farmer; $25,000/11,075 (parents); b. Barbour 1842, son of John and Lucinda (Sinsel) Williamson; living Barbour 1870.

WILSON, Albert Gallatin
Enl. Co. H, 31st Va. Inf. 5-14-61; des. 7-61; drafted 3-65, never inducted. $4,000/402 (parents); b. Barbour 1839; Democrat; m. Roanna Jane Jones 1872; living Barbour 1880. Son of Isaiah and Deborah (Yoke) Wilson, b. Barbour; grandson of William and Jane (Booth) Wilson; great-grandson of William and Elisabeth (Friend) Wilson, b. Hardy Co., W. Va. settled Barbour; great-great-great-grandson of William and Elisabeth (Black) Wilson, immigrants from Scotland, settled Hardy Co.

WILSON, David
Enl. Co. H, 31st Va. Inf. 5-14-61; on roll to 10-63. Tenant; $0/155; b. Barbour 1825; m. Amanda Jane Carter 1845; moved to Upshur Co., W. Va. after war where d. 1917. Son of John and Ann (Keys) Wilson; father b. Barbour; grandson of William and Jane (Booth) Wilson.

WILSON, William
Enl. Co. E, 62nd Va. Mtd. Inf. 8-26-62; des. 10-5-64; took oath 11-29-64 and released; NFR. Farmer; $2,000/1,383; b. Barbour 1829, brother of David.

WILSON, Henry
Sympathizer; killed by men of Co. A, 6th W. Va. Inf. 1-5-63; brother-in-law *Benjamin Ekis served Co. K, 6th W. Va. Inf. (USA). Farmer and German

Baptist preacher; $3,700/786; b. Randolph Co., W. Va. 1809; m. Hester Ekis. Son of Thomas Wilson.

WILSON, Johnson William
Enl. Co. H, 31st Va. Inf. 5-18-61; KIA McDowell 5-9-62; father-in-law *John Nicola and brother-in-law *Jacob Nicola Confederate sympathizers. Farmer; $3,700/786 (parents); b. Barbour 1833, son of Henry and Hester (Ekis) Wilson; German Baptist; m. Catherine Nicola 1856.

WILSON, D. B. F. "Doc"
Enl. Co. K, 31st Va. Inf. 5-18-61; prom. to sgt.; killed while arresting deserter Bedford Co., Va. 9-3-63. Farmer; $3,700/786 (parents); b. Barbour 1839, brother of Johnson; German Baptist.

WILSON, Thomas
Enl. Co. K, 31st Va. Inf. 5-1-61; prom. to sgt.; wd. Gaines Mill 6-27-62; POW Gettysburg 7-3-63; paroled 5-20-65. Farmer; $3,700/786 (parents); b. Barbour 1840, brother of Johnson; German Baptist; m. Mary Hesley 1883; post-war German Baptist minister; d. 1883.

WILT, Peter
Enl. Co. K, 31st Va. Inf. 5-29-61; wd. in leg Port Republic 6-9-62; des. and took oath 11-29-64. Farmer; $200/155; b. Allegany Co., Md. 1819; Methodist-Protestant Church; m. Catherine Wilson 1839; moved to Tucker Co., W. Va. after war where living 1884.

WILT, John H.
Enl. Co. K, 31st Va. Inf. 5-29-61; wd. Winchester 5-25-62; prom. to cpl. 8-62, serving as regimental color-bearer; wd. left arm Rappahannock River 8-21-62; hospitalized to end of war. Farmer; $200/155 (parents); b. Barbour 1842, son of Peter and Catherine (Wilson) Wilt; Methodist-Protestant Church; m. Nancy Philips 1867; moved to Tucker Co., W. Va. 1870's where d. 1910.

WISE, Randolph
Enl. Co. F, 31st Va. Inf. 5-24-61; wd. in left arm Second Bull Run 9-1-62; arm later amputated; disch. 10-24-63; re-enlisted Co. C, 19th Va. Cav. 11-12-63; POW Craigsville, Md. 7-11-64; exch. 3-65; POW Beverly, W. Va. 5-18-65; paroled 5-22-65; step-father John Rollins served Co. I, 10th W. Va. Inf. (USA), KIA. Farm laborer; $0/0; b. Randolph Co., W. Va. 1843; m. Mary C. ____; returned to Randolph Co. after war; d. Tucker Co., W. Va. 1888. Son of Frederick and Sarah (Mace) Wise; father b. Hardy Co., W. Va.; grandson of Christian Wise, b. Hardy Co.

WOODFORD, John Howe
Sympathizer; president pro-secessionist meeting Philippi 3-7-61; sons *Asa and *John Harvey Unionists; son-in-law *Robert Talbott Confederate sympathizer. Farmer; $54,000/23,200; b. Rockingham Co., Va. 1796; came to Barbour 1804; Democrat; m. Nancy Minear 1819; d. Barbour 1881. Son of William and Hannah (Moss) Woodford. Cf. Unionists.

WOODFORD, Jacob
Sympathizer; president pro-secessionist meeting Hackers Creek, Barbour 1-61; brother-in-law *John Robinson Unionist. Farmer; $10,000/1,154 (parents); b. Rockingham Co., Va. 1799, brother of John Howe; m. Mary Robinson 1819; d. Barbour 1892.

WOODFORD, John H.
Enl. Co. H, 31st Va. Inf. 5-14-61; des. 1863; NFR; brothers *James and *Robinson Unionists. Farmer; $10,000/1,154 (parents); b. Barbour 1838, son of Jacob and Mary (Robinson) Woodford.

WOODFORD, Benjamin Holley
Enl. Co. E, 62nd Va. Mtd. Inf. 8-26-62; prom. to sgt.; wd. Stephenson's Depot 9-8-64; on roll to 12-64. Farmer; $10,000/1,154 (parents); b. Barbour 1843, brother of John H.; Democrat; m. Mary Elisabeth Hudgson 1870; d. Barbour 1923.

WOODS, Samuel
Elec. to Richmond Convention 2-61 where voted for Ordinance of Secession; fled Philippi 6-3-61; indicted for treason 9-20-61; Com. Capt., Quartermasters Corps; sister *Sarah Jane Holt Confederate sympathizer; brothers-in-law *Charles and *William Holt served Confederate Army. Attorney; $14,600/1,154; b. Quebec Province, Canada 1822, brother of Sarah Jane (Woods) Holt; Methodist-Episcopal Church; moved to Pa. 1830's; settled Barbour 1849 where m. *Isabella Neeson 1849; Democrat; d. Barbour 1897.

WOODS, Isabella (Neeson)
Sympathizer; home burned 2-8-62; refugee in Waynesboro, Va.; brother James Confederate sympathizer, represented Marion Co., W. Va. in Virginia legislature during war. $14,600/1,154; b. N.Y. 1824, wife of Samuel Woods; Methodist-Episcopal Church; d. Barbour 1895. Daughter of John and Margaret (McKendrick) Neeson, immigrants from Ireland.

WRIGHT, Richard
Enl. Co. C, 19th Va. Cav.; POW Gilmer Co., W. Va. 9-20-63; d. of typhoid fever Rock Island Prison, Ill. 2-21-64; brother *John served Co. B, 2nd W. Va. Inf.

(USA). Farmer; $800/242 (parents); b. Rockbridge Co., Va. 1843. Son of William and Angeline Wright. Cf. Unionists.

WYMER, Samuel
Enl. Co. H, 31st Va. Inf. 5-29-61; d. of disease 10-17-61. Farm laborer; $0/0; b. Pendleton Co., W. Va. 1840. Son of John and Hester Ann (Syford) Wymer; parents b. Pendleton Co., W. Va.; settled Barbour 1840's; grandson of Jacob and Sarah (Seybert) Wymer, b. Pendleton Co.; great-grandson of George and Elinor Wymer; George b. Pa., settled Pendleton Co.

YEAGER, George
Listed Barbour Light Horse; Com. Capt., Barbour Home Guard. Cf. Unionists.

YOKE, Henson L.
Enl. Co. H, 62nd Va. Mtd. Inf. 9-1-62; prom. to Lt.; POW Randolph Co., W. Va. 12-6-63; released Camp Chase, Ohio 5-10-65; brothers John, William and Isaac and brother-in-law *Daniel Vanscoy served Union army. Farm laborer; $0/0; b. Barbour 1833; m. Sarah Jane Wilson Simpson 1870; d. Barbour 1885. Son of Elias and Hannah (Kelley) Yoke; father b. Hardy Co., W. Va.; grandson of John and Margaret (Carpenter) Yoke; grandfather b. Pa., settled Barbour from Hardy Co.

YOKE, William J.
Enl. Co. D, 20th Va. Cav. 4-1-64; drowned Potts Creek, Va., 5-14-64. Farmer; $1,000/247; b. Barbour 1845. Son of Jeremiah and Elisabeth (Jones) Yoke; grandson of John and Margaret (Carpenter) Yoke.

ZINN, Anthony
Listed Barbour Light Horse. Farmer; $1,500/529 (parents); b. Barbour 1839; m. Margaret Berger 1862; d. Barbour 1863. Son of Peter and Catherine (Heatherly) Zinn; father b. Harrison Co., W. Va.; grandson of Peter and Rachel (Heatherly) Zinn; grandfather b. Preston Co., W. Va.; great-grandson of George and Mary (Saylor) Zinn, immigrants from Switzerland.

ZINN, James Simpson
Listed Barbour Light Horse; brother-in-law *Bartholomew O'Neal Unionist. Farmer; $1,500/529 (parents); b. Barbour 1842, brother of Anthony; m. Mary O'Neal 1862; d. Barbour 1864.

ZINN, Lucinda Ann (Gawthorpe)
Sympathizer; husband Unionist; brother James served Co. A, 20th Va. Cav. (CSA); brother Thomas served 133rd W. Va. Mil., taken prisoner by 20th Va. Cav.; brother-in-law *Israel Sears served Co. C, 6th W. Va . Cav. (USA).

$4,670/920; b. Taylor Co., W. Va. 1835; Baptist; m. *Alpheus Zinn 1854; living Barbour 1880. Daughter of James and Hulda (Waldo) Gawthorpe; father b. Hampshire Co., W. Va.; granddaughter of Thomas and Elisabeth (Hiatt) Gawthorpe, settled Taylor Co. 1770's; great-granddaughter of James Gawthorpe, immigrant from England.

APPENDIX A

UNITS IN WHICH BARBOUR'S UNION AND CONFEDERATE SOLDIERS SERVED

Exclusive of militia, a total of 907 men from Barbour served in the armed forces during the Civil War, a figure representing forty-seven percent of all males of military age living in the county. Nearly all were volunteers, only a handful having been drafted in the final months of the conflict. While no unit of either the Union or Confederate army was composed exclusively of Barbour men, nine companies – three Union and six Confederate – were raised primarily in the county. These were Company H of the 10th West Virginia Infantry, Company F of the 15th West Virginia Infantry, the Barbour Home Guard, the Barbour Light Horse, Companies H and K of the 31st Virginia Infantry, Companies E and H of the 62nd Virginia Mounted Infantry and Company D of the 20th Virginia Cavalry. Ninety percent of all Confederate and nearly half of the Union soldiers who joined the army from Barbour served in these units. The rest served in two dozen other regiments of the two armies.

The following lists show the number of Barbour men who served in each of these and gives a breakdown of deaths, desertions, transfers and early discharges for incapacitating wounds or illness. The figures for Total Enlisted exceeds the actual number of soldiers from Barbour as fifty-six Union and seventy-five Confederate servicemen enlisted in two or more regiments. Non-combat deaths were due almost entirely to disease, only two men dying as a result of accidents. Because of incomplete records for Confederate servicemen, it's likely that many more Confederate soldiers died during the war than are counted here. Not included among Union desertions are six men serving with the 6th West Virginia Cavalry who left their regiment in Kansas after the war when it was sent West to suppress a Sioux uprising.

UNION SOLDIERS

	2nd W. Va. Inf./ 5th W. Va. Cav.*	3rd W. Va. Inf./ 6th W. Va. Cav.*
Enlisted	13	29
Combat deaths	1	2
Non-combat deaths	2	
Taken prisoner	5	4
Deserted	1	
Discharged		3
Transferred	2	

	6th W. Va. Inf.	7th W. Va. Inf.
Enlisted	55	19
Combat deaths		4
Non-combat deaths	2	1
Taken prisoner		1
Deserted		2
Discharged		2
Transferred	3	

	10th W. Va. Inf.	12th W. Va. Inf.
Enlisted	86	10
Combat deaths	9	2
Non-combat deaths	12	
Taken prisoner	6	
Deserted	3	
Discharged	6	
Transferred		

	15th W. Va. Inf.	17th W. Va. Inf.
Enlisted	109	50
Combat deaths	7	
Non-combat deaths	9	
Taken prisoner	5	
Deserted	2	
Discharged	7	1
Transferred		

	1st W. Va. Cav.	3rd W. Va. Cav.
Enlisted	10	16
Combat deaths		
Non-combat deaths		2
Taken prisoner		3
Deserted	1	
Discharged		
Transferred		

	4th W. Va. Cav.	1st W. Va. Art.
Enlisted	24	18
Combat deaths		1
Non-combat deaths	2	2
Taken prisoner		3
Deserted		
Discharged		1
Transferred	2	

	Home Guard	Other**	Totals
Enlisted	66	18	523
Combat deaths	3		29
Non-combat deaths	2	1	35
Taken prisoner			27
Deserted			9
Discharged	1		22
Transferred	1	1	8

CONFEDERATE SOLDIERS

	25th Va. Inf.	31st Va. Inf.
Enlisted	11	153
Combat deaths	1	22
Non-combat deaths	1	9
Taken prisoner	2	36
Deserted	1	65
Discharged	4	17
Transferred	3	4

	62nd Va. Mtd. Inf.***	11th Va. Cav.
Enlisted	130	6
Combat deaths	6	1
Non-combat deaths	11	
Taken prisoner	29	2
Deserted	35	1
Discharged	2	1
Transferred	9	

	14th Va. Cav.	17th Va. Cav.
Enlisted	5	4
Combat deaths	1	
Non-combat deaths	1	
Taken prisoner	3	1
Deserted		
Discharged		
Transferred		

	18th Va. Cav.	19th Va. Cav.
Enlisted	6	8
Combat deaths	2	
Non-combat deaths		2
Taken prisoner	3	4
Deserted		1
Discharged		1
Transferred		2

	20th Va. Cav.	46th Va. Cav.+
Enlisted	71	10
Combat deaths	1	
Non-combat deaths	5	
Taken prisoner	22	3
Deserted	13	4
Discharged		
Transferred	1	2

	Barbour Light Horse	Other++	Totals
Enlisted	74	4	482
Combat deaths			34
Non-combat deaths			29
Taken Prisoner	1		106
Deserted		1	121
Discharged			24
Transferred			21

*The 2nd and 3rd West Virginia Infantry were formed in 1861. In 1863, both regiments were mounted and re-designated the 5th and 6th West Virginia Cavalry. The veterans of the two regiments who re-enlisted after their initial three-year terms expired in 1864 were consolidated into the 6th West Virginia Cavalry.

**These were the 1st, 11th and 14th West Virginia Infantry, the 4th Pennsylvania Cavalry, the 4th Pennsylvania Artillery, the 15th Ohio Infantry, the 1st U.S. Cavalry, the 9th U.S. Artillery and the 45th Colored Infantry.

***The regiment was initially organized as the 1st Partisan Rangers. In December, 1862 it was re-designated the 62nd Virginia Mounted Infantry.

+In 1865 the 46th and 47th Battalions Virginia Cavalry were consolidated into the 26th Virginia Cavalry.

++These were the 13th Virginia Infantry, the Virginia State Line and McClanahan's Battery.

APPENDIX B

BATTLES AND ENGAGEMENTS REFERENCED IN UNION AND CONFEDERATE BIOGRAPHIES

Regiments in which Barbour Soldiers Served

	Union	Confederate
Philippi, W. Va. June 3, 1861		Barbour Light Horse; Barbour Greys;* Mountain Guards;* Letcher Guards*
Laurel Hill, W. Va. July 7, 1861	2nd W. Va. Inf.	25th Va. Inf. 31st Va. Inf.
Rich Mountain, W. Va. July 11, 1861		25th Va. Inf.
Greenbrier, W. Va. October 3, 1861		25th Va. Inf. 31st Va. Inf.
Alleghany, W. Va. December 13, 1861		25th Va. Inf. 31st Va. Inf.
McDowell, Va. May 8, 1862	2nd W. Va. Inf. 3rd W. Va. Inf. 1st W. Va. Cav.	25th Va. Inf. 31st Va. Inf.
Cross Keys, Va. June 8, 1861	2nd W. Va. Inf. 3rd W. Va. Inf..	25th Va. Inf. 31st Va. Inf.
Port Republic, Va. June 9, 1861		25th Va. Inf. 31st Va. Inf.
Gaines Mill, Va. June 27, 1862		25th Va. Inf. 31st Va. Inf.
Cedar Mountain, Va. August 9, 1862	1st W. Va. Cav.	25th Va. Inf. 31st Va. Inf.

Freemans Ford, Va. August 22, 1862	2nd W. Va. Inf. 3rd W. Va. Inf.	25th Va. Inf. 31st Va. Inf.
Second Bull Run, Va. August 29, 1862	2nd W. Va. Inf. 3rd W. Va. Inf. 1st W. Va. Cav. 3rd W. Va. Cav.	25th Va. Inf. 31st Va. Inf.
Buckhannon, W. Va. August 30, 1862	10th W. Va. Inf. Bat. E, 1st W. Va. Art.	
Sommerville Ford, Va. September 14, 1862		25th Va. Inf. 31st Va. Inf.
Antietam, Md. September 17, 1862	7th W. Va. Inf.	25th Va.. Inf. 31st Va. Inf.

Moorefield, W. Va.
April 4, 1863
	Bat. E, 1st
	  W. Va. Art.
		62nd Va.
		  Mtd. Inf.
		18th Va. Cav.

Jones-Imboden Raid, W. Va. April-May, 1863	6th W. Va. Inf.	25th Va. Inf. 31st Va. Inf. 62nd Va. Mtd. Inf. 11th Va. Cav. 18th Va. Cav.
Fredericksburg, Va. December 13, 1862	7th W. Va. Inf.	25th Va. Inf. 31st Va. Inf.
Chancelorsville, Va. May 1 to 5, 1863	7th W. Va. Inf.	25th Va. Inf. 31st Va. Inf.
Winchester, Va. June 15 to 18, 1863	12th W. Va. Inf. 1st W. Va. Cav. 3rd W. Va. Cav.	25th Va. Inf. 31st Va. Inf. 11th Va. Cav. 14th Va. Cav.
Martinsburg, W. Va. July 1, 1863	Bat. F, 1st W. Va. Art.	

Gettysburg, Pa. July 1 to 3, 1863	7th W. Va. Inf. 1st W. Va. Cav. 3rd W. Va. Cav.	25th Va. Inf. 31st Va. Inf. 62nd Va. Mtd. Inf. 11th Va. Cav. 14th Va. Cav. 17th Va. Cav. 18th Va. Cav.
Beverly, W. Va. July 2 to 4, 1863	10th W. Va. Inf.	19th Va. Cav. 20th Va. Cav.

Williamsport, Md.
July 7, 1863
	Bat E, 1st
	  W. Va. Art.
		62nd Va..
		   Mtd. Inf.
		14th Va. Cav.
		18th Va. Cav.

Rocky Gap, W. Va. August 26, 1863	2nd W. Va. Inf. 3rd W. Va. Inf. 10th W. Va. Inf.	
Bulltown, W. Va. October 13, 1863	6th W. Va. Inf.	19th Va. Cav. 20th Va. Cav. 46th Va. Cav.
Droop Mountain, W. Va. November 6, 1863	2nd W. Va. Inf. 3rd W. Va. Inf. 10th W. Va. Inf. 3rd W. Va. Cav.	14th Va. Cav. 17th Va. Cav. 19th Va. Cav. 20th Va. Cav. 46th Va. Cav.
Mine Run, Va. November 27, 1863	7th W. Va. Inf.	25th Va. Inf. 31st Va. Inf. 11th Va. Cav.
Covington, W. Va. December 19, 1863	2nd W. Va. Inf.	14th Va. Cav.
Wilderness, Va. May 6, 1864	7th W. Va. Inf.	25th Va. Inf. 31st Va. Inf. 11th Va. Cav.
Raid on Dublin, Va. May 5 to 19, 1864	1st W. Va. Cav. 3rd W. Va. Cav.	62nd Va. Mtd. Inf. 18th Va. Cav. 19th Va. Cav. 20th Va. Cav. 46th Va. Cav.

Cloyd Mountain, W. Va. May 9, 1864	15th W. Va. Inf. 5th W. Va. Cav.	14th Va. Cav.
Spotsylvania, Va. May 12, 1864	7th W. Va. Inf.	25th Va. Inf. 31st Va. Inf.
New Market, Va. May 15, 1864	12th W. Va. Inf.	62nd Va. Mtd. Inf. 18th Va. Cav.
Mechanicsville, Va. May 30, 1864	7th W. Va. Inf.	25th Va. Inf. 31st Va. Inf.
Piedmont, Va. June 4, 1864	12th W. Va. Inf. 15th W. Va. Inf. 1st W. Va. Cav. 3rd W. Va. Cav. 5th W. Va. Cav.	62nd Va. Mtd. Inf. 14th Va. Cav. 17th Va. Cav. 18th Va. Cav. 19th Va. Cav. 20th Va. Cav. 46th Va. Cav.
Lexington, Va. June 10, 1864	12th W. Va. Inf. 15th W. Va. Inf. 1st W. Va. Cav. 3rd W. Va. Cav. 5th W. Va. Cav.	62nd Va. Mtd. Inf. 14th Va. Cav. 17th Va. Cav. 18th Va. Cav. 19th Va. Cav. 20th Va. Cav. 46th Va. Cav.
Lynchburg, Va. June 18, 1864	12th W. Va. Inf. 15th W. Va. Inf. 1st W. Va. Cav. 3rd W. Va. Cav. 5th W. Va. Cav.	25th Va. Inf. 31st Va. Inf. 62nd Va. Mtd. Inf. 14th Va. Cav. 17th Va. Cav. 18th Va. Cav. 19th Va. Cav. 20th Va. Cav. 46th Va. Cav.
Cold Harbor, Va. June 27, 1864	7th W. Va. Inf.	25th Va. Inf. 31st Va. Inf. 62nd Va. Mtd. Inf.

Monocasy River, Md. July 15, 1864		25th Va. Inf. 31st Va. Inf. 62nd Va. Mtd. Inf. 14th Va. Cav. 17th Va. Cav. 18th Va. Cav. 19th Va. Cav. 20th Va. Cav. 46th Va. Cav.
Snickers Ferry, Va. July 17, 1864	1st W. Va. Inf. 10th W. Va. Inf. 12th W. Va. Inf. 15th W. Va. Inf. 1st W. Va. Cav. 3rd W. Va. Cav. Bat. E, 1st W. Va. Art.	25th Va. Inf. 31st Va. Inf.
Belle Grove, Va. July 19, 1864		25th Va. Inf. 31st Va. Inf.
Kernstown, Va. July 24, 1864	10th W. Va. Inf. 12th W. Va. Inf. 15th W. Va. Inf. 1st W. Va. Cav. Bat E, 1st W. Va. Art.	25th Va. Inf. 31st Va. Inf. 62nd Va. Mtd. Inf. 18th Va. Cav. 19th Va. Cav. 20th Va. Cav. 46th Va. Cav.
Moorefield, W. Va. August 7, 1864	1st W. Va. Cav. 3rd W. Va. Cav.	17th Va. Cav.
Berryville, Va. September 3, 1864	10th W. Va. Inf. 12th W. Va. Inf. 15th W. Va. Inf. 1st W. Va. Cav. 3rd W. Va. Cav.	25th Va. Inf. 31st Va. Inf. 62nd Va. Mtd. Inf. 18th Va. Cav. 19th Va. Cav. 20th Va. Cav. 46th Va. Cav.

Stephensons Depot, Va. September 5, 1864	1st W. Va. Cav. 3rd W. Va. Cav.	62nd Va. Mtd. Inf. 18th Va. Cav. 19th Va. Cav. 20th Va. Cav. 46th Va. Cav.
Winchester, Va. September 19, 1864	10th W. Va. Inf. 12th W. Va. Inf. 15th W. Va. Inf. 1st W. Va. Cav. 3rd W. Va. Cav.	25th Va. Inf. 31st Va. Inf. 62nd Va. Mtd. Inf. 14th Va. Cav. 17th Va. Cav. 18th Va. Cav. 19th Va. Cav. 20th Va. Cav. 46th Va. Cav.
Fishers Hill, Va. September 23, 1864	10th W. Va. Inf. 12th W. Va. Inf. 15th W. Va. Inf. 1st W. Va. Cav. 3rd W. Va. Cav.	25th Va. Inf. 31st Va. Inf. 62nd Va. Mtd. Inf. 14th Va. Cav. 17th Va. Cav. 18th Va. Cav. 19th Va. Cav. 20th Va. Cav. 46th Va. Cav.
Hobbs Hill, Va. October 13, 1864	10th W. Va. Inf. 12th W. Va. Inf. 15th W. Va. Inf.	
Cedar Creek, Va. October 19, 1864	10th W. Va. Inf. 12th W. Va. Inf. 15th W. Va. Inf.	25th Va. Inf. 31st Va. Inf. 11th Va. Cav. 14th Va. Cav. 19th Va. Cav. 20th Va. Cav. 46th Va. Cav.
Beverly, W. Va. October 29 to 31, 1864		Elements of 62nd Va. Mtd. Inf., 18th, 19th, and 20th Va. Cav.

Nineveh, Va. November 12, 1864	1st W. Va. Cav. 3rd W. Va. Cav.	14th Va. Cav. 17th Va. Cav.
New Creek, W. Va. November 28, 1864	5th W. Va. Cav. 6th W. Va. Cav. Bat. E, 1st W. Va. Art. Bat. H, 1st W. Va. Art.	11th Va. Cav. 14th Va. Cav. 18th Va. Cav.
Liberty Mills, Va. December 22, 1864	1st W. Va. Cav. 3rd W. Va. Cav.	
Waynesboro, Va. December 28, 1864	1st W. Va. Cav. 3rd W. Va. Cav.	62nd Va. Mtd. Inf. 19th Va. Cav. 20th Va. Cav. 46th Va. Cav.
Hatchers Run, Va. February 7, 1865	7th W. Va. Inf.	25th Va. Inf. 31st Va. Inf.
Mount Crawford, Va. March 1, 1865	1st W. Va. Cav. 3rd W. Va. Cav.	62nd Va. Mtd. Inf. 11th Va. Cav.
Fort Stedman, Va. March 25, 1865		25th Va. Inf. 31st Va. Inf.
Petersburg, Va. April 2, 1865	7th W. Va. Inf. 10th W. Va. Inf. 12th W. Va. Inf. 15th W. Va. Inf.	
Appomattox, Va. April 9, 1865	7th W. Va. Inf. 10th W. Va. Inf. 12th W. Va. Inf. 15th W. Va. Inf. 1st W. Va. Cav. 3rd W. Va. Cav.	25th Va. Inf. 31st Va. Inf. 11th Va. Cav. 14th Va. Cav. 17th Va. Cav.

*The 25th and 31st Virginia Infantry regiments were organized after the Battle of Philippi, the Barbour Greys and Mountain Guards becoming Companies H and K of the 31st, the Letcher Guards Company A of the 25th.

APPENDIX C

WAR-RELATED DEATHS

	Unionists	Confederates	Total
Soldiers killed in action	29	34	63
Soldiers died of disease	21	16	37
Soldiers died in prison	14	13	27
Civilians killed	1	5	6
Civilians died in prison		6	6
Totals	65	74	139
Other civilian war-related deaths			3
Total Barbour war-related deaths			142

www.ingramcontent.com/pod-product-compliance
Lightning Source LLC
Chambersburg PA
CBHW051642230426
43669CB00013B/2410